THE AIRBORNE

Other National Historical Society Publications:

THE IMAGE OF WAR: 1861-1865

TOUCHED BY FIRE: A PHOTOGRAPHIC PORTRAIT OF THE CIVIL WAR

WAR OF THE REBELLION: OFFICIAL RECORDS
OF THE UNION AND CONFEDERATE ARMIES

OFFICIAL RECORDS OF THE UNION AND CONFEDERATE NAVIES
IN THE WAR OF THE REBELLION

HISTORICAL TIMES ILLUSTRATED ENCYCLOPEDIA OF THE CIVIL WAR

CONFEDERATE VETERAN

THE WEST POINT MILITARY HISTORY SERIES

IMPACT: THE ARMY AIR FORCES' CONFIDENTIAL HISTORY
OF WORLD WAR II

HISTORY OF UNITED STATES NAVAL OPERATIONS IN WORLD WAR II
by Samuel Eliot Morison

HISTORY OF THE ARMED FORCES IN WORLD WAR II
by Janusz Piekalkiewicz

A TRAVELLER'S GUIDE TO GREAT BRITAIN SERIES

MAKING OF BRITAIN SERIES

THE ARCHITECTURAL TREASURES OF EARLY AMERICA

For information about National Historical Society Publications, write:
The National Historical Society, 2245 Kohn Road, Box 8200,
Harrisburg, Pa 17105

THE ELITE
The World's Crack Fighting Men

THE AIRBORNE

Ashley Brown, Editor

Jonathan Reed, Editor

Editorial Board

Lisa Mullins, Managing Editor, NHS edition

A Publication of
THE NATIONAL HISTORICAL SOCIETY

Published in Great Britain in 1986 by Orbis Publishing

Library of Congress Cataloging-in-Publication Data
The Airborne / Ashley Brown, editor ; Jonathan Reed, editor.
    p.   cm.—(The Elite : the world's crack fighting men ; v. 11)
  ISBN 0-918678-49-8
  1. Airborne troops—History—20th century.   I. Brown, Ashley.
II. Reed, Jonathan.   III. Series: Elite (Harrisburg, Pa.) ; v. 11.
UD480.A37   1990
358.4—dc20   89-12164
                                                   CIP

CONTENTS

INTRODUCTION

From their introduction early in this century, the men of THE AIRBORNE have shown something extra in the realm of daring and resourcefulness. They began in Europe in the 1930s, but it took the coming of global war a decade later for their full potential to be realized. Then, when Germany brought warfare out of the skies, and when the Allies in turn brought the war back to them in 1944, THE AIRBORNE reigned supreme. It is no accident that in January 1946, Washington selected the 82d Airborne to lead the victory parade, for the contribution of the parachutists to final triumph was inestimable.

It has been the same since, whether in Korea or Vietnam, Afghanistan, or elsewhere. The special training, the special weapons and skills of THE AIRBORNE, have continued to set them apart, as their stories tell so eloquently. Witness the exploits of No. 1 USAAF Air Commando in Burma in 1944. Look at the story of the 101st Airborne—the "Screaming Eagles"—at Hamburger Hill in 1969. Fly through the night skies in silence with Britain's Glider Pilot Regiment, ferrying commandos and supplies over enemy lines on one-way flights in aircraft never intended to return.

Or, for the really daring, become a Pathfinder, part of a platoon of the 5th Airborne Brigade, whose mission it is to parachute into a combat zone even before the main drop force, to reconnoiter and mark drop sites for those to follow—a few men alone, dropping out of dark skies, entirely on their own. For heroism, hit the silk with the British 1st Airborne Division in the heroic, but abortive, Market Garden campaign in August 1944. Witness one of the most spectacular airborne operations of World War II as the 503d Parachute Infantry Regiment drop into Corregidor in 1945, spearheading MacArthur's return to the Philippines.

Americans, Russians, Germans, Scandanavians, the British, and more, all demonstrate in their AIRBORNE what it is that makes men a part of THE ELITE.

SOVIET AIRBORNE ORGANISATION

The Soviet Armed Forces were the pioneers of paratroop and air landing formations, with four such units in existence by 1932. Despite a series of failed operations during World War II, the result of a lack of sufficient officers and heavy equipment, the Soviet Air Assault Force (VDV) was retained after 1945. The airborne arm was placed under the control of the ground forces, and General V.F. Margelov began an extensive modernisation programme.

In the wake of the Cuban Missile Crisis of 1962, Soviet planners placed the VDV under the direct control of the Ministry of Defence, to operate at the discretion of the Soviet High Command in the event of a conflict. This reorganisation provided Western observers with the first real indication that the airborne arm would play a crucial role in expanding Soviet capabilities worldwide.

The VDV currently fields eight known divisions. One of these – the 106th Guards Air Assault Division – is based in the Tula-Ryazan area, 100 miles south of Moscow, and is responsible for training new recruits. The seven other divisions are the 6th, 76th, 102nd, 103rd, 104th and 107th Guards Air Assault Divisions, and the 44th Guards Airborne Division. Above: The sleeve badge of an Air Assault Division.

AIRBORNE ARMOURY

When a new weapon is added to the Soviet arsenal, the combat-ready paratroopers are the first to test its operational capability

THE SOVIET AIRBORNE ARM has experienced violent reversals of fortune since its formation in 1929, but today it forms a vital and formidable component of the Soviet Army. Parachute troops were first deployed in a military exercise in 1930; six years later came a famous demonstration, before foreign attaches, in which some 1500 men were dropped. After that, however, little was heard of these troops, and it is surmised that most of their senior officers vanished during Stalin's purge of the army in 1936-37, thus removing the driving power from the airborne arm. While parachute troops were used in three operations against the Germans in 1943-44, all three ended disastrously, principally because the Soviet paratroops were relying almost entirely on what light weapons they could carry, with no heavy support back-up.

In 1956, however, the Tushino Air Display revealed to the world that a totally new Soviet airborne arm had been organised, and in the last three decades it has been built up into the largest and probably best-equipped airborne force in the world. The men are all volunteers, and their bases are buried away deep inside Russia, providing Western observers with little opportunity to assess these elite troops. Their strength is not known with any degree of accuracy, but it is estimated that there are as many as 75,000 men organised into 8 airborne divisions. The Soviet Air Force has ample transport aircraft available, and it is probable that two, or even three, divisions could be lifted at short notice and moved for distances up to 3000km. The standard transport for parachute troops is the Antonov An-12 Cub, a turbo-prop with a range of 4600km at 620 kilometres per hour when carrying 100 fully equipped paratroopers. Alternatively, the An-12 can lift

Left: Bayonet fixed, an airborne officer carries out weapons drill. Above left: Sighting an AGS-17 automatic grenade launcher. Above right: A Soviet para advances, carrying the anti-armour punch of the airborne troops – the RPG-16 rocket launcher. Below: A paratrooper unit penetrates the 'enemy' flank during a night exercise.

loads of up to 15,000kg, and according to Soviet sources some 117 of these machines are required to lift one airborne regiment and its equipment.

An airborne division consists of three airborne regiments, together with engineer, signal, anti-tank missile, maintenance, resupply and medical battalions, an artillery support regiment, a reconnaissance company, a chemical defence company and parachute rigging company. However, this appears to be an 'ideal' composition, and the actual make-up of a division would depend very much on the type of operation envisaged. In Soviet doctrine there are two basic types of airborne operation: the parachute assault, carried out by specialist troops, or the helicopter assault, normally carried out by ordinary motor-rifle troops. The handbooks emphasise the bold use of parachute forces to probe deeply into an enemy's lines after an initial nuclear exchange, to support a conventional armoured attack by advance landings on communications centres, river crossings or other tactically important points, to decoy reserves away from an impending advance, to take out enemy nuclear delivery systems, or to disrupt command and communications networks behind enemy lines.

Judging from the few photographs which have been seen in the West over the past 30 years, it would seem probable that the Soviet airborne soldier, being accorded the 'guards' status, is among the first o receive new weapons; it is notable that the first AK-74 rifle, the first RPG-16 anti-tank rocket launcher and the first AGS-17 grenade launcher were all seen in the hands of parachute troops before they were issued to the remainder of the Soviet Army. On the basis of this, Western observers can only speculate as to the range of new weapons possessed by the paratroopers, weapons that have not yet appeared in the public eye.

The basic combat weapon of the parachutist is the AK-74 rifle. This was first seen in 1978, and by 1980 had spread to the remainder of the Soviet Army. The AK-74 is based on the well-known AK-47 Kalashnikov design, the major difference being its 5.45mm calibre and the addition of a combined muzzle-brake and compensator on the end of the barrel. This, it is believed, is intended to reduce the recoil and barrel climb during automatic fire, though evidence from Soviet military medical journals indicates that the blast from the muzzle brake is hazardous to soldiers on each side of the weapon. The 5.45mm cartridge is comparable to the NATO 5.56mm round, but it has a bullet of peculiar design with a truncated steel core inside a cupro-nickel envelope. The flat tip of the core leaves a hollow space inside the nose of the bullet, so that when it strikes, the tip usually folds over and the bullet then follows a curved path, leaving a severe wound cavity. Tracer and armour-piercing bullets are also provided, though these are more likely to be used with machine guns.

There are two variants of the AK-74 rifle, the most

The plastic magazine and hollow stock of the AK-74 (top left) provides the Soviet airborne troops with a weapon that is light and easy to carry (main picture). Far left: The anti-tank RPG-18 rocket launcher (bottom), able to penetrate 250mm of armour plate, shown here with its American equivalent – the M72 LAW (top).

common being the AKS-74, which is the standard weapon with the addition of a folding tubular steel stock, and is frequently seen in the hands of parachute troops. The second, less common, is the short AKR sub-machine gun version. This has a very short barrel (200mm long instead of 400mm) and a folding stock similar to that of the AKS-74. A bulbous flash-hider on the muzzle helps to reduce the gas pressure in the operating piston. So far, this weapon has only been seen in Afghanistan, but there seems little doubt that it is standard among drivers and similar technical troops within the airborne division.

The 5.45mm machine gun, used as the squad automatic weapon, is the RPK-74 model. This is similar to the earlier 7.62mm RPK gun, and is what the West would call a 'machine rifle', being no more than a heavier version of the AK-74 rifle with the addition of a bipod, a larger magazine, and a heavier and longer barrel. The barrel cannot be removed and replaced when it gets hot, which suggests that it would only be used in short bursts and not for sustained supporting fire. The magazine takes 40 rounds, but the gun will also accept the standard 30-round rifle magazine.

Although the RPK-74 is adequate as the squad weapon, it is obvious that something with more power and range is required as the company support machine gun, and here the standard 7.62mm PKM is used – a compact belt-fed gun with a bipod and quick-change barrel, allowing it to be used for long bursts of fire. Catering for the requirement of an even longer-ranging weapon, the 12.7mm NSV heavy machine gun is provided on a scale of two per parachute company. The NSV is replacing the old DShK 12.7mm weapon as the standard Soviet heavy machine gun, and it can be used as a ground weapon or in the air defence role. It fires from a 50-round belt at about 700 rounds per minute, and delivers accurate fire to a range of almost 2km.

Heavy support is provided by a company, deploying six 82mm mortars. The model used is the 'New M37', a lightened version

In the event of a conflict, the main deployment of the airborne forces would take the form of operational missions. Regiments, and possibly division-sized units, would be used in airborne assaults to secure key objectives up to 300km behind NATO lines. These would then be held by the paratroopers until the arrival of the main Soviet force. For the Soviets, the most important operational mission would be the insertion of small units in the enemy rear or flank. Such missions are known as *desants*, and would involve the destruction of nuclear weapons and installations by units varying in size from a regiment to small sabotage squads. These units would also co-operate with Soviet long-range patrols in seizing routes to facilitate the main advance, as well as gathering intelligence on enemy deployments. Airborne assaults and *desants* are not intended to fight independently of the main ground forces, but they do have the potential for causing massive disruption behind NATO lines. In 1979, the use of the 105th Guards Airborne Division in securing Kabul, the capital of Afghanistan, showed how effective airborne troops could be in conjunction with a larger force.

Soviet airborne troops can also be employed in a strategic role, to establish a new theatre of operations or to secure bases of strategic value. The importance of Soviet paratroopers in this context is illustrated by the fact that all but one of the divisions (the 44th Guards Airborne) are maintained at Category 1 readiness in peacetime.

AIRBORNE TACTICS

Underlying Soviet airborne tactics is the belief that a large airborne assault would be doomed to failure against an alerted enemy, unless it was preceded by a massive bombardment of the defences. For this purpose, air strikes, artillery or nuclear/biological/chemical (NBC) weapons would be used to weaken or eliminate enemy defences.

The drops would most likely occur under cover of darkness, with the An-12 Cubs flying along routes cleared of anti-aircraft defences, and supported by Soviet fighters such as the MiG-27.

The drop zones would be located at a maximum distance of 5000m from the target, with up to six zones allocated to each division. These areas would be marked by pathfinders from each division's reconnaissance company, whose personnel are well versed in the art of precision parachuting. Electronic and visual beacons would also be used to identify the drop zones to the pilots of the An-12s.

After the initial wave has landed, along with its heavy equipment, the zone would be secured in readiness for the next wave. The paras would then increase the territory under their control using circular patrols, supported by air strikes and artillery fire. In the main, however, the airborne troops would have to rely on their own weapons and combat skills to secure the area.

Having secured their objective, the paratroopers would have to await the arrival of heavy Soviet forces before they could be relieved. While they themselves possess relatively few heavy weapons, the airborne troops provide the Soviet armed forces with a vital asset – that of mobility.

of a design introduced 50 years ago. A conventional drop-fired muzzle-loading mortar, it fires a 3kg bomb to a range of 3km, and a well-practised crew can reach a rate of some 20 rounds per minute. For transport on the ground it can be split into three components (barrel, baseplate and bipod), and when assembled for action weighs about 56kg.

The airborne regiment has a heavy support mortar company which is armed with six 120mm M43 mortars. This is another elderly design, being little more than an improvement on a 1938 model, but age is no bar to efficiency in this type of weapon and the M43 is an excellent mortar. Smooth-bored, muzzle-loaded and drop-fired, it sends its 15kg bomb to a maximum range of 5.7km and can reach a rate of fire of 15 rounds per minute. Although of the usual pattern – baseplate, barrel and bipod – there is also a lightweight trailer that transports the mortar without the need for dismantling, and it can then be towed by a light vehicle or manhandled.

In the past, rifle squads were also given a number of light 50mm mortars, but these have now been superseded by an entirely different short-range weapon – the AGS-17 automatic grenade launcher. This resembles a stubby machine gun, is mounted on a tripod, and fires a powerful 30mm grenade projectile fed into the gun by means of a 30-round belt. The high explosive grenade weighs 275g and carries a charge of RDX high explosive surrounded by several hundred steel balls to provide powerful blast and fragmentation effect. The weapon has a rate of fire of about 65 rounds per minute and can send its grenades to a range of 1500m with considerable accuracy.

The most serious threat to an airborne operation comes from armour deployed against it, since most paratroopers have to operate with light weapons. However, as this factor led to the downfall of the wartime Soviet airborne actions, the new Soviet organisation has taken positive steps to ensure that ample anti-armour weapons are provided.

The basic anti-tank weapon, at the lowest level throughout the Soviet Army, is the well-known RPG-7 rocket launcher. A one-man shoulder-fired weapon, the RPG-7 is a combination of recoilless gun and rocket missile; the missile is a finned rocket carrying an over-calibre shaped charge warhead, and is launched from its 40mm firing tube by a small recoilless charge. After flying a few metres through the air, the rocket motor ignites and accelerates the missile towards its target. The RPG-7 weighs only 9kg complete with its rocket, with a range of 500m against stationary targets and 300m against moving targets. The warhead is ignited by a piezo-electric fuze that is activated upon striking the target, and the resulting shaped charge detonation is capable of penetrating over 300mm of solid steel armour.

In the past four years, evidence of a new and improved weapon has come to light. This is known as the RPG-16, and is an enlarged and more powerful

version of the RPG-7. This weapon has a 58mm launcher tube and fires an oversized warhead with tandem shaped charges – two shaped charges, one of which detonates and makes the first penetration of the target, while the second then detonates and either deepens or widens the hole. The RPG-16 has a range of 800m against stationary targets, and probably half that against moving targets. Although no figure for penetration has been published, it seems safe to assume that the RPG-16 can defeat 500mm of armour plate.

A third light anti-tank weapon operated by Soviet troops is the RPG-18. While there is no positive evidence of its adoption by airborne forces, it seems likely that the RPG-18 forms part of their equipment – being a light throwaway device that can be carried by individual members of an airborne infantry squad. In fact, it is no more than a copy of the American M72 66mm LAW, a telescoped launch tube with a pre-packed shaped-charge rocket carried inside it. When required, the end caps are flung off, the tube extended – which automatically cocks the weapon and raises the sight – and the soldier fires it by use of a simple trigger. The rocket is launched, and the empty tube is then thrown away. The RPG-18 has a maximum range of about 200m and can penetrate 250mm of armour plate. These anti-tank weapons can also be used for other purposes: the RPG-7 has a fragmentation rocket which can be fired instead of the standard anti-armour warhead, and all three of the weapons can produce a useful anti-personnel effect from their shaped-charge warheads. An RPG rocket delivered against a pillbox or emplaced machine-gun post, for example, would be extremely effective.

To keep the armoured opposition at arm's length, the airborne troops are provided with heavy weapons

The main drawback with these rocket launchers is that they are only effective at short range; not due to any defect in the warhead, but because the projectile moves at a relatively low speed. The rocket's trajectory is therefore curved rather than flat, and this factor presents the firer with enormous difficulties when concentrating on a moving target. It is for this reason that different ranges against moving and stationary targets are quoted, and even these would be the maximum that can be expected from a highly trained soldier under ideal conditions. A panting, out of breath paratrooper who has just dropped from the sky, and is the focus of attention for several people with firearms, will be unlikely to perform perfectly.

In order to keep the armoured opposition at arm's length, the airborne troops are provided with heavier weapons. The most recent weapon, of which practically nothing is known in the West, is an 85mm gun. This has replaced the old SD-44 85mm anti-tank and general support gun, a conventional split-trail weapon with an auxiliary propulsion motor attached to the trail that allowed the gun to be motored about without the need of a towing vehicle. It is probable that the new gun also uses auxiliary propulsion, and sources indicate that the weapon is a lightweight smoothbore, firing a fin-stabilised discarding sabot solid projectile similar to the projectiles used in Soviet tank guns. If this is the case, it would be reasonable to expect that it would be able to defeat 250mm of armour at 1000m range.

The rifle companies are each provided with two 82mm B-10 recoilless guns for anti-tank defence.

Emphasising the importance attached to the airborne arm, the eight divisions operate independently of the Soviet Army chain of command, coming under the direct control of the Ministry of Defence. This elite status is confirmed by their distinctive uniform (main picture), incorporating a blue beret and shoulder boards, and a rigorous training programme at the Ryazan airborne school that amalgamates the pursuit of physical and intellectual excellence. The subjects covered include language instruction (top left), parachute packing (centre) and exhaustive academic studies designed to give the students a comprehensive education (left).

OFFICER TRAINING

The armed forces of the Soviet Union run many tank, air, artillery and general service schools, but the Ryazan Leninist Kommosol higher airborne command school – twice awarded the Order of the Red Banner – is the only establishment that trains airborne command officers.

All prospective candidates are required to pass a rigorous entrance examination in mathematics, physics, literature and Russian language before gaining admittance to the school.

The students are then introduced to the various types of military hardware – receiving instruction both in their use and maintenance. Future officers must become well-versed in communications, hand-to-hand combat and demolition techniques. Special consideration is given to airborne training, and officers must demonstrate their ability to jump – day or night – into any environment. A full understanding of the parachute equipment is also required, with officers learning how to rig the apparatus to handle heavy military hardware such as the BMD airborne combat vehicle.

In addition to an exhaustive physical training programme, great attention is paid to the development of sport parachuting, and many students of the school have gone on to become world-record holders. By encouraging such standards of excellence in the pursuit of sport, the Ryazan airborne school has ensured that its pupils reach the peak of physical fitness.

This is an elderly weapon, but, like all recoilless guns, is light and easily carried by two men. It is a smooth bore weapon, firing a fin-stabilised projectile, and two shells are available, one a shaped charge anti-armour shell and the other a high explosive shell for general support. The shaped-charge shell will defeat 240mm of armour plate, but since the velocity is relatively low, hits cannot be guaranteed at ranges above 500m. For general support with the high explosive shell, however, the B-10 has a range of 4.5km.

The battalion anti-tank company is provided with three 107mm B-11 recoilless guns. These are larger versions of the B-10 design, firing heavier projectiles to a greater range. The shaped-charge bomb will defeat about 380mm of armour plate and has a practical range of about 500m, while the 13kg high explosive bomb can be fired to a maximum range of 6.6km.

The divisional anti-tank missile battalion is equipped with an indeterminate number of missiles; indeterminate, too, is the precise type used, since battalions are undergoing something of an upheaval as new weapons replace old. What little evidence is available seems to indicate that the AT-4 Spigot and AT-5 Spandrel missiles are now replacing the earlier AT-2 Swatter and AT-3 Sagger models. The AT-4 appears to be a semi-automatic guidance weapon very similar to the Western Milan. There is a ground-emplaced firing post with sight and control unit, to which a pre-packed launch tube containing the missile is clipped. The operator takes aim and fires the missile, which trails a wire behind it. The sight unit is kept aimed at the target by the firer; an infra-red detector in the sight spots a flare in the tail of the missile; measures its displacement from the axis of the sight, and then commands the missile, down the wire, to fly into the sight line. Thus, provided the operator keeps the sight laid on the target throughout the engagement, the missile will conform to his sight line and hit the target. We have no figures for the performance of Spigot, but the comparable Western weapon, Milan, has a 95 per cent hit probability and Spigot should perform similarly. The missile carries a 120mm shaped charge warhead capable of defeating over 500mm of armour plate, and it has a maximum range (governed by the length of trailing wire) of 2500m. Airborne units also carry the Spigot missile launcher on the turret of the BMD-1 combat vehicle; in this application the launcher unit appears to be somewhat differently configured, with the sight unit much lower so that the operator can use the weapon with the minimum of exposure from the turret hatch.

The AT-5 Spandrel has only recently been introduced, and very little is known about it. It is carried in a bank of five launchers on the turret of the BRDM-2 armoured reconnaissance vehicle, and appears to be of somewhat larger calibre than the AT-4. We have no positive identification in Soviet airborne formations, but since the BRDM-2 is used as an air-defence missile carrier, it seems likely that the anti-tank version will eventually form one of the component elements of airborne armament.

Finally, the tank destroyer battalion of the airborne division deploys 31 self-propelled ASU-85 guns. These are full-tracked vehicles weighing some 15 tonnes each, and armed with a D-70 85mm rifled gun in a limited-traverse mount at the front of an armoured superstructure. The gun fires high velocity armour-piercing projectiles which would probably defeat 300mm of armour at 1000m range, and, in addition, it can fire high explosive fragmentation shells for general support and demolition tasks. The ASU-85 also mounts a heavy machine gun, smoke grenade dischargers, and is fitted with infra-red night sights and driving equipment to give it a

During his four years at Ryazan airborne school, the student's life is hard – but never dull. A day's activities may vary from hand-to-hand combat drills (below) and maintenance classes on the BMD airborne combat vehicle (right), to the exacting art of sport parachuting (far right).

Above: Airborne forces are trained to fight in any terrain, with particular emphasis given to the techniques of mountain warfare. Below: Learning how to perform routine maintenance on a BMD.

Below left: Soviet airborne troops are among the few units specially trained in street fighting. Below: An AKS-74 rifle and reserve parachute strapped to his chest, a para reads off his checklist prior to a practice jump.

15

ANTONOV AN-12

Called the Cub-B by NATO (its exact designation is unknown), the Antonov An-12 is based on the older An-10 civil design, its rear fuselage expanded to incorporate a full-width rear ramp and loading doors. The fuselage is pressurised and air-conditioned, and the fuel is carried in 22 compartments located in the wings. The normal capacity is 3981 gallons, allowing a maximum range of 4600km with a full payload of 15,000kg. The standard flightcrew comprises two pilots, a navigator, a radio/radar operator, an engineer and a tail gunner.

In the paratroop role, 100 soldiers can be seated along the sides and centre of the cargo bay. During an air drop, the rear doors are folded upwards and all of the paras would be out of the aircraft within one minute.

The Antonov An-12 is also capable of transporting the PT-76 amphibious tank and airborne combat vehicles such as the BMD, ASU-85 guns, ZSU-23/4 anti-aircraft vehicles, and a variety of surface-to-air missile launchers. Over 500 of these aircraft remain in service, and a small number have been supplied with electronic surveillance equipment in order to monitor signals from NATO ships, aircraft and ground forces.

The Cub-C represents a more extensive modification, and has been equipped as an electronic counter-measures (ECM) aircraft. In this model, the tail turret of the Cub-B has been replaced by a large radar dome. The Antonov An-12 is powered by four Ivchyenko A1-20M single-shaft turbo props, providing a maximum speed of 777 kilometres per hour. Cruising speed, however, is 620 kilometres per hour with a full payload. The aircraft's service ceiling is 33,460ft.

Below: The SA-7 'Grail' rocket launcher fires a 2.5kg warhead to a maximum range of 5km, though its effectiveness is limited to relatively slow moving aircraft. Main picture: Their 73mm guns aimed skywards, a column of BMDs – each capable of carrying an airborne squad – advances through open terrain.

24-hour battlefield capability. With a top speed of about 45 kilometres per hour, the ASU-85 has an operating range of some 250km on one tank of fuel and is usually equipped with auxiliary fuel tanks on the rear of the hull to give additional endurance.

Air defence is catered for on three levels; the most basic weapon is the twin 23mm ZU-23 automatic cannon. This is carried on a light two-wheeled trailer, and consists of two 23mm guns each with a rate of fire of some 900 rounds per minute. The guns are belt fed and fire either high-explosive incendi-

ary or armour-piercing incendiary shells to a maximum altitude of 2500m. The ZU-23 can also be used in the ground role as a high-volume support weapon.

The most recent information, however, suggests that these guns are being rapidly phased out of airborne service and replaced with something entirely different – the SA-9 Gaskin surface-to-air-missile system, known in the Soviet Army as ZRK-BD. This is a self-propelled missile system, carried on the wheeled BRDM-2 chassis, with four missiles in launcher canisters mounted above the turret. Each

missile weighs about 30kg, reaches a speed of Mach 1.5 in flight, and has a range of 6500m. The warhead is equipped with an infra-red seeker unit and a proximity fuze which will detonate the explosive content when within 1.5m of its target. Although it is possible to link these launchers to radar for 24-hour coverage, the system that is deployed with airborne divisions is strictly a fair-weather weapon, relying upon the use of optical sights to acquire the target, and then upon the heat-seeking capability of the missiles to engage successfully.

Dropped from an An-12 Cub transport, an army vehicle (below centre) relies upon a vast array of parachutes to slow its descent before the retro rockets are ignited. Bottom (left to right): ASU-85 assault guns parade through Red Square. Trim vanes raised to increase stability, BMDs demonstrate their amphibious capability.

Heavily armed, with a flexible organisation that allows rapid deployment of units varying in size from a squad to a division, the airborne forces are likely to remain at the forefront of Soviet military strategy. Below: An ASU-57 self-propelled assault gun is manoeuvred onto an airmobile platform before being placed aboard the An-12 transport. Although the An-12 still comprises the backbone of the force's aircraft, the introduction of improved, heavier weapons such as the ASU-85 has been accompanied by moves to replace the An-12 with the Ilyushin Il-76 heavy cargo airlifter. The result of this is a gradual shift away from conventional paratroop operations, towards an airborne strategy that makes more extensive use of air-landing and parachute techniques.

The third type of air defence weapon is the Strela-2, known in the West as the SA-7 Grail. This is a shoulder-fired rocket that appears to be based on the American Redeye system. The operator places the launcher on his shoulder, and, taking aim at the target through a simple optical sight, presses the trigger to its first stage. The missile's infra-red seeker head is now operational, and as soon as it has acquired its target an audible signal is sounded to alert the operator. He then presses the trigger to its second stage which fires the rocket. The missile has a maximum range of about 5km and is programmed to self-destruct if the target has not been reached after 15 seconds of flight. The warhead is high explosive and has an impact fuze.

The final element in the equipment of the airborne forces is mobility, and for this the BMD airborne combat vehicle was designed. The BMD went into service in 1970, and although it was not publicly seen until 1973, it was still far ahead of anything which the West was capable of producing at that time. These vehicles are airportable, fully amphibious and can also be parachute dropped – each airborne division is equipped with 330.

The Soviet airborne forces are among the best equipped troops in the world

The BMD is a tracked vehicle with a welded steel hull. The driver sits centrally at the front; on his left is the vehicle commander and on his right is the machine gunner, who operates two 7.62mm machine guns that are set into the hull and fire forward. Behind this compartment is the turret, armed with a 73mm smoothbore gun that fires a fin-stabilised shaped-charge projectile with rocket boost. This gun is fed by a 40-round automatic magazine to the right and rear of the gunner. In the early models, the BMD had a launch ramp above the gun barrel to accommodate the Sagger anti-tank guided missile, but this is now being replaced by a launcher post for the Spandrel missile, mounted on the right side of the turret. There is also a 7.62mm machine gun mounted loosely on the turret for air defence or ground shooting. One variant model, the BMD-81-1, mounts a high-velocity 30mm cannon in the turret in place of the 73mm gun, and although little is known about this weapon, Western experts believe that it uses discarding-sabot

armour-piercing ammunition suitable for the destruction of enemy light armoured vehicles.

There is a second variant model that is seen in airborne formations; this is a command vehicle which has no turret, the body being enclosed and provided with communication equipment and other command facilities.

Behind the turret of the BMD is an open compartment with a concertina-style cover that opens forward, revealing seats for six men, plus room for ammunition, stores and an automatic grenade launcher. Beneath this compartment is the V-6 diesel engine and the transmission. The vehicle weighs 6700kg in combat order, can travel at 80 kilometres per hour on roads, 10 kilometres per hour in water (propelled by two water-jet units), and has a range of 320km.

The Soviet airborne forces are among the best equipped troops in the world, and the ample provision of transport aircraft ensures that they can be deployed over considerable distances at very short notice. All their equipment is air-droppable, either in containers (for smaller items), or on shock platforms suspended by parachute in the case of artillery and vehicles. These platforms are released from the aircraft by parachute, descend steadily and are arrested close to the ground by the firing of retro-rockets attached to the parachute suspensions. A weight, dangling 20m beneath the platform, strikes the ground and ignites the rockets, which then slow the final descent. According to reports the eventual contact with the ground is so controlled that vehicle springs and suspension are barely deflected.

Soviet airborne forces, and their equipment, have been seen in action in Afghanistan, though not in the airborne role. As with other armies, the Soviets look upon their airborne troops as elite infantry who can be used in the normal ground role if necessary, and it is in this role that they have been employed in Afghanistan. Whether there is a future for airborne troops in the face of modern air defence systems is a question which is often debated; whatever the answer, the Soviets have a well equipped and highly motivated fighting force at their disposal.

THE AUTHOR Ian Hogg is an authority on smallarms, modern weapons systems and equipment, and the technology of warfare.

ALL-AMERICAN
AIRBORNE

In July 1943, paras from the 82nd Airborne Division stormed the Axis defences on Sicily and snatched victory from the jaws of defeat

'DISASTERS THAT LED TO VICTORY.' That describes the night parachute drops by two regiments of the American 82nd Airborne Division on Sicily in July 1943. Spread far and wide by gale-force winds and fired on by friendly guns, the paratroopers might have thought that this, their first combat jump, was doomed to failure. Instead, they fought hard and accomplished results out of all proportion to the small size of their force. By assuring the swift conquest of Sicily, the paras gave the Allies the stepping-stone they needed in order to cross the Mediterranean from North Africa to Italy.

The task of ousting Axis forces from Sicily had fallen to a combined British-American force under the overall command of General Dwight D. Eisenhower. The assault was timed for early July 1943, and could be expected to encounter stiff resistance from Axis forces under the command of General Alfredo Guzzoni. Guzzoni had 10 Italian and two German divisions at his disposal, amounting to over 200,000 troops. Six divisions had been deployed to defend the coast, with the remaining six held in mobile reserve. The latter included the seasoned 'Hermann Göring' Panzer Division, equipped with Panzerkampfwagen Mk IIIs, IVs and VIs.

'This worked out well, but bayonet practice at 2am was a little too unique to bring enthusiasm'

The Allied plan for Operation Husky was formulated by Eisenhower, and called for night landings by American paratroopers and British glidermen. These would precede the main amphibious landings that were scheduled for 10 July. The airborne troops would seize key terrain and bridges in an attempt to prevent enemy forces from dislodging the amphibious troops. The British gliderborne troops from the 1st Air Landing Brigade would lead off, coming down a few kilometres south of Syracuse, on the east coast of Sicily. This stage of the assault, known as Operation Ladbroke, was intended to wreak havoc on enemy defences prior to the landing of General Bernard L. Montgomery's British Eighth Army. The American paratroopers of the 82nd Airborne Division would begin their descent towards Sicily's southern coast soon after the British glidermen. A formation of C-47 troop carriers would drop the paras behind beaches on the southwest shore. A few hours later, at dawn on 10 July, the three divisions of General George S. Patton's US Seventh Army would storm these beaches. The 1st Infantry Division would come ashore near Gela. Fourteen miles to the southeast, the 45th Infantry Division would land near Scoglitti. The landing beach of the 3rd Infantry Division was farther west, at Licata.

Commanded by Major-General Matthew B. Ridgway, the 82nd Airborne Division arrived in Morocco in mid-May 1943 and began training immediately. Although pushed to the limit of their endurance, the paras displayed a keen sense of humour. One trooper later wrote: 'All this worked out well, but bayonet practice at 2am was a little too unique to bring enthusiasm.'

In June, after careful consideration, Major-General Ridgway chose the 505th Parachute Infantry Regiment for the honour of the night drop. He reinforced the three battalions of the 505th with the 3rd Battalion, 504th Parachute Infantry Regiment. These four infantry battalions, together with supporting engineers, artillery, and other arms, comprised the 505th Combat Team (505 CT). Comprising over 3000 paratroopers, the force was commanded by Colonel James M. Gavin.

In early June, one month before the drop, Colonel Gavin took off on a night reconnaissance of the proposed landing zone. Together with two of his battalion commanders, Gavin flew over the planned route. The checkpoints of Linosa and Malta showed up clearly in the moonlight. Gavin was relieved – that would make navigation easier on jump night.

The planned drop zone for the 505th Combat Team was based on the landings of Patton's seaborne divisions. By capturing the high ground behind the beaches allocated to the 1st and 45th Infantry Divisions, the four battalions of the combat team would be placed in a commanding position. The paras would be situated to the rear of the Axis coastal defences, enabling them to shield Patton's forces from any counter-attacks launched by General Guzzoni's mobile reserves.

In preparation for the drop, 18 makeshift airfields were constructed in an arc around Kairouan, Tunisia, only 250 miles west of Sicily. Transport units arrived with their C-47s and gliders, and British and

Previous page: While a jumpmaster prepares to leap from the door of a C-47 transport during pre-invasion exercises at Oujda (right), an 'All-American' para surveys the barren Moroccan terrain during a brief respite from the arduous training programme. Top, far right: Transport pilots from the Troop Carrier Command listen attentively to the pre-mission briefing. Once the combat team's artillery has been hung underneath the C-47s (above right), the paras use the 'buddy system' to check their equipment (bottom right) before boarding the carriers (right). Below right: An airborne soldier exudes the confidence that characterised the 82nd Airborne Division. Below: Major-General James Gavin, the commander of the 82nd Airborne. In February 1945, when this picture was taken, Gavin was the youngest major-general in the US Army.

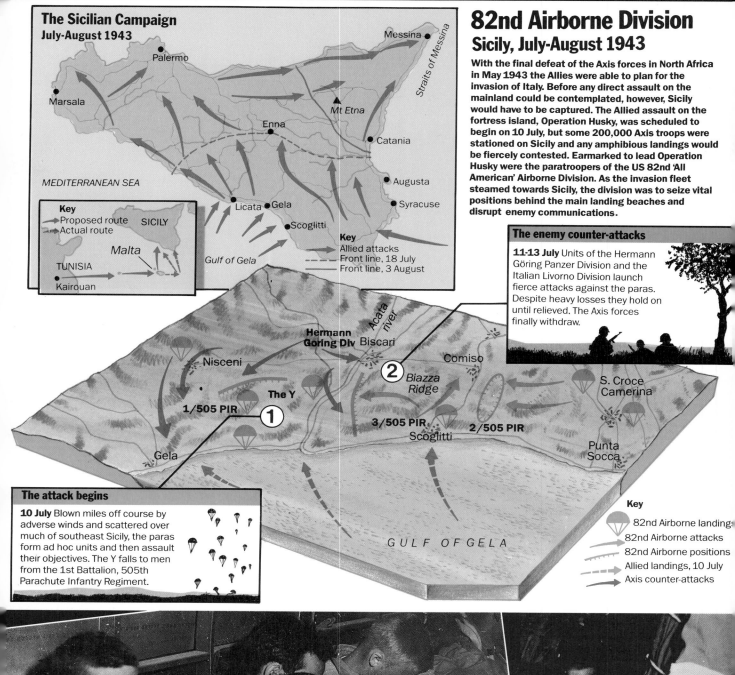

The Sicilian Campaign
July-August 1943

Messina
Palermo
Marsala
Straits of Messina
Mt Etna
Enna
Catania
MEDITERRANEAN SEA
Augusta
Licata · Gela
Syracuse
Scoglitti

Key
→ Proposed route
⇢ Actual route
SICILY
Malta
TUNISIA
Kairouan

Gulf of Gela

Key
Allied attacks
Front line, 18 July
Front line, 3 August

82nd Airborne Division
Sicily, July-August 1943

With the final defeat of the Axis forces in North Africa in May 1943 the Allies were able to plan for the invasion of Italy. Before any direct assault on the mainland could be contemplated, however, Sicily would have to be captured. The Allied assault on the fortress island, Operation Husky, was scheduled to begin on 10 July, but some 200,000 Axis troops were stationed on Sicily and any amphibious landings would be fiercely contested. Earmarked to lead Operation Husky were the paratroopers of the US 82nd 'All American' Airborne Division. As the invasion fleet steamed towards Sicily, the division was to seize vital positions behind the main landing beaches and disrupt enemy communications.

The enemy counter-attacks

11-13 July Units of the Hermann Göring Panzer Division and the Italian Livorno Division launch fierce attacks against the paras. Despite heavy losses they hold on until relieved. The Axis forces finally withdraw.

Acata river
Hermann Goring Div Biscari
Nisceni
Comiso
② *Biazza Ridge*
The Y
S. Croce Camerina
1/505 PIR
①
3/505 PIR
2/505 PIR
Scoglitti
Gela
Punta Socca

The attack begins

10 July Blown miles off course by adverse winds and scattered over much of southeast Sicily, the paras form ad hoc units and then assault their objectives. The Y falls to men from the 1st Battalion, 505th Parachute Infantry Regiment.

GULF OF GELA

Key
🪂 82nd Airborne landing
→ 82nd Airborne attacks
— 82nd Airborne positions
⇢ Allied landings, 10 July
→ Axis counter-attacks

American troops moved into bivouac areas nearby. The training continued relentlessly, both day and night. According to one veteran of the 82nd, the men were now ready for action: 'With the body hardened and the mind still filled with the disagreeable training area, anticipation for the future and combat could not have been keener. Morale was at a peak.'

The battalion commanders briefed their men on the flight route, drop zone, and objectives. One key target, a critical road junction east of Gela, was dubbed 'The Y'. It was protected by 16 pillbox positions whose guns were sited to provide interlocking bands of fire. The enemy position was duplicated on the ground at Kairouan, and the paratroopers spent several days and nights perfecting their plan of attack.

On the morning of 9 July, the men of Gavin's 505th Combat Team made ready for their trip to Sicily. Following supper at 1600, the paras carried out last-minute weapons and equipment checks before being transported to the airfields. While the heavy weapons and the 75mm pack howitzers of the parachute artillery were hung in parapacks on the belly racks of the C-47s, the airborne troops waited for the signal to chute up. The new 2.36in rocket launchers were hung with care – in close-quarters combat, these bazookas were the paras' only defence against enemy armour.

Jumpmasters lined up their troops in single file and helped them into the C-47 transports. Just as the engines of Colonel Gavin's aircraft were revving up for take-off, an airman from the weather station ran across the airstrip. 'Is Colonel Gavin here?' he inquired after reaching the C-47. Gavin leaned out of the door only to hear the following words, 'I was told to tell you that the wind is going to be 35 miles per hour, west to east. They thought you would want to know.' This was not welcome news. In training, jumps had been called off when the winds rose above 15 miles per hour due to an unacceptably high number of injuries.

The flight plan for the 266 C-47s was simple. From Kairouan, the formation would fly east across the Mediterranean at low level. After flying over Malta, the formation would dogleg to the left towards Sicily. As far as navigation was concerned, it was a piece of cake. Once the aircraft had taken off, however, the wind took over, blowing the formations off course. As the C-47s bounced and bucked in the low-level turbulence, navigators and jumpmasters watched for checkpoints. But none came up. The formation was dispersed and blown off course. Instead of reaching their target in an orderly stream, the aircraft arrived over Sicily singly and in small groups over the entire southeast and southern coasts. Time to jump. The red light came on. The paras clicked the snap fasteners of their parachute static lines onto the cable, and jumpmasters ran through the equipment check. Once the men had sounded off OK, the jumpmasters stood in the door and awaited the green light.

Dotted over the dark countryside below, gun flashes signalled the start of the pre-invasion bombardment. All over southern Sicily, green lights winked in the C-47s. Gavin and the other jumpmasters of the 505th Combat Team leapt into the darkness of the propeller blast, leading their men on the 800ft drop to the ground. In less than four hours, the main assault force would hit the beaches. Gavin had planned to have a compact force of four battalions concentrated around the Gela drop zone. Instead, thanks to the high winds, his combat team was strewn over a 65-mile swathe of southern Sicily.

Left: Lieutenant-Colonel Kouns urges his men to uphold the fine traditions of the 82nd. Far left: Emplaned in a C-47 en route to Sicily, paras of the 82nd Airborne Division wait for the signal that will send them into action, jumping out of their transports into the skies over Sicily (below right).

WHY SICILY?

At the time of the Casablanca Conference in January 1943, the Allies in North Africa were squeezing Axis forces into Tunisia. Logistical problems had resulted in the delay of a cross-Channel attack in Europe, and Churchill and Roosevelt therefore decided to concentrate the enormous resources that were gathered in the Mediterranean theatre against Italy.

This strategy was to be pursued once the Axis powers had been defeated in North Africa, and its advantages were three-fold. First, German strength from the eastern Front would be diverted into Italy, enabling Stalin to complete the destruction of the German Sixth Army. Second, there was the possibility of knocking Italy out of the war. And finally, control of the Mediterranean would speed the flow of supplies to Southeast Asia, in addition to threatening German forces in the Balkans.

Since Italy was too far from the North African coast for sustained air and logistical operations in support of an invasion force, Sicily was chosen as the objective for an amphibious landing. Sardinia was rejected on the grounds that enemy forces left on Sicily would still be in a position to hamper the passage of Allied convoys in the Mediterranean.

Well over a tenth of Gavin's force, 414 paratroopers, dropped near the east coast. Slapping down hard behind the British beaches, elements of the 3rd Battalion, 505th Parachute Infantry Regiment, aided the British landings and fought side by side with them for several days. The remainder of the battalion landed much closer to the drop zone, coming down near Biazza Ridge. Most of the 1st Battalion, 505th Parachute Infantry Regiment, and the 3rd Battalion, 504th Parachute Infantry Regiment, were strung out in small groups on the high ground to the east of Gela. Many injuries had been incurred during the drop, and casualties mounted once contact with the German and Italian forces, now on full alert, had been made. However, the paras fought hard and created confusion among the defenders by cutting every communications wire they could find. The 2nd Battalion, under the command of Major Mark Alexander, landed more than 15 miles east of the Gela drop zone. The unit assembled in good order, with few casualties, and got to work almost immediately. The paras stormed the high ground overlooking the beaches and attacked Italian pillboxes and defensive positions. By noon on the second day, 11 July, they had captured the towns of Santa Croce Camerina and Vittoria.

The sound of rifle and machine-gun fire echoed through the hills as the paras stormed enemy positions

Twenty miles east of the drop zone, Colonel Gavin, in command of more than 3000 paratroopers, found himself with only five when he got out of his chute and looked around. Within an hour, however, his small force numbered more than 20 fighters. All around the horizon were gunflashes and the sounds of small-arms fire. Gavin did what he had learned 20 years earlier as a cadet at West Point: when in doubt, head towards the sound of the guns. He and his men headed west towards the heaviest firing.

Nine miles east of Gela, elements of Gavin's combat team were engaged in heavy fighting. Part of the 3rd Battalion, 504th Parachute Infantry Regiment, had set up a position commanding the main road from Niscemi to Biscari. The paras held their ground for three days and prevented the movement of German reinforcements to the Allied beachheads.

By daylight on 10 July, parts of Lieutenant-Colonel Arthur Gorham's 1st Battalion had assembled into a 95-man force. The unit prepared itself for an attack on the combat team's primary objective – the Y. Led by Gorham and Captain Edwin Sayre, the paras stormed the pillboxes and captured their target after a furious firefight. They held the position all morning, greeting scouts from the 1st Infantry Division when they walked into sight at about 1130 hours.

General Guzzoni's reaction to the Allied landings was swift. From his command post in Enna, 35 miles north of Gela, he ordered immediate counter-attacks against the American and British troops that were ashore at Gela and Syracuse. However, the paras had cut many telephone lines during the previous night and this prevented the Axis units from receiving their orders until late morning. In the Gela area, the earliest counter-attacks were made by the Italian 'Livorno' Division on the west, and the German Hermann Göring Panzer Division from the north and east. After both had been halted in their tracks by the paras' dogged resistance, Axis forces withdrew northwards and regrouped for a fresh assault the following day.

By mid-morning on 11 July, Colonel Gavin had mustered a force of 250 paras and was approaching Biazza Ridge. A platoon from the 45th Infantry Division warned Gavin that German troops were already entrenched on the high ground. If the enemy advanced south towards the beach at Scoglitti, the 45th Division would be in grave danger. Gavin ordered his men to attack. The sound of rifle and machine-gun fire echoed through the hills as the paras stormed

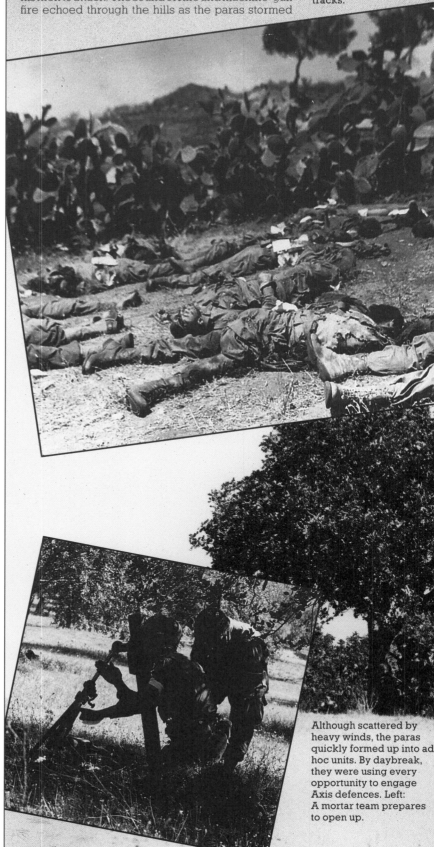

Below: The bloody carnage of war. On Biazza Ridge, many paras fell victim to the German heavy armour before sheer bravery and determination stopped the enemy advance in its tracks.

Although scattered by heavy winds, the paras quickly formed up into ad hoc units. By daybreak, they were using every opportunity to engage Axis defences. Left: A mortar team prepares to open up.

enemy positions and took the ridge after fierce close-quarters fighting. However, the attack drew heavy German mortar and artillery fire. This was followed by a counter-attack by panzers armed with 88mm guns. To their dismay, the paratroopers found that their puny bazookas could not penetrate the Tigers' heavy armour.

A naval gunfire liaison officer had jumped with Gavin the first night, and the commander of the 505th Combat Team now took advantage of this fact. He instructed the officer to call for a trial round from one of the Allied ships moored offshore. It slammed in on a German tank position with incredible precision. More rounds followed, and the tide of battle

began to turn. Soon after 1700, the ridge was reinforced by more troops and six Sherman M4 tanks from the 45th Division. Gavin counter-attacked just before nightfall. Screaming and yelling, the paratroopers charged the enemy and captured a Tiger tank before overrunning German mortar positions. The Germans fled. However, the darkness that descended on Gavin's triumph was to be the cloak of disaster for the remaining battalions of the 82nd Airborne Division's other regiment – the 504th.

Several hours earlier, on the morning of 11 July, General Ridgway had sent a message to Kairouan. It informed the commander of the 504th Parachute Infantry Regiment, Colonel Reuben Tucker, that his two reinforced battalions were to parachute onto the Farello airstrip, near Gela, that same night. Ridgway had then sought assurances from the navy that its ships would not fire on the columns of C-47s as they made their way towards Sicily's southern shore. During the course of the day, however, German aircraft had made several large strikes against the beachheads and ships. At 2240, only minutes after the last of the enemy bombers had withdrawn, the stream of C-47s carrying Tucker's regiment reached the shoreline in good formation. In the darkness, a gunner mistakenly thought the Germans were returning and opened fire. Others followed suit, until the entire formation was being blasted by Allied fire.

'Everywhere, the Germans and Italians saw small groups of troopers coming out of the night'

When the guns finally ceased firing, 23 of Tucker's planes had been lost, blowing up in the air or crashing into land or water. By the following night, Colonel Tucker was able to assemble only 550 of the 2000 men who had taken off with him. However, despite the loss of 318 paras killed or wounded, Tucker had the bulk of his unit assembled and ready to fight by the morning of 13 July. On 19 July, with the beachheads firmly secured, Patton pushed westwards with the 82nd Airborne Division and the 2nd Armored Division, leaving Montgomery's Eighth Army to advance northwards.

By 18 August, the Axis forces had escaped across the Strait of Messina to Italy, leaving behind almost 159,000 casualties and prisoners. In contrast, the total American and British casualties were less than 20,000. The 82nd Airborne Division lost 206 men killed, 810 wounded and 12 missing in action. Colonel Gavin later paid the following tribute to the men under his command:

> 'The American trooper has the mental and physical courage to try anything, asking and expecting no odds. Everywhere, the Germans and Italians saw small groups of troopers coming out of the night. The panic of not knowing how many were coming, or from where, had its demoralising psychological effect.'

By preventing Axis mobile reserves, particularly the Hermann Göring Panzer Division, from reaching the Allied beachheads, the paratroopers played a crucial role in the success of Operation Husky. In Sicily, the fighting spirit of the 82nd Airborne Division set standards of the highest order.

THE AUTHOR F. Clifton Berry, Jr writes from Washington on military subjects. In the mid-1950s, he served in the 82nd Airborne Division as a paratroop officer in the 325th and 505th Parachute Infantry Regiments.

BROADWAY BURMA

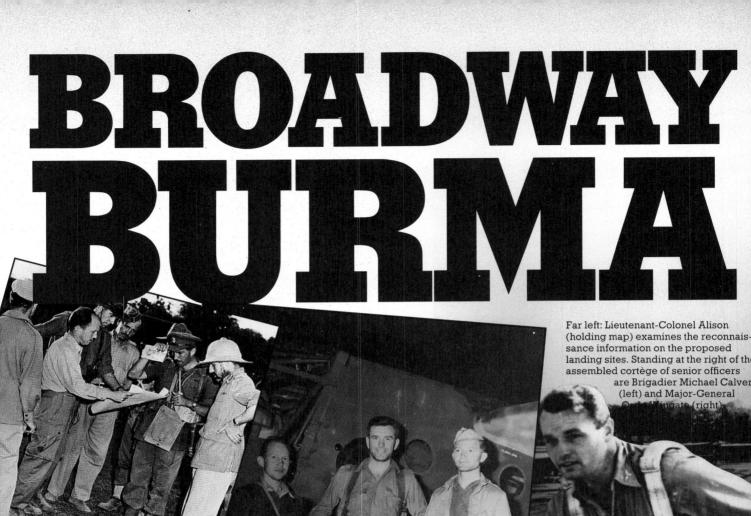

Far left: Lieutenant-Colonel Alison (holding map) examines the reconnaissance information on the proposed landing sites. Standing at the right of the assembled cortège of senior officers are Brigadier Michael Calvert (left) and Major-General Orde Wingate (right)

In March 1944, the men of No.1 Air Commando created military history by pioneering the techniques of airborne invasion

IT'S JUST A FIELD covered with buffalo grass, in the midst of a jungle where it has slept for countless years under the Burmese sun. Marked on no map, it was unknown and nameless until the necessities of war gave it sudden importance. Then one night, many men in gliders slipped like mammoth eagles down through the hazy moonlight, making history in aerial warfare and giving to it the name of "Broadway Burma."'

Written by a colonel in the United States Army Air Force (USAAF), these words describe the airborne invasion of Burma in March 1944. The success of Operation Thursday, as it was codenamed, relied on one remarkable unit. This unit was No. 1 Air Commando, USAAF.

In February 1943, Major-General Orde Wingate's hastily formed Long Range Penetration (LRP) brigades had been sent into Burma to harass the Japanese lines of communication in the north of the country. By creating alarm and confusion, it was hoped that the Japanese would be discouraged from invading India. Known as the Chindits after a mythical dragon, this combined British, Gurkha and Burmese force had been trained to fight as raiders and guerrillas. After six weeks of operations, having fulfilled their role in a series of hit-and-run raids, Wingate's force crossed back into India and China. Although the Chindits had lost one third of their number to disease and the enemy, Wingate was convinced that the light infantry brigades, supported and supplied by the air, could survive behind enemy lines. However, he also appreciated that a method of evacuating the wounded back to India had to be worked out if the Chindit operations were to be repeated.

Wingate accompanied Winston Churchill to the Quebec Conference with the US President, Franklin D. Roosevelt, in the autumn of 1943, and managed to convince both leaders of the importance of air support in the Burma operations. He was introduced to General Henry 'Hap' Arnold, the Commanding General USAAF, who was impressed with Wingate's ideas. Arnold, however, went even further and envisaged providing the air-landing force with increased firepower in the form of fighter-bombers

Above, far left: Alison, Lieutenant-Colonel Scott (centre) and a glider pilot from No.1 Air Commando pose for the camera immediately prior to take-off. Left: Lieutenant-Colonel Cochran, seen here on the wing-tip of his P-51 Mustang. Above: Ready to roll. A row of gliders at Lalaghat airfield reveals the enormous scale of Operation Thursday.

Left: Wearing his characteristic sun helmet, Major-General Wingate briefs some of the Chindits and pilots on the mission that lies ahead of them.

and medium bombers. Once the concept of No. 1 Air Commando Force had been agreed upon, Arnold set the ball rolling by recruiting leaders for this revolutionary fighting unit.

His first choice was Lieutenant-Colonel Philip Cochran, a confident, aggressive and imaginative officer who had already amassed a distinguished combat record as a fighter pilot in North Africa. Second on Arnold's list was Lieutenant-Colonel John Alison. Like Cochran, Alison had distinguished himself in action when flying with the famous 'Flying Tigers' in China. While Cochran was an outspoken and extrovert leader of men, Alison was a more disciplined and articulate type, thoroughly versed in the planning and administration that was an essential part of successful operations. General Arnold appointed both men as 'co-commanders'.

Cochran and Alison had carte blanche orders from General Arnold to procure the necessary equipment and personnel for their new command. They chose the best available. Major Grant Mahoney, an 'ace' in the Pacific Theatre, was selected to lead the fighter section and, as pilots were brought into the unit, they in turn recommended others. Following flight training in North Carolina, Cochran and the first elements of No. 1 Air

Commando arrived at Delhi, India, on 13 November 1943. While the crews of the Transport Squadron practised the 'snatching' of loaded Waco gliders off the ground, the pilots of the Fighter Squadron engaged their P-51 Mustangs in mock dogfights to practise their aerial skills.

The Air Commando's first combat mission was flown on 3 February 1944, led by Cochran himself, and the B-25H Mitchell Bomber Squadron joined the fight one week later. Lieutenant-Colonel R. Smith, the commanding officer of the Bomber Squadron, later described the tactics his aircrews adopted when attacking the Japanese lines of communication in northern Burma:

Main picture: A flight of four Mustangs 'buzzes' one of the home bases in Assam, India, having returned from a patrol over Broadway. A B-25 medium bomber can also be seen coming in to land on the 'dry sod' fair-weather airfield. All of the aircraft are emblazoned with five stripes on their fuselage – the official marking of No. 1 Air Commando.

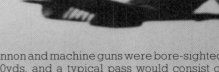

'Our cannon and machine guns were bore-sighted for 1000yds, and a typical pass would consist of three cannon rounds at approximately 1500, 1000 and 500yds, interspersed with bursts of machine gun fire ... Most attacks were made at between 200 and 250 miles per hour ... most of us could hit a target the size of a one-car garage.'

By the end of February 1944, the fighters, bombers and transports of No. 1 Air Commando had been dispersed to forward airfields in India. On 29 February, gliders were called in to assist elements of the Chindits' 16th Brigade in crossing the Chindwin River. Two gliders, carrying folding boats and outboard engines, landed on a sand bar. After being unloaded, they were 'snatched' by a C-47 transport and returned to base.

In early March 1944, the Japanese crossed the Chindwin River and began heading for Imphal and Kohima. The situation demanded an urgent response, and several reconnaisance missions were flown by B-25s in an effort to find suitable landing sites for the Allied forces. The task of spearheading

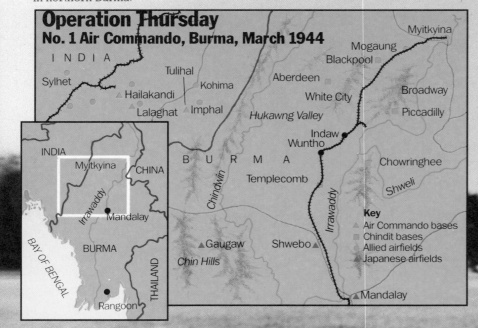

Operation Thursday
No. 1 Air Commando, Burma, March 1944

INDIA

Sylhet

Tulihal
Kohima

Hailakandi

Lalaghat Imphal

Hukawng Valley

Myitkyina

Mogaung
Blackpool

Aberdeen

White City

Broadway

Piccadilly

Indaw
Wuntho

BURMA

Chowringhee

Templecomb

Shweli

Chindwin

Irrawaddy

INDIA

Myitkyina CHINA

Irrawaddy

Mandalay

BAY OF BENGAL

BURMA

Chin Hills

Gaugaw

Shwebo

Mandalay

THAILAND

Rangoon

Key
▲ Air Commando bases
■ Chindit bases
● Allied airfields
▲ Japanese airfields

the British airborne operations against the Japanese lines of communication was given to the 77th Indian Infantry Brigade, under the command of Brigadier Michael Calvert. The method chosen was an assault glider landing, with the Waco gliders being towed by C-47 pilots from No. 1 Air Commando.

By 6 March, the gliders were assembled at Lalaghat airfield, 100 miles inside the Indian border. Cochran concluded his mission briefing with the words: 'Nothing you've ever done, nothing you are ever going to do, counts now. Only the next few hours. Tonight you are going to find your souls.' Two jungle clearings had been designated as the landing sites. The first, known as 'Piccadilly', was east of the Irrawaddy Valley, while the second, codenamed 'Broadway', lay to the west. Cochran despatched Lieutenant Russhon to reconnoitre both landing sites, and the lieutenant returned from his mission just as the British troops were climbing aboard the gliders. His report indicated that a landing at Piccadilly would be impossible due to the area being blocked by logs. This caused great consternation all round, but Calvert informed Cochran that he would be content to see the whole of his brigade land at Broadway. Wingate agreed to the proposed change in plan and gave the go-ahead for the transports and gliders to take-off.

The first wave of gliders, carrying the 1st King's (Liverpool) Regiment and Calvert's tactical headquarters, arrived at Broadway. However, huge semi-circular ditches, two to three feet deep, had been formed when monsoon floods had deposited teak logs from the Rangoon sawmills on the landing site. Lieutenant-Colonel Alison had arrived in the first wave to act as an air-traffic controller, and together with Calvert he started to organise the placing of

In addition to resupply, evacuation and fire support, the men of No. 1 Air Commando also took over responsibility for the retrieval of damaged aircraft. When a C-47 transport came unstuck on swampy ground behind the Japanese lines, Captain Charles Herzog (above, third from right) flew in a reclamation crew under the command of Chief Warrant Officer Herbert Carr (standing, sixth from right). With the help of Chindits and Burmese farmers, the transport was swiftly repaired and flown back to base.

flares to mark the ditches. But their task was immense. As the main body of gliders started to land, many collided with their immobile predecessors. Initially, neither Calvert nor Alison was able to contact base and warn Wingate of the situation. Eventually, Calvert got through and transmitted the signal 'Soya-Link' to prevent the despatching of further consignments.

On 7 March, a dawn count revealed that 37 Waco gliders had landed with the loss of 31 men, 27 of whom were Chindits. A further 33 men required evacuation by the Air Commando's light plane squadrons because of injuries incurred during the night landings. On the positive side, 539 Chindits, three mules and 29,000lb of stores had been brought to earth safely. Calvert sent off the reassuring signal 'Pork-Sausage' to signify that the airborne invasion could continue.

The 1st King's Regiment, commanded by Lieutenant-Colonel Scott, was given two main responsibilities. The first of these was to conduct wide-ranging patrols that would provide ample warning of any encroachment by the enemy. Second, the regiment was instructed to clear Broadway of immobile gliders and help with the construction of a 4700ft runway in preparation for the arrival of the Dakotas. This task was carried out under the supervision of Lieutenant Brockett, an Air Commando engineer who, together with his bulldozer, had landed by glider in the first wave. The men worked ceaselessly, and by 1730 hours the first flight of six Dakotas, carrying Wingate in the leading aircraft, was able to land. A further 67 fully loaded RAF and USAAF Dakotas landed that night, carrying the remainder of the King's Regiment, several Bofors light anti-aircraft guns, and the advance party of the 3/9th Gurkha Rifles.

Also on 7 March, an alternative landing site – codenamed 'Chowrinchee' – was opened east of the Irrawaddy River. Its development was slow, however, and by 9 March it was closed due to Japanese attacks. Meanwhile, 120 Dakotas were landing each night at Broadway. By 12 March, the two landing sites had together received a total of 9000 personnel, 175 horses, 1283 mules, 509,000lb of stores and two troops of anti-aircraft and field guns. Once the landings had been completed, the Chindit column moved off into the jungle and fanned out to attack Japanese lines of communication. A garrison battalion – the 3/9 Gurkha Rifles and a troop of 25-pounder guns – stayed behind to man Broadway's defences. In the space of seven days, a defended airfield had been constructed 200 miles behind enemy lines. From here, a total of five brigades could be supported and reinforced.

While the landings at Broadway and Chowrinchee had been taking place, the remainder of Cochran's aircrew were far from idle. In fact, the series of

resounding victories that Cochran's pilots had scored over the Japanese Air Force gave the Allies almost complete dominance of the skies over Burma. Unarmed transport aircraft were able to deliver stores and men to units on the ground and evacuate casualties without fear of being attacked by enemy aircraft. This dominance in the air was later to prove crucial to the success of the British Fourteenth Army, commanded by General William Slim.

Cochran had appreciated that the greatest threat to the airborne invasion would come from enemy fighters. He was therefore determined to seek out and destroy Japanese aircraft before, and during, the airborne operation. On the fourth day of the

invasion, when intelligence reported that the Japanese were massing aircraft in the Shwebo area of central Burma, the fighter aircraft of No. 1 Air Commando went into action. Arming each of his P-51 Mustangs with one 500lb bomb, Major Grant Mahoney led a 21-fighter formation in a wide sweep of the area. After pounding Mandalay airfield and dropping their auxiliary fuel tanks as incendiaries, the Mustangs spotted more than 60 enemy aircraft, including heavy bombers, at the airfields of Onbauk and Shwebo. Japanese Oscar fighters were circling overhead, but Mahoney was undeterred – he ordered his pilots to ignore the fighters and concentrate on the bombers. The Mustangs swooped down and began to strafe their targets. Five bombers exploded during one attack, and the Japanese groundcrew were sent into a state of total confusion. Avoiding a dogfight with the Oscars, Mahoney's formation set course back to base.

Meanwhile, Cochran had been listening in on the radio net and realised that the presence of an enemy bomber fleet was too good an opportunity to miss. Having been given exact details by Mahoney, Cochran ordered the mobilisation of all 12 of his B-25 Mitchell medium bombers at Hailikandi base, 100 miles inside the Indian border. The pilots of the Air Commando were superb all-rounders and, within 45 minutes of the Mustang pilots arriving back at base, many of the pilots exchanged their charges for bombers and set off again for the enemy airfield, 300 miles away. Lieutenant-Colonel R. Smith, and his deputy, Walter Radovitch, were two such pilots. Having spent six hours in the cockpit of their fighters, both Smith and Radovitch were in the air again without even having time for a cup of coffee!

The bombers arrived back over their target just as the sun was setting, and once again the Japanese were caught completely by surprise. Coming in at 1000ft, they employed fragmentation and incendiary bombs to pound the

enemy airfield. Twelve Mitsubishi Ki-21 bombers were destroyed, and the 75mm cannon of the Mitchells claimed several gasoline trucks and an oil storage depot. In the course of one day, an Air Commando assault force of 21 fighters and 12 bombers had destroyed a total of 48 enemy aircraft. Major-General George Stratemeyer, commander of the USAAF in the Indian-Burma sector, reported: 'In one mission, this US unit has obliterated nearly one fifth of the known Japanese air force in Burma.'

This destruction of the potential air threat to the second Chindit expedition was only part of Cochran's task. The Air Commando was instructed to use its fighters and bombers on all types of interdiction missions to interrupt and destroy Japanese communications – preventing an enemy build-up against the air-landed troops.

On 13 March, two days after the completion of Operation Thursday, Japanese fighters and ground forces discovered Broadway and attempted to dislodge the Chindits in a series of attacks. From this point on, the pilots of No. 1 Air Commando made their landings and take-offs in the face of heavy mortar and machine-gun fire. The Chindits, however, were performing the role that had been asked of them. Over half of the Japanese 5th Air Division was being diverted from its main task – that of supporting the ground troops invading India.

The Chindits were fighting over a vast area – from Bhamo, east of the Irrawaddy River, to Mogaung in the north – and the Air Commando provided vital air-artillery support during clashes with Japanese ground forces. In addition, the prompt evacuation of wounded from the jungle battlefields to the base hospital in

Far right: At one of the Assam airfields in India, groundcrew fasten a drop-tank under the wing of a Mustang. Once armed with its 500lb bomb (far right, below) the fighter will be ready for a long-range mission against Japanese lines of communication. Bottom right: Chindits coax a recalcitrant mule into one of the C-47 transports prior to taking off for Broadway. Below: As dawn breaks on 7 March, men who arrived at Broadway in the first wave prepare to clear the landing site of aircraft rendered immobile by unforeseen obstacles.

THE REAL FLIP CORKIN

In 1941, Lieutenant Philip Cochran (above right) took command of the 65th Fighter Squadron based at Groton, Connecticut. It was here that he became acquainted with the cartoonist Milton Caniff, who decided to base one of his characters on the maverick young lieutenant. The result was Colonel 'Flip Corkin' (above left).

In 1942, Cochran was posted to Casablanca but later flew south, insisting that: 'I've got to see a man about a dogfight.' Landing at an airfield in western Tunisia, Major Cochran proceeded to organise the remnants of two P-40 squadrons which, in Cochran's own words, 'were getting their rumps shot off.' Sixty-one missions later, Cochran returned to the US with a host of medals. With characteristic humour, Cochran made light of his new-found fame: 'Most of the time, it was a toss-up between a court-martial and a decoration.'

Cochran's adventures often became mixed up with those of Flip Corkin – on 17 March 1944, 'Flip' announced that he was planning an airborne invasion of Burma; one day later, the success of Operation Thursday was announced! Caniff maintained that he would sit in his studio and imagine an operation for Flip Corkin that seemed impossible. But that is precisely what Cochran excelled at – turning the impossible into the possible.

the Assam region of India was a tremendous fillip to Chindit morale.

Over 100 miles to the southwest of Broadway, a defensive stronghold, known as 'White City', had been set up by Brigadier Calvert's 77th Brigade as a block to the Japanese forces that were opposing General Stilwell's Chinese-American Army. This area rapidly became the fulcrum of the Chindit opposition to the Japanese in north Burma; and thus the enemy's main target. The Japanese 24th Independent Mixed Brigade bombarded White City with air strikes, artillery and mortar fire by day, and Japanese infantry attacked the perimeter defences at least three times each night. Throughout the siege, Calvert's forces were supplied by the RAF transport squadrons. The Mustang and B-25 pilots flew in to the stronghold every morning and evening, bombing and strafing enemy artillery and troop concentrations on the way in. After a second block had been wedged behind the Japanese forces, Calvert launched his counter-attack. When 27 of Mahoney's Mustangs decimated a Japanese troop concentration that was massing for a 'Banzai' attack, the enemy brigade crumbled and fled south.

Lightning struck on 24 March when Major-General Wingate was killed en route to his headquarters at Sylhet, India. He had boarded an Air Commando B-35H at Broadway, but never completed his journey – the bomber ran into the side of a hill and exploded, killing all on board. The Chindit operations continued, however, supported as always by the redoubtable men of No. 1 Air Commando.

By the end of the first month of operations, the pilots under Cochran and Alison had built up an impressive set of combat statistics. The Dakota transports and Waco gliders had flown in a total of 220 tons of supplies, and light planes had evacuated over 1200 casualties. The assault force had destroyed 50 enemy aircraft, four trains, eight bridges, 38 warehouses and seven ammunition sites. Gradually, however, the roles of the Chindits and the Air Commando began to change. General Arnold had

Below: A B-25 Mitchell medium bomber carries out a raid on Japanese supply and ammunition dumps. Such attacks, combined with hit-and-run raids on enemy lines of communication, enabled the pilots of No.1 Air Commando to lend invaluable support to the Chindits fighting within the Japanese perimeter. Against telephone lines, Cochran used a technique he had perfected in North Africa. Old landing gear struts were first attached to cables hooked onto the bomb shackles of the P-51 Mustangs. The pilots then weaved between the telephone posts, hooking the wires around the struts and wrenching them out of place. During Operation Thursday, the men of No.1 Air Commando wrote themselves into the annals of history. As the United States Army Air Force report stated: 'For the first time in military history, the backbone of an invasion was based on airpower which became the supply column, the artillery and the ambulance for the evacuation of casualties.'

created four additional air commando units, but was forced to withdraw his support for the Burma airborne operation due to pressure from the British and Indian High Command. Cochran was posted to Europe and Alison to the Philippines, and Colonel Gaty took over the command of the reorganised No. 1 Air Commando Group.

Under the command of Lieutenant-General Stilwell, the Chindits fought on for a further four months, but without the hitherto intimate support of No. 1 Commando. Starved of any reinforcements, they were eventually withdrawn from the order of battle. However, this should not detract from the decisive effect that airborne operations had achieved in Burma. One general in the Japanese Imperial Army later stated that:

'The penetration of Operation Thursday and the LRP phase that followed into northern Burma, caused the failure of the Japanese Army to complete its Imphal operation ... The airborne raiding force ... eventually became the reason for the total Japanese abandonment of northern Burma.'

Under the dual leadership of Cochran and Alison, the Air Commando had performed an invaluable role in re-supplying Allied ground forces, in addition to attacking enemy airfields, troop concentrations and supply lines, and evacuating thousands of wounded servicemen to hospitals in India. By early October 1944, British forces had established bridgeheads across the Chindwin River and, when the British Fourteenth Army began to advance westwards towards Mandalay, General Slim employed the same airborne techniques that had been pioneered by Cochran, Alison and the men of No. 1 Air Commando.

THE AUTHOR Brigadier Michael Calvert, DSO, commanded the 77th Indian Infantry Brigade in Burma during the siege of White City in 1944. Calvert was awarded the DSO and Bar and the American Silver Star for the capture of Mogaung during the same campaign.

HELL AT DAK TO

THE 173RD AIRBORNE BRIGADE

The 173rd Airborne Brigade was formed on 26 March 1963 and was the first major US Army ground combat unit to be deployed to Vietnam, arriving at Vung Tau on 5 May 1965. Headquartered at Bien Hoa, it made several fighting excursions into War Zone D during June and July, and in August moved to Pleiku in the Central Highlands on its first mobile-response 'fire brigade' mission – the brigade's intended role in the Vietnam conflict. Initially, the fighting arm of the brigade consisted of the 1st and 2nd Battalions of the 503rd Infantry (Airborne), but during the war it was expanded to incorporate all four battalions of the 503rd.

The brigade's first major battle of the war was fought against the Viet Cong in War Zone D in November 1965. In the autumn of 1966, the US initiated large-scale search and destroy operations and the 173rd was deployed as part of Operation Attleboro – the largest US campaign of the war to date.

In early 1967 the 173rd was involved in further operations north of Saigon, and on 22 February the brigade's 2nd Battalion made the first combat jump of the war as part of Operation Junction City. During the 1968 Tet Offensive the 173rd served in a general fire-brigade role. In 1969, as part of the policy of Vietnamization, the 173rd worked with the 22nd and 23rd ARVN Divisions in II Corps Tactical Zone. After more than seven years of combat, the brigade finally left Vietnam in August 1971.

Above: An insignia of the 173rd Airborne.

Previous page: Men of the
Battalion, 503rd Infantry,
begin their assault up the
slopes of Hill 875 on the final
day of the battle.

Left: The grim face of war in
the Central Highlands.
Bottom: Paras of the 173rd
Airborne deploy from a
helicopter. Below: A Viet
Cong is taken prisoner.

At Dak To, paratroopers of the 173rd Airborne Brigade absorbed a series of relentless enemy attacks before launching their final assault against the NVA on Hill 875

DROPPING STEADILY through the dense blanket of low cloud, the giant four-engine C-130 transport aircraft began the run-in to the airstrip at Dak To, a God-forsaken little place in the heart of the Central Highlands of South Vietnam, some 15 miles east of the juncture of the border with Laos and Cambodia. Conditions for the airlift were not good. As the aircraft emerged from the cloud cover their pilots were confronted with a dark and forbidding landscape of towering, jagged peaks rising ominously from the swirling ground fog that enshrouded the valleys below. It was a bad place for an airlift and it was a bad place to fight.

Packed into the bellies of the C-130s were two battalions of paratroopers of the US 173rd Airborne Brigade, a recently formed, tough and professional fighting formation that had earned itself the nickname 'The Herd' on account of the close camaraderie that ran through the unit. The 173rd had been the first major US Army combat unit to land in Vietnam, and the men were already veterans of a great many operations against the Viet Cong and the North Vietnamese Army (NVA). In keeping with US Airborne traditions, they liked to fight, despite the high level of casualties that resulted from such an aggressive spirit. The 173rd won a lot of battles, but they also lost a lot of men.

The difficult airlift into Dak To was made on 17 June 1967, a year that would go down in the annals of the Vietnam War as 'the year of the big battles'. The 173rd had already taken part in Operations Cedar Falls and Junction City earlier in the year – massive search and destroy operations in War Zones C and D north of Saigon – and now they were involved in the battle for the Highlands. For the paras of the 173rd the year would culminate in the ferocious struggle for Hill 875, a battle that would rank alongside the exploits of their forbears in the 503rd Infantry (Airborne), who had made the legendary combat jump on the island fortress of Corregidor during the Pacific campaign against the Japanese during World War II.

Five days after the airlift the Herd was in action. In the early morning of 22 June the men of Company A of the 2nd Battalion, 503rd Infantry, broke camp and moved out from their night position. Progress was slow as they pushed forward through dense jungle choked with tall bamboo. As they made their way down a precipitous ridgeline towards the brigade command post at Dak To, the squad walking point ran into a wall of North Vietnamese machine-gun fire. Hitting the dirt, they immediately called in fire support from artillery and US Air Force planes but the incoming barrage of bombs, napalm and 105mm shells failed to dislodge the entrenched NVA forces. Two platoons were ordered to take on the enemy firing positions, while the remainder of the company scrambled back up the ridge to cut a landing zone (LZ) for a helicopter extraction. Soon, all contact with the assault platoons was lost.

Meanwhile, Companies B and C of the 2nd Battalion were sent forward to reinforce their embattled comrades. Company B was choppered into a nearby clearing in the forest, but came under heavy fire as it tried to make its way towards the sounds of the raging firefight. Company C was luckier and managed to

reach the battle area by early afternoon, but it too was pinned down by the weight of fire from concealed NVA bunkers and trench systems. On the 23rd the battle eased, and the relief companies were able to move into the area where the two forward platoons of Company A had fought their last engagement. There, in a ghostly wasteland of mist, splintered trees and the smouldering debris of war, they found the bodies of 76 of their fellow paratroopers. It was a bloody and sobering foretaste of what was yet to come in the struggle for the area around Dak To.

A week later, US and allied forces were strengthened in the Highlands when the remainder of the 173rd, along with the 3rd Brigade of the 1st Air Cavalry and three battalions of South Vietnamese (ARVN) troops, were transported into Kontum City, 25 miles south of Dak To. Several months of hard patrolling of the area followed. The monsoon season brought torrential rain and thick fog, reducing roads and tracks to a sea of mud, and for much of the time supplies and ammunition had to be ferried in by air. The area was crawling with North Vietnamese forces. While the American units came and went in helicopter assaults and slogged it out on gruelling foot patrols, the NVA were well dug in and fought from hidden, well-prepared complexes of fortified bunkers in the depths of the jungle. Casualties among the 173rd mounted steadily.

In mid-August, after three months of jungle operations, the weary 173rd was pulled back to the coastal town of Tuy Hoa, where command of the brigade was assumed by Brigadier-General Leo H. Schweiter. However, during October, US intelligence detected a gradual build-up of enemy troop deployment in Kontum province – the NVA was moving the bulk of its regiments from bases along the Cambodian bor-

COMBAT JUMP

At 0825 on the morning of 22 February 1967 the first aircraft of a flight of 16 C-130 transports rose into the air from the runway at Bien Hoa airbase. On board were 845 paratroopers of the 173rd Airborne en route to War Zone C north of Saigon. The 173rd was deployed as part of the forces engaged in Operation Junction City and the men were to be dropped into position on the right flank of a massive 'horseshoe' cordon.

The decision to drop the 173rd, rather than take the paras in by helicopter, had been the idea of Lieutenant-Colonel Robert H. Sigholtz, commander of the airborne task force. Sigholtz argued that he could have his whole force in the field and combat ready within 10 minutes; if they came in in helicopters it would take at least two hours and 120 helicopter sorties.

At 0900 the 173rd began its jump. First to go was Brigadier-General John R. Deane, leading his men on the first combat jump of the Vietnam War. The C-130s crossed the drop zone, marked with coloured smoke by a forward airborne controller, at the prescribed 20-second intervals and the complete drop went according to plan. The brigade reported only 11 minor injuries and no troopers were wounded during the descent. The first combat jump of the Vietnam War was an unqualified success.

Above: Troops of the 173rd Airborne move through the jungle after the combat jump of 22 February.

der and other remote areas of the Highlands in readiness for a campaign in the province. Lieutenant-General William B. Rosson, commanding US Field Force, responded by strengthening his own forces in the area to counter the enemy expansion. Among the forces deployed to Dak To, which had now become the main logistic centre in the area, was the 4th Battalion, 503rd Infantry of the 173rd, under the command of Lieutenant-Colonel James H. Johnson. The 4th Battalion was airlifted in on 1 November.

Johnson and his men were immediately ordered to cover the area to the west of Dak To, and the battalion made its way to Ben Het, some 10 miles away, where a fire support base was established to cover ground operations. Then, probing out to the southwest, Companies A, C and D moved out on divergent axes to try and locate the NVA. Each man lugged a 50lb rucksack with several days' supply of C-rations, 500 rounds of 5.56mm ammunition, fragmentation and smoke grenades, 200 rounds of 7.62mm for the 'pig' – the M60 machine gun – his M16 rifle and three canteens of water. Several days of exhausting patrolling turned up very little, but on 6 November signs of enemy presence in the immediate vicinity began to materialise. In the early morning of the 6th, Company D, under the command of Captain Thomas Baird, moved onto the ridgeline of a feature known as Ngok Kom Leat. At 1130 hours the point squad spotted an NVA communications wire disappearing up a track and into the jungle. Baird requested permission from Lieutenant-Colonel Johnson, overseeing operations from a command helicopter above, to follow the cable. As Company D moved up the trail after the wire they soon came upon further signs of recent enemy activity. Baird drew his men into a defensive perimeter to counter the possibility of an NVA ambush and the company advanced cautiously, squad by squad. Suddenly, the harsh chatter of automatic fire greeted the forward elements as they proceeded up the hill.

Fire was immediately brought to bear on the assault wave and the NVA force was repelled

Baird immediately secured his rear and flanks, and then called for air support and 105mm artillery fire from the base back at Ben Het. The leading 2nd Platoon then pulled back to complete the defensive formation and, as they did so, the enemy launched an attack. Fifteen to 20 North Vietnamese soldiers poured out of the trees behind a barrage of automatic fire and several paras dropped, wounded or killed. Fire was immediately brought to bear on the assault wave and the NVA force was repelled. Minutes later, the enemy came at the 173rd again, this time from a different direction. Again the Americans' firepower pushed them back. Pin-point air strikes with napalm, 250lb bombs and cannon fire effectively kept their

Above: The agony of the 173rd. On Hill 875 the men of the 2nd Battalion, 503rd Infantry, suffered horrendous casualties as they fought to save their positions from being over-run by wave after wave of determined NVA assaults.

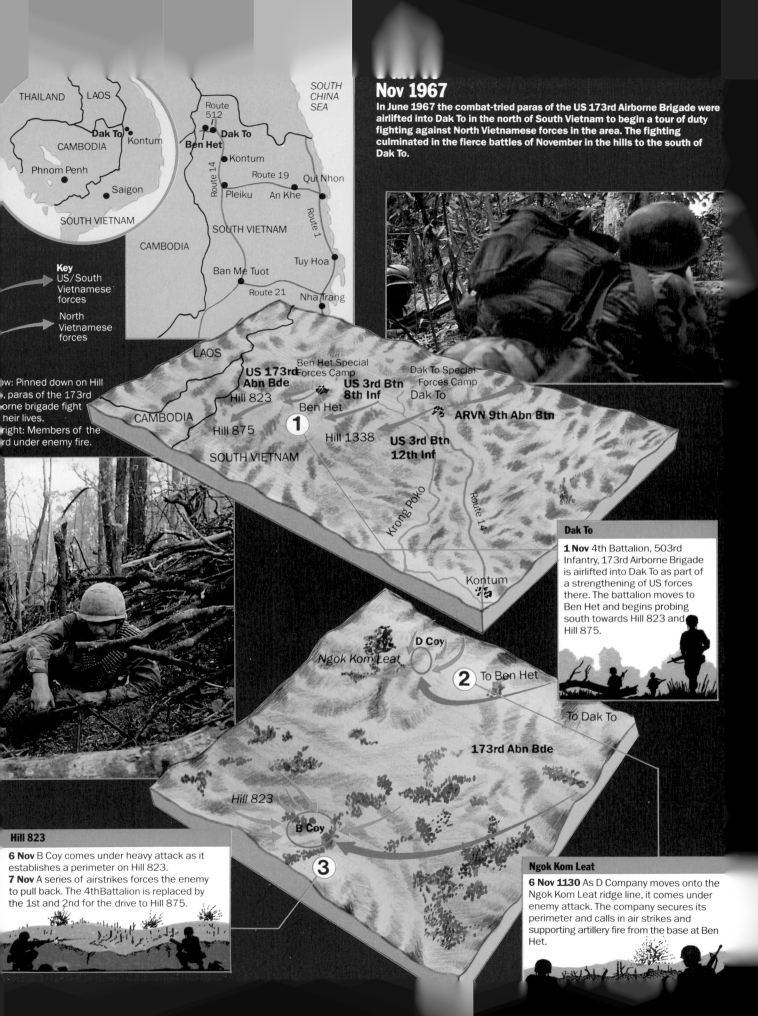

Nov 1967

In June 1967 the combat-tried paras of the US 173rd Airborne Brigade were airlifted into Dak To in the north of South Vietnam to begin a tour of duty fighting against North Vietnamese forces in the area. The fighting culminated in the fierce battles of November in the hills to the south of Dak To.

THAILAND
LAOS
Dak To
Kontum
CAMBODIA
Phnom Penh
Saigon
SOUTH VIETNAM

Route 512
Ben Het
Dak To
Kontum
Route 14
Route 19
Qui Nhon
Pleiku
An Khe
Route 1
SOUTH VIETNAM
CAMBODIA
Ban Me Tuot
Tuy Hoa
Route 21
Nha Trang

SOUTH CHINA SEA

Key
US/South Vietnamese forces
North Vietnamese forces

ow: Pinned down on Hill
, paras of the 173rd
orne brigade fight
heir lives.
right: Members of the
rd under enemy fire.

LAOS
US 173rd Abn Bde
Hill 823
Ben Het Special Forces Camp
US 3rd Btn 8th Inf
Ben Het
Dak To Special Forces Camp
Dak To
CAMBODIA
Hill 875
Hill 1338
US 3rd Btn 12th Inf
ARVN 9th Abn Btn
SOUTH VIETNAM
Krong Poko
Route 14
Kontum
1

D Coy
Ngok Kom Leat
2 To Ben Het
To Dak To
173rd Abn Bde
Hill 823
B Coy
3

Dak To

1 Nov 4th Battalion, 503rd Infantry, 173rd Airborne Brigade is airlifted into Dak To as part of a strengthening of US forces there. The battalion moves to Ben Het and begins probing south towards Hill 823 and Hill 875.

Hill 823

6 Nov B Coy comes under heavy attack as it establishes a perimeter on Hill 823.
7 Nov A series of airstrikes forces the enemy to pull back. The 4thBattalion is replaced by the 1st and 2nd for the drive to Hill 875.

Ngok Kom Leat

6 Nov 1130 As D Company moves onto the Ngok Kom Leat ridge line, it comes under enemy attack. The company secures its perimeter and calls in air strikes and supporting artillery fire from the base at Ben Het.

heads down for a while, but in the middle of the afternoon the NVA resumed their attack. For the next hour the NVA piled on the pressure, but the company perimeter held firm.

Meanwhile, as Company D fought off the NVA on Ngok Kom Leat, Company B, under Captain George Baldridge, had moved forward by helicopter to establish another fire support base, on top of Hill 823. This dominant feature was situated some 1500yds south of the Company D positions, across a deep valley. On landing, Baldridge and his men found the remains of a number of NVA soldiers, annihilated by the artillery bombardment that had been used to clear the LZ for the company's insertion. Rapidly, Baldridge positioned his men in a defensive peri- meter to guard the approaches to the summit of 823 from surprise attack. Hardly had the men got them- selves organised when an observation post on the western slope, manned by two paras of the 3rd Platoon, was wiped out by a violent volley of close- range smallarms fire. A relief force despatched down the hill was similarly decimated. Baldridge called for mortar fire and plastered the western slope with 60mm and 81mm rounds as the NVA pressed home their attack, charging up the hill and engaging the 3rd Platoon fox-holes on the crest at close quarters. For 20 minutes, the 173rd poured everything it had onto the advancing enemy and the attack finally crumpled. A lull in the fighting enabled the company to reorganise; gaps in the perimeter were plugged and the wounded tended.

At 1515 hours the NVA were back, but a well-sited M60 and a 90mm recoilless rifle, firing from a bomb crater, tore the heart out of this second thrust. The two assaults had left Company B with seven dead and 13 wounded. At 1530 the mortars came. Lieutenant- Colonel Johnson, circling the hill in his command helicopter, watched as the bombs ripped into the company lines. When Baldridge took a chunk of shrapnel from a round exploding close to his com- mand post, leaving the company temporarily leader- less, Johnson moved in and dropped off the battalion executive officer and two other officers under a hail of enemy fire.

The attack was met by a furious barrage of smallarms fire which tore into the company

The NVA were now harassing the company peri- meter on 823 from both the west and the east, making movement within the position extremely hazardous. Their forward elements were within grenade range of the pinned-down paras and any activity was greeted by a shower of grenades and AK47 fire. In one position a trooper, hearing enemy movement in the bamboo ahead, cautiously stuck his head out only to see an NVA soldier five yards away. A swift round from an M79 grenade launcher took out this threat, but the incident marked the beginning of a terrifying night of close-quarters combat around the edge of the perimeter. All through the night, in the eerie, harsh light of illuminating flares, the NVA probed the US defences with small teams of men creeping up and blasting the paratroopers' fox-holes.

With the first streaks of dawn came the full fury of American firepower and reinforcements to the grim and exhausted men of the 173rd. Gaggles of helicop- ter gunships raked the enemy positions while F-100s pounded the slopes of Hill 823 with bombs and napalm, some rounds striking home close to the company positions. Under this deluge of fire, the

NVA beat a hasty retreat down the hill and Company B was reinforced. In the aftermath of the battles on Ngok Kom Leat and Hill 823, Brigadier-General Schweiter moved the remaining battalions of the 173rd at Tuy Hoa up to Kontum and into the area of operations. The battle-weary men of the 4th Batta- lion, 503rd Infantry, were pulled back and replaced with fresh troops from the 1st Battalion, and the 2nd Battalion was brought into the steadily escalating battle around Dak To on 12 November. The following day the 2nd Battalion was back in action.

For the first time since the battle had started, the 2nd Battalion was able to get its casualties clear

In the early evening of the 13th, the battalion's Company B was checking out a possible position to leaguer for the night when it spotted two concealed NVA bunkers. Bringing up the 90mm recoilless rifle that the hapless paras had been humping over the difficult terrain, some 20 rounds of canister ammuni- tion were unleashed into the enemy positions. The attack was met by a furious barrage of smallarms fire which tore into the company as the men struggled to adopt a defensive position. NVA infantry stormed out of the bamboo thickets, and Company B was en- gulfed in a tidal wave of rocket fire and grenade explosions. The situation was chaotic. In amongst the bamboo it was impossible to see the enemy and shouted orders were drowned by the roar of the raging battle. Support soon arrived in the form of Company A, but throughout the night the two com- panies were attacked with grenades, smallarms and heavy machine guns at close range. When morning came, the NVA withdrew from a battlefield strewn with the bodies of American and NVA soldiers.

Four days later, the action around Dak To flared up yet again. The stage was set for the final round of the 1967 battle for the Highlands – the assault on Hill 875. On 18 November a large complex of enemy bunkers, manned by troops of the 174th NVA Regiment, was discovered by a Special Forces Montagnard patrol on the slopes of 875, some 12 miles west of Dak To. The patrol made a hurried withdrawal and Lieute- nant-Colonel James Stevenson, commanding the 2nd Battalion, 503rd Infantry, was tasked with clear- ing the formidable positions. On the morning of the 19th, Companies C and D of his battalion moved on the hill. They soon encountered heavy North Viet- namese fire and then, in mid-morning, the NVA regiment launched wave after wave of assault troops against the two companies. Diving for cover, the 173rd fought to hold off the attack as the green-clad NVA regulars rushed its positions in small groups. Casualties were heavy. At the bottom of the slope, Company A – the reserve force – was cutting out a landing zone for resupply and casualty evacuation. As they hacked at the bamboo and scrub, they too were suddenly engulfed in a furious flanking assault. Two platoons were literally chopped to pieces by the weight of the NVA attack. With their six-man command group wiped out in the savage hand-to- hand fighting, the remnants of the shattered com- pany crawled up the hill to join the perimeter manned by Companies C and D.

As the embattled 173rd struggled to organise a

Right: Troopers of the 2nd Battalion, 503rd Infantry, search NVA bunkers after the taking of Hill 875. Far right: A helicopter lifts in supplies to the men of the 173rd.

consolidated defence, disaster struck from an unexpected quarter. An off-target US Air Force bomb detonated at tree-top level above the defenders, pulverising the battalion below. Some 20 men were blown to smithereens and another 30 grievously wounded. With no LZ available, the wounded remained where they had fallen and only one medic had survived to deal with the horrendous carnage.

Throughout the night, the paras struggled for survival as the battle raged relentlessly around their tiny, battle-torn perimeter, strewn with the dead and dying. At daybreak on the morning of the 20th, Lieutenant-Colonel Johnson's veterans of Hill 823 re-entered the battle and that night they made it up the slope to the beleaguered 2nd Battalion's positions. A landing zone was hacked out of the jungle, and, for the first time since the battle had started, the 2nd Battalion was able to get its casualties clear.

The next day saw a massive artillery and air effort against the enemy investing the hill. For a solid seven hours, napalm, cannon fire and high explosives blasted the slopes into a wasteland of craters and shattered trees. In the early afternoon, the paras of the 173rd prepared themselves to launch a counter-attack against the NVA. At 1500 hours the men began to advance at a snail's pace, under heavy fire from the massively fortified enemy bunkers which had survived the fury of the day's bombardment. Despite a resolute North Vietnamese defence, the 173rd made progress and on 22 November the final assault on Hill 875 was initiated. As the paras advanced towards the crest of the hill, they were surprised at the lack of resistance – the NVA had departed. Reaching the summit at 1155 hours the men of the 173rd celebrated their hard-won victory.

The climax of the battle of Dak To was to go down as one of the bloodiest engagements of the whole Vietnam War. Throughout the battle the 173rd had sustained heavy losses, but the ability of the NVA to launch further major offensive operations in the Central Highlands had been, if only temporarily, curtailed by the efforts of the men of the Herd.

THE AUTHOR Jonathan Reed is a historian with a special interest in revolutionary warfare and modern counter-insurgency techniques, and has contributed articles to a number of military publications.

Bottom left: A Marine helicopter airlifts supplies into an artillery firebase high in the A Shau Valley. Top: A gaggle of UH-1H Hueys responds to an urgent call for reinforcement. Below right: Paras from the 101st Airborne pour their fire into suspected NVA positions.

During the controversial battle for Hamburger Hill, the paras of the US 101st Airborne Division fought with a tenacity that stunned the enemy

FOR THE MEN of Lieutenant-Colonel Weldon Honeycutt's 3rd Battalion, 187th Infantry (3/187), there seemed nothing particularly significant about the morning of 11 May 1969. As part of 3 Brigade, US 101st Airborne Division (Airmobile), they were out in the boondock again – on patrol in the rough and isolated terrain of South Vietnam. As Company B, 3/187, threaded its way along the narrow mountain tracks that led up a heavily forested ridge, the soldier on point looked on ahead and checked the route. The company was orientating itself towards a feature marked on the US military maps as Hill 937. Known to the Vietnamese as Dong Ap Bia, the area would soon

be known to the world as Hamburger Hill.

3 Brigade had flown into the A Shau Valley the previous day, carried aboard 65 of the airmobile division's UH-1H Huey helicopters. It was not a discreet arrival, and any North Vietnamese forces in the area would certainly have been alerted to the presence of the 'Screaming Eagles'. But the brigade split up into company-size units and moved out to comb the valley for enemy troop concentrations or supply dumps. The A Shau Valley, near the border with Laos in northwest South Vietnam, was a prime infiltration route for the North Vietnamese heading across from the Ho Chi Minh Trail to attack the populous coastal region around Hue. 3 Brigade's mission, codenamed Operation Apache Snow, was

SCREAMING EAGLES

all-time low. By 1969, it could no longer be assumed that an American soldier would be prepared, unquestioningly, to fight the enemy to the best of his ability when ordered to do so. It was difficult to go on fighting when a sense of purpose was lacking and, it was rumoured, US withdrawal from Vietnam was on its way. For many, personal survival had become the only goal. No-one wanted to be the last US soldier killed in Vietnam.

When the fighting started on 11 May, it was predictably sudden. As Company B pressed cautiously forward through the forest towards Hill 937, a burst of automatic fire ripped through the dense vegetation. Some men were hit; others dived for cover and struggled to return fire against the invisible enemy. In the heat of the moment, it was almost impossible to identify a target, but clearly North Vietnamese forces were present in some strength. Any move forward drew an instant stream of smallarms and machine-gun fire. Although Company B was pinned down, it had performed its primary function of locating the North Vietnamese. Following standard US procedure in Vietnam, the company commander now called on the air force and 3 Brigade's artillery, located at the fire support base at Ta Bat, to destroy the enemy. The company withdrew to what was reckoned a safe distance and waited for the onslaught to begin. The hillsides where the enemy positions lay were soon an inferno of napalm bursts and explosions as the USAF laid on a tactical air strike. Shell fire also poured in. It seemed unlikely that any body of men would stay put in the face of such a barrage, but the next probings by Company B again encountered smallarms fire. The enemy had not budged.

For the commander of 3 Brigade, Colonel Joseph B. Conmy Jr, and battalion commander, Lieutenant-Colonel Honeycutt, the fact that the North Vietnamese were holding their ground seemed to offer

o disrupt the build-up of enemy strength in this area and pre-empt the possibility of a strike towards the coast.

Previous operations of this kind had frequently failed to make substantial contact with the enemy, but this knowledge offered little reassurance to the men as they advanced through the eight-foot high elephant grass of the valley floor, and then up into the forest that carpeted the surrounding mountain ridges. Fear was a constant companion for the soldier on patrol in Vietnam, never knowing when a mine, a more primitive booby trap, or a sudden ambush might drop him stone dead. But the soldiers were also accompanied by a gut feeling that was even more disturbing – a sense of failure and defeat that had reduced the morale of the US Army to an

101ST AIRBORNE DIVISION (AIRMOBILE)

The US 101st Airborne Division – nicknamed the 'Screaming Eagles' – had been one of the most famous paratroop formations of World War II. As soon as the large-scale commitment of the US Army to Vietnam began in the summer of 1965, therefore, the division's 1 Brigade was drafted to Cam Ranh. Time and time again, the crack paratroopers proved their worth during the desperate struggle with forces from the North Vietnamese Army and Viet Cong.

In 1967, the US High Command decided to transfer the division's remaining two brigades to Vietnam, and to make the 101st Airborne the second 'airmobile' formation in the US Army. To attain this airmobile status, a division had to possess its own fully integrated helicopter fleet, capable of providing the transport, medevac, close air support and reconnaissance needs of the entire formation. When the order to move to Vietnam arrived, both 2 and 3 Brigades of the 101st Airborne Division were well under strength. As a direct result of this, when the two units arrived in Vietnam in December 1967, a large proportion of their personnel had been drafted in from other army units. Many of these men had no paratroop training. The division experienced delays before sufficient helicopters and trained flying personnel could be gathered together to meet requirements. The title 'Airmobile' was added to the division's official designation in August 1968, but a full three-battalion aviation group of 400 helicopters was not in action with the unit until mid-1969.

The 101st Airborne Division performed creditably throughout the difficult

period of withdrawal from combat in Vietnam, and fully vindicated the airmobile concept as applied to the Vietnam battlefield.

an exciting – and unexpected – opportunity to inflict heavy losses. Normally, even if contact had been established, the lightly equipped and mobile enemy would have disappeared before much damage could be done. By the following day, 12 May, Honeycutt had committed all four companies of his battalion to the struggle for Hill 937. Intelligence reports suggested that the position was probably the headquarters of the 29th North Vietnamese Army (NVA) Regiment. This was a prize worth fighting for.

Company B spent the daylight hours of 12 May preparing a landing zone for medevac helicopters, while the other companies moved into place. The pounding of the North Vietnamese by air strikes and artillery fire continued throughout the day and the following night. On 13 May, everything was ready for an infantry assault on Hill 937.

With Companies A and D left in reserve, Companies B and C set out to advance from the northwest, working their way cautiously up to the forward slopes. After about half an hour, the companies suddenly ran into intense enemy fire. The North Vietnamese were dug in to almost invulnerable emplacements that had come through the barrage of napalm and high explosives virtually unscathed. The openings of these bunkers were at ground level, overhung by vegetation for concealment, and afforded the NVA interlocking fields of fire that covered every approach up the mountain slopes. The two US companies were soon bogged down, unable to force a way forward. They eventually withdrew, having taken casualties of four dead and 33 wounded.

Nerves were beginning to jangle, but the men stuck grimly to their task and actually broke through

The following day, 14 May, witnessed another frustrating struggle for the men of the 3rd Battalion. This time, Companies B, C and D went up the hill separately, on different lines of advance. For the soldiers of Company B, it was already the third time they had walked forward into enemy fire since the action started. Nerves were beginning to jangle, but the men stuck grimly to their task and actually broke through a line of North Vietnamese fortifications to reach the crest of a ridge that lay between them and the top of the hill. But it was all to no avail. Company C ran into serious difficulties and was forced to withdraw, its commander wounded. Company B could not stay forward without adequate support and once again the men had to pull back.

Colonel Conmy and Lieutenant-Colonel Honeycutt were still determined that the chance to hammer the North Vietnamese should be seized, and preparations began immediately for another assault on 15 May. Honeycutt withdrew the badly mauled Company C to rest, and replaced it with Company A. So far, this unit had not been involved in the fighting. Meanwhile, Conmy ordered the 1st Battalion, 506th Infantry (1/506), another of the 101st Airborne's constituent formations, to move round to the west of the North Vietnamese position, between Hill 937 and the Laotian border. This deployment would cut off the enemy's line of escape and bring pressure to bear from another direction on their defences.

Throughout the night of 14/15 May, AC-47 gunships circled relentlessly, pouring fire from their 7.62mm miniguns down onto the North Vietnamese positions. This spectacular sight must have com-

Above: Wearing the thick flak jackets that had been issued in the desperate hope of reducing casualties, paratroopers of the 101st Airborne Division disembark from a Huey during the battle for Hamburger Hill. Once clear of the chopper, the paras will search for cover from the storm of fire coming from bunkers that the North Vietnamese Army had burrowed into the sides of Hill 937. Right: Doubled over by pain, a wounded para is rushed towards a waiting medevac helicopter.

forted the embattled US troops but, despite the softening up, the next day's fighting was to prove even more savage than before. Companies A and B moved off together and skilfully worked their way forward. At the same time, divisional helicopters ghosted in overhead, unleashing salvoes of rockets into the hillside in front of their advance. Bunker after bunker was overrun, and the crest of Hill 937 itself seemed almost within their grasp. But then disaster struck. The co-ordination of air strikes, helicopter support and artillery barrages was a desperately complex operation over the congested battlefield, with the chance of scoring 'own goals' an ever-present threat. Now, when victory at last seemed in sight, a helicopter gunship presumed it was attacking an NVA position and poured rocket fire down into the exposed ranks of Company B on the open hillside. There was havoc as men fell on all sides with atrocious wounds. Soldiers struggled to move their wounded comrades back to safety, while others retreated in shock and confusion. The attack fell apart; the job would have to be done all over again.

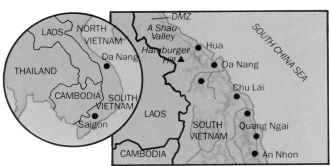

101st Airborne Division (Airmobile)

Hamburger Hill, 10-20 May 1969

Early in May 1969, the US 101st Airborne Division was tasked with blocking the movement of NVA forces from Laos along the A Shau Valley into South Vietnam. The operation, codenamed Apache Snow, began on 10 May. The division's 3rd Brigade deployed by helicopter near Hill 937, known as Hamburger Hill, and began a series of assaults on NVA defensive positions in the area.

Into the A Shau Valley

10-14 May The 3rd Brigade, 101st Airborne Division airlifts onto landing zones in the A Shau Valley below Hamburger Hill to attack NVA positions.

Key
- US attacks, 10-14 May
- US attacks, 15 May
- US attacks, 16-20 May
- NVA defences
- Initial landing zone

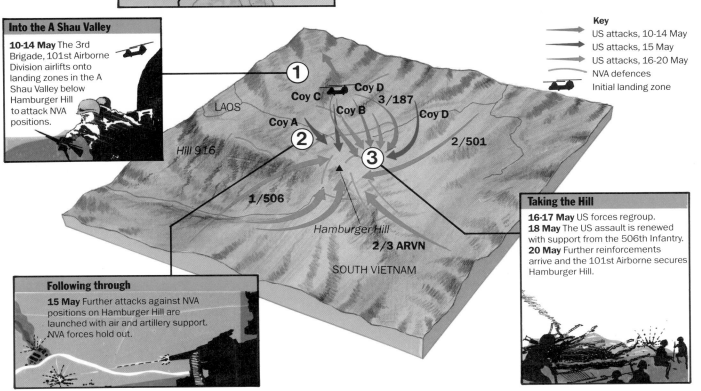

Taking the Hill

16-17 May US forces regroup.
18 May The US assault is renewed with support from the 506th Infantry.
20 May Further reinforcements arrive and the 101st Airborne secures Hamburger Hill.

Following through

15 May Further attacks against NVA positions on Hamburger Hill are launched with air and artillery support. NVA forces hold out.

During the nightmarish struggle for Hamburger Hill, the paras of the 101st Airborne Division found themselves embroiled in one of the bloodiest battles of the Vietnam War. From the shelter of their carefully constructed bunker system, the North Vietnamese Army regulars were able to direct a constant stream of mortar and machine-gun fire against the advancing American troops. Despite horrendous casualties and sinking morale, the paras fought for 10 days before taking the hill in a co-ordinated four-battalion assault. Right: Medics help an airborne trooper who has been hit in the face by fragments of a hand grenade. Far right: Supporting a dazed and wounded colleague on his shoulder, a para from the 101st looks to the skies for an incoming medevac helicopter.

By this time, the battle for Hill 937 had become a focus of attention, both for the media and the military. The commander of the 101st Airborne, Major-General Melvin Zais, had flown to the scene in an observation helicopter to follow the action on the spot. Meanwhile, journalists sought out interviews with men ready to gripe about American lives being wasted in the effort to take Hamburger Hill – the soldiers' nickname for a feature that had chewed up so many men to mincemeat.

Both Conmy and Honeycutt remained convinced that the hill had to be overrun, whatever the cost. The option of blasting the hill into oblivion with a B-52 strike was mooted but rejected. Conmy later explained: 'If I backed away the distance necessary to launch a B-52 strike [the enemy] would disappear in the dark of the night and attack us somewhere else.' Honeycutt had been wounded three times already, the third time on 15 May when a rocket-propelled grenade (RPG) struck his command post, but he refused evacuation and now set about planning yet another infantry assault. The commanders agreed that only a simultaneous attack by two battalions could reach the summit, and so Honeycutt's men took a well-earned break from the offensive on 16 and 17 May while 1/506 slogged its way forward from the western side of the hill. By 18 May it had reached a sufficiently advanced position, and the two battalions were ready for a co-ordinated assault from the north and the west.

For 36 hours, the North Vietnamese had been subjected to a ceaseless barrage of tactical air strikes and artillery fire, yet their resistance was still fierce. For the men of 3/187, it took every reserve of courage and nerve to advance once again where so many of their buddies had already fallen. For some soldiers it was their fifth assault on the hill – how long could their luck hold? The advance was cautious but relentless, through a nightmare war landscape of shell-blasted trees and churned up earth. Suddenly a man would stumble on a Claymore mine, sending a stream of lethal steel pellets lashing across the

Below: Drenched by a driving rainstorm, a paratrooper works furiously to save the life of a wounded colleague from the 101st. Below, far right: Grimacing with pain, a young para approaches breaking-point as he waits for the medevac chopper that will take him to the field hospital, away from the hell of Hamburger Hill. Images such as these, depicting the horrors of Vietnam, had a profound influence on public opinion in the US.

advancing troops; or a burst of automatic fire apparently out of nowhere, would cut a soldier down. Medevac helicopters were soon busy, themselves coming under heavy fire as they ferried badly wounded men back to the care of overworked surgical teams to the rear.

But the advance did not lose its momentum, and by midday the troops of 3/187 were inside the North Vietnamese defensive perimeter. The terrain within the enemy defences was booby-trapped with mines and grenades that took their toll of the attacking force, but once again, victory was in sight. Then, in the early afternoon, it began to rain – a heavy, steaming tropical rain that turned the bomb- and shell-torn earth of the denuded slopes into a quagmire. Already physically drained by the effort of the day's fighting, the US troops stumbled and slithered on the treacherous slopes, sinking down into the soft mud or slipping backwards with every step. NVA mortars and RPGs exploded all around them, and smallarms fire converged on their ranks from every direction. It was a débâcle. The assault was abandoned and the men retreated down the hill as best they could. They were a desperate sight as they appeared through the downpour – mudcaked, sodden and exhausted, supporting the walking wounded between them. The battalion had lost 14 killed and 64 wounded during the day. Morale reached rock-bottom.

To the divisonal, brigade and battalion commanders, the situation still seemed favourable – the enemy was surrounded and there remained the possibility of bringing up fresh units until the NVA defences finally cracked. 1/506 had made substantial progress on 18 May, and Zais ordered another divisional unit, the 2nd Battalion, 501st Infantry, together with a battalion of the South Vietnamese Army, to be helilifted into the battle zone, to the east of the mountain.

To the troops in the front line, however, things appeared a little differently. All the cynicism that had accumulated through the years of the Vietnam War finally surfaced in a bitter resentment that became

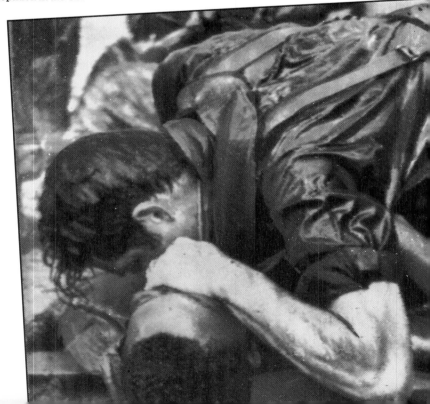

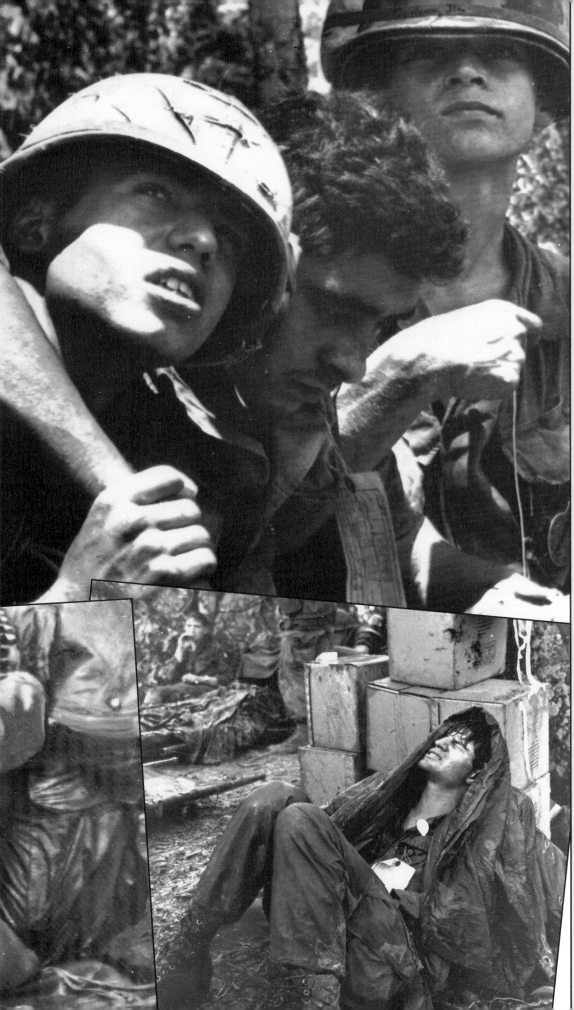

WAS IT WORTH IT?

The battle for Hamburger Hill caused an outcry in the United States, with Senator Edward Kennedy describing it as 'senseless and irresponsible'. Yet despite many similar criticisms, Major-General Melvin Zais, the commander of the 101st Airborne Division, defended the action vigorously. General Zais agreed that Hill 937 had 'no military value whatsoever' as an area of land but argued that: 'the enemy had to be engaged wherever he was found if the mission was to be accomplished.'

The main drawback of Zais' military doctrine was that it no longer conformed to US strategy as laid down by the administration of President Richard Nixon, and by General Creighton W. Abrams, the commander of US forces in Vietnam. The days of the 'body count', in which the US Army waged a war of attrition in Vietnam aimed at killing as many of the enemy as possible, were at an end. By 1969, the aim was to contain the enemy using tactics that avoided infantry engagements and therefore minimised US casualties.

The hostile reaction of US public opinion to the battle for Hamburger Hill undoubtedly accelerated moves towards the removal of American troops from an active combat role in Vietnam. President Nixon made it abundantly clear to General Abrams that no further operations involving such losses would be tolerated. On 9 June 1969 Nixon announced that the first withdrawals of US troops from Vietnam would take place the following August. As so often happened in Vietnam, a military victory on the ground had led only to calls for the war to end by the American public.

900,000lb of bombs, 152,000lb of napalm and 21,73[?] artillery shells had been expended. It had also bee[n] costly in lives: American losses were around 60 dea[d] and 300 wounded. The search through the Nort[h] Vietnamese bunker complex revealed a horrifi[c] carnage – 630 bodies were recovered. From th[e] casualty figures, this was clearly an American vic[-] tory of considerable proportions. But the action left [a] legacy of bitterness. When, having destroyed th[e] enemy bunkers, the Americans abandoned the hi[ll] only one week after taking it, a message scrawled o[n] cardboard was left on the scene by an anonymou[s] soldier. It read: 'Hamburger Hill. Was it worth it?'

Through all the controversy, however, the qualit[y] of the performance of the men of the 101st Airborn[e] and especially that of the 3rd Battalion, 187th Infan[-] try, was unquestionable. 3 Brigade won the Pres[-] idential Unit Citation, and Colonel Conmy gav[e] moving testimony to the courage of his men:

'No matter how tough the job is, the America[n] soldier gets the job done. He might hate the he[ll] out of it but he never quits… In Hamburger Hil[l] they might have grumbled, but my God, the[y] were there when the chips were down! The[y] eventually went up that hill and took it.'

THE AUTHOR R.G. Grant graduated in Modern Histor[y] from Trinity College, Oxford. He has written exten[-] sively on the military campaigns of the 20th century.

focused on Colonel Honeycutt. A wounded soldier, using the colonel's codename, is reported to have said of Honeycutt: 'That damned "Blackjack" won't stop until he kills every damn one of us.' This indictment of Honeycutt apparently summed up a general feeling that the objective was futile and a waste of lives. But there was no avoiding it – the troops would have to go in one more time.

Nothing is more difficult for a soldier than to fight when he is consumed with doubts about the compe- tence of his officers or the necessity of his task. But for all the griping, on the morning of 20 May the men of the 101st Airborne went up the hill again. Once more, the main thrust came from 3/187, now reinforced by two companies from the 2nd Battalion, 506th Infantry. After 10 days of air strikes, artillery bombardment and infantry assaults, the North Vietnamese resist- ance was at last worn down. The US troops advanced almost unmolested as supporting artillery and mor- tar fire rained down ahead of them – the noise level was so high that radio contact became impossible. By noon, 3/187 had reached the crest of the hill. Now they had to fight from bunker to bunker, clearing out remaining nests of North Vietnamese troops that were prepared to fight to the last. 1/506 soon joined in, having broken through from the west. During the afternoon, the last vestiges of resistance were eli- minated. By nightfall, Hamburger Hill was in Amer- ican hands.

The hill had cost a great deal in munitions: some

Right: Objective secured, a para surveys the A Shau Valley from his vantage point atop Hill 937. Above: Victory belonged to the 101st, but at what price?

GLOBAL STRIKE FORCE

Geared to hit the enemy hard and fast, 5 Airborne Brigade can call upon a wealth of combat-ready units during its out-of-area operations

BRITAIN'S AIRBORNE rapid deployment force, 5 Airborne Brigade, came into being just six years after its predecessor, 16 Parachute Brigade, was disbanded in 1977. The Falklands conflict of 1982 had shown the need for an airborne assault force, and 5 Airborne Brigade was formed precisely for this purpose. The unit has a general war role as a strategic reserve, but it is also an invaluable insurance policy against the unexpected in peacetime. Its chief responsibilities in out-of-area (OOA) operations include rapid reinforcement of dependent territories (for example, the Falkland Islands), the protected evacuation of United Kingdom nationals from overseas trouble spots, assistance to friendly governments, international peace-keeping operations and rapid response to emergencies.

The brigade has been organised to operate at a variety of levels, from the deployment of a single rifle company group with a battalion HQ, to a full brigade under the command of the Joint Headquarters (JHQ) in Aldershot. By early 1987, 5 Airborne Brigade comprised: the 2nd Battalion, King Edward VII's Own Goorkha Rifles; the 2nd Battalion, The Parachute Regiment (2 Para); 3 Para; The Life Guards; the 7th Regiment, Royal Horse Artillery; 36 Engineer Regiment; the 3rd Battalion, The Queen's Regiment; and 5 Airborne Brigade Logistic Regiment.

5 Airborne Brigade has been fortunate in having a succession of three commanding officers who have had a profound influence on the unit. The first commander, Brigadier Tony Jeapes, had been the CO of 22nd Special Air Service (22 SAS) Regiment,

and he handed over to Brigadier Robert Corbett. Corbett was an Irish Guards officer who had served for five years in the original 16 Parachute Brigade, and had commanded its Pathfinder Company. He had also commanded the 1st Battalion, Irish Guards Battle Group, in the British Army of the Rhine (BAOR). Jeapes, who handed over to Corbett in March 1985, had given the brigade its unique identity and was instrumental in setting up the unit's strategic and tactical doctrines. Corbett, on the other hand, brought his expertise to bear on the brigade's armour, as well as conducting experiments with new concepts in tactical air assault. The current commander, Brigadier David Chaundler, took up his assignment in January 1987, having previously led 2 Para in the Falklands campaign.

The JHQ in Aldershot has been set up to co-ordinate any major OOA deployment, and it controls elements of all three services through its tri-service permanent staff. If an OOA deployment takes place, the JHQ will exercise overall control of operations through one of the three four-star operational commanders in Britain: the Commander, UK Land Forces (UKLF), near High Wycombe; the Air Officer Commanding (AOC), RAF Strike Command, at Salisbury; or the Commander-in-Chief Fleet, at Northwood. The choice of commander would obviously depend on the nature of the operation. At a lower level, command on the ground would be exercised by a two or three-star commander working from his Joint Force Headquarters (JFHQ) in the operational area. The JHQ's permanent staff forms the Permanent Planning Group (PPG), a team of 16 staff officers and men whose job is to maintain and update contingency plans, prepare operational plans for live deployments and work out exercise scenarios and plans. They receive their intelligence from the various government agencies and move, once activated, to the headquarters of the JHQ commander concerned: Northwood, Salisbury or High Wycombe.

The objective was to set up a secure base from which the force could operate

Three years of planning and exercises finally led to the first real test of the brigade's ability to carry out its task in the rapid reinforcement role. This was Exercise 'Saif Sareea' (Arabic for Swift Sword), and it took place in Oman, in November 1986. The scenario was classically simple: a friendly country had been invaded and had asked for immediate assistance from the UK. The JHQ was activated under Air Chief Marshal Sir Peter Harding, AOC Strike Command. As the Leading Parachute Battalion Group (LPBG), 2 Para was deployed with Brigade HQ and the JFHQ, under Lieutenant-General Mike Gray, to a forward mounting base on Masirah Island, off the coast of Oman. Supported by Royal Air Force (RAF) Tornadoes and Omani Jaguars, Hunters and Strikemasters, the LPBG carried out a parachute assault into an airhead that was then rapidly reinforced by troops air-landed into the area. Simultaneously, 40 Commando, Royal Marines, went in by sea. The two forces, airborne and amphibious, met up with Omani armoured and infantry units and the entire force, under the tactical control of 5 Airborne Brigade, went on to engage and destroy the 'invaders'.

Exercise Saif Sareea demonstrated an unusual departure for British Airborne Forces. Instead of a mass descent by the whole of 2 Para, only a weak battalion of some 360 men (including members of the

Previous page: Trained by parachute jumping instructors from the Royal Air Force, members of 5 Airborne Brigade (above) deplane from a C-130 Hercules. Below: Setting up a GPMG position.

Sultan of Oman's Parachute Regiment) was dropped at first light on 26 November. First in, however, had been a 90-man Pathfinder Group, dropped from low level at last light the previous afternoon. This small force conducted a recce of the Drop Zone (DZ) and marked it for the main drop and subsequent reinforcement. The reinforcements were then air-landed before the full force headed off towards its objectives.

Exercise 'Purple Victory', which took place in the north of England in November 1985, tested the brigade's ability to enter hostile territory and carry out a 'protected evacuation' of British subjects. This was followed by a series of mopping-up operations against local 'guerrilla' forces and a full-scale brigade-strength heliborne attack on an 'enemy' battalion. This involved parachuting two battalion groups onto Corby Pike DZ on consecutive nights. The objective was to set up a secure base from which the force could operate and from where the 'hostages' could be evacuated safely. 2 Para went in first, followed by 3 Para. The base was a disused runway at Ouston, Northumberland, into which the majority of support troops, helicopters and armour was deployed by air-landing. Re-supply was carried out partly by air-landing and, when the runway began to break up under the sustained pounding of C-130 Hercules aircraft, by parachute. Purple Victory emphasised the importance of having a parachute reinforcement and re-supply capability.

It has been known since the early 1940s that transport aircraft, flying straight and level at low speed over a paratroop DZ, are highly vulnerable to enemy air defences. This threat is even more dangerous in an age of surface-to-air missiles. In addition, the troops themselves remain vulnerable; both when hanging below their parachute canopies, and when they are scattered and disorganised on the DZ immediately after landing. 5 Airborne Brigade's new tactical doctrine seeks to reduce, if not eliminate completely, some of the traditional risks of airborne warfare.

Top left: As a platoon field commander directs operations, members of 2 Para deploy around a 0.5in Browning machine gun (below).

5 AIRBORNE BRIGADE

5 Infantry Brigade was formed in 1805 during the Napoleonic Wars, and has the distinction of being the only brigade in the British Army to have been in continuous existence since that time.

Between 1977 and 1982 it was known as the 8th Field Force, designated for home defence in the event of a war. During this period, two significant events coincided with the disbanding of 16 Parachute Brigade. The first of these was the Entebbe raid in 1976, and the second was the deployment of the 2e Régiment Etranger de Parachutistes, French Foreign Legion, to Kolwezi in 1978.

Britain realised that the loss of 16 Parachute Brigade would prevent her from carrying out any similar missions. To redress the situation, a single parachute battalion with limited support was added to the 8th Field Force to create the Parachute Contingency Force (PCF) for out-of-area (OOA) operations. When it was decided that an enhanced OOA capability was required, the formation was reinforced by a second parachute battalion.

In January 1982 the formation became 5 Infantry Brigade once again. The loss of 16 Parachute Brigade had seemed acceptable in the light of Britain's gradual withdrawal from her overseas commitments, but the Falklands conflict of 1982 resulted in a complete reversal of policy. Eighteen months after the capture of Port Stanley, it was therefore announced that an existing formation, 5 Infantry Brigade, would be converted to the airborne role and renamed 5 Airborne Brigade. The new unit was formed on 14 November 1983.
Above: The insignia of 5 Airborne Brigade.

Above: Rapid deployment. Members of 5 Airborne emerge from the belly of a C-130 onto the dust-strewn airstrip at Al-Mahata during Exercise 'Swift Sword'.

Top right: With the platoon's Land Rovers stationed to the rear, a two-man Milan anti-tank team prepares to fire during the exercise in Oman.

Brigadier Jeapes realised that the elements of surprise and concentration are too precious to be wasted by a scattered drop, and the brigade's current doctrine is that troops should be air-landed in cohesive groups wherever possible – fully organised and ready to go as soon as they step off the aircraft's ramp. However, Britain has only a limited long-range self-deployment capability for her helicopters, which means that airstrips must be captured wherever possible. Deployment of the entire brigade by parachute is seen as a last resort.

It is generally assumed that 22 SAS will be a part of most operational brigade deployments. The regiment's High-Altitude Low-Opening (HALO) parachute capability would allow special forces teams to be inserted covertly, carrying out recce missions or attacking specific targets before the brigade arrives. Whether or not the HALO-trained brigade pathfinders would accompany the SAS would depend very much on the type of operation concerned. Although the pathfinders are trained to remain undetected before the main force arrives, the risk of the operation being compromised may force them to go in at low level as little as 30 minutes before the main drop. They would mark the DZ for the main force before joining up to form the core of the brigade's patrol effort, working alongside the battalions' recce or patrol companies.

Another alternative to the straight parachute or parachute/air-landing assault is the Entebbe-style assault. During a recent realistic training exercise, a company of paras was tasked to 'hit' an airfield in the UK. A single C-130 made a surprise landing in pitch darkness and ground to a halt near the airport installations. Within seconds, the force had deplaned. In the space of 20 minutes, the paras destroyed the control tower and other airfield equip-

ment with Milan missiles and re-embarked, their aircraft having taken off for its own safety and then returned to extract the assault force.

More recently, the 2nd Battalion, King Edward VII's Own Goorkha Rifles, tried a larger-scale version of the Entebbe-style assault as part of another 'protected evacuation'. The battalion achieved the same spectacular success as the paras. It now seems very likely that the brigade's armour (two squadrons equipped with FV721 Fox wheeled combat reconnaissance vehicles, and one with FV101 Scorpions), would be landed in the same way. Various other re-supply and delivery techniques are either available or under trial, however. These include Low-Altitude Parachute-Extraction System (LAPES), Ultra-Low-Level Aerial Delivery (ULLAD), and traditional para-dropping techniques using Medium-

Top left: Brigadier Robert Corbett (centre of picture), the former commander of 5 Airborne Brigade, holds an Orders Group with the other commanding officers within the brigade. Far left: A Chinook helicopter delivers a consignment of 105mm ammunition to one of 7 RHA's gun positions. Left: Flying a low-altitude approach path, a C-130 Hercules airdrops a Medium-Stress Platform (MSP). The key to 5 Airborne Brigade's mobility rests in the capable hands of the Royal Air Force (RAF) Hercules fleet at RAF Lyneham, Wiltshire. The four squadrons responsible for Transport Support operations are Nos.24, 30, 47 and 70. There is also a Special Forces Flight whose crews specialise in the techniques required for HALO parachute operations. There are three distinct types of Hercules, and of these the C.Mk 3s are equipped with a low-power, short-range radar that enables pilots to maintain a 4000ft horizontal separation between aircraft. Carrying up to 90 parachutists, the Hercules are able to fly over the drop zone at intervals of only 15 seconds – ideally suited to the tactical doctrine of surprise and concentration upon which the rapid deployment capability of 5 Airborne Brigade depends. Below: Members of 63 Squadron, Royal Corps of Transport, disconnect a Land Rover from an MSP.

Stress Platforms (MSPs). The latter are used for 7 RHA's 105mm Light Guns and the brigade's Land Rovers, while Heavy-Stress Platforms (HSPs) are required for the heavy plant of 9 Para Squadron, Royal Engineers. The Life Guards' Scorpion and Fox armoured vehicles are dropped using a modified MSP, the Unit Suspended Platform. This entails securing the vehicle firmly to the platform's base, and the parachute to the vehicle's own lifting points. The subsequent savings in weight and space mean that a single C-130 can carry two armoured vehicles for para-dropping.

The brigade is quite candid about its inability to take on a stronger, more heavily equipped enemy. The Life Guards provide a recce capability with rapid mobility for a small number of men if required, together with substantial fire support during assault and defence. However, they cannot realistically be expected to defeat heavy armoured forces. The brigade has insisted on retaining both Milan anti-tank missiles and the now venerable 120mm BAT L6 Wombat recoilless anti-tank gun in its inventory. The latter is still effective and can cover the 400m 'dead zone' created by Milan's minimum effective range. It possesses a greater rate of fire than the Milan, and is far cheaper to use in the 'bunker-busting' role. Nobody denies, however, that the brigade would have to go in against comparatively light defences in order to secure a foothold for heavier reinforcements or be certain of getting in and out quickly and safely. In the former, it would act as a spearhead, tasked with securing an airhead for a rapid build-up by air. Alternatively, the brigade might be ordered to secure a sea port that would allow substantial reinforcement by heavy armour or a major evacuation of large numbers of civilians.

The logistical set-up of 5 Airborne Brigade is light and mobile. The 5 Airborne Brigade Logistic Battalion, comprising 63 Squadron, Royal Corps of Transport, 82 Company, Royal Army Ordnance Corps, and 10 Field Workshop, Royal Electrical and Mechanical Engineers, has the ability to deploy an airborne force at 'no notice' and sustain it at second-line level for seven days before the arrival of third-line support. The Logistic Battalion would set up a Brigade Maintenance Area (BMA) within the captured air-

THE SHAPE OF THE FUTURE

By the early 1990s, Britain's airborne forces intend to add a new tactical assault parachute to their inventory. This will replace the popular, although obsolescent, PX1Mk4 that is currently used. Manufactured by Irvin (Great Britain) Ltd, the PX1Mk4 is certainly the world's most reliable parachute – but it does have its drawbacks. It demands too low an airspeed and too high a dropping altitude (650ft at 130 knots) for modern airborne operations.

A series of secret trials is believed to have taken place at the Aircraft Development Centre at Boscombe Down in the early months of 1987. A number of new designs were evaluated, including two submitted by British manufacturers (Irvin and GQ Parachutes), a French company and an American or Canadian firm. Published figures for the GQ 8 Metre Parachute suggest the capability of dropping a fully equipped paratrooper weighing 360lb, together with his equipment, from as low as 300ft at 150 knots. Experts believe that all of the competing designs roughly match this performance. The secret of their reliability is the new Aeroconical canopy, initially fitted to the ejector seats of fighter pilots. The aeroconical shape facilitates very fast canopy development with acceptable 'g-loadings' on the parachutist. More importantly, the new design eliminates the danger of 'post-inflation' collapse and significant height loss before opening. The new shape is very different from the old 'mushroom' of the PX1Mk4, and a row of four symmetrical slots eliminates the oscillation that could cause casualties in high winds.

Two major benefits will result from the adoption of the new design – the para will remain in the air for only 13.5 seconds when jumping from 300ft, and the aircraft will be able to cross the Drop Zone much faster, making it less vulnerable to ground fire and surface-to-air missiles.

head. From here, the medics of 23 Para Field Ambulance and the brigade's Gazelle helicopters from 658 Squadron, Army Air Corps, together with the armour, engineers and gunners, would be able to offer full support.

Apart from 658 Squadron, Army Air Corps, the brigade has no tactical rotary wing assets. These would be supplied by the RAF's Pumas and Chinooks, or by the Sea Kings and Wessex helicopters of 846 and 845 Naval Air Squadrons. This remains a major problem, as there is no doubt that troop-carrying helicopters proved a major advantage during Purple Victory and Saif Sareea. At present, a lightning deployment could leave the brigade bereft of battlefield transport until either the navy arrived, or enough C-130s could be spared to airlift the required helicopters close enough to the operational area for a long-range self-ferry flight.

One of 5 Airborne Brigade's major assets is 7 RHA. With 18 105mm Light Guns on strength, artillery support is virtually guaranteed to be flexible and highly effective. The regiment was formerly part of 16 Parachute Brigade, and possesses a wealth of airborne experience that can be brought to bear during operations. The 105mm Light Gun is unrivalled in its combination of firepower, range and mobility. One troop of 7 RHA – P Troop – provides air

defence with Javelin shoulder-launched SAMs. The brigade is unique within the British Army in using the old but much-loved M2 0.5in Browning heavy machine gun for both fire support and air defence. Each battalion has six of these in its machine-gun platoon for supporting fire, along with its sustained-fire 7.62mm General Purpose Machine Gun (GPMGs). There is also one GPMG and one Bren light machine gun in each rifle section to thicken up supporting fire and provide extra air defence. Only the Goorkhas, however, in their role as airhead guard force, have special air defence mountings for the 0.5in guns. If necessary, the brigade can also count on the Rapier SAMs of 32 Air Defence Battery, Royal Artillery, and 19 Squadron, RAF Regiment.

The brigade is not a tool for poker players – it is a weapon, pure and simple

The armour support from the Life Guards is invaluable. The ability to deploy quickly and carry out distant recces cannot be overestimated, and nor can the fire support provided by the Fox's 30mm Rarden cannon and the Scorpion's 76mm gun. Interestingly enough, this combination of weapons was used to support paratroopers for the first time during 2 Para's battle for Wireless Ridge on the Falkland Islands.

The man who commanded 2 Para then, Lieutenant-Colonel David Chaundler, took over as 5 Airborne Brigade commander in January 1987. Chaundler has been able to draw on Brigadier Corbett's unique experience (for an airborne commander) of having commanded an armour-heavy battle group in BAOR that contained two squadrons of Chieftain main battle tanks. To Corbett must go the credit for imaginative use of armour assets within the brigade, and developing a highly effective doctrine for their deployment in support of the parachute and air-landing battalions.

One of the most interesting logistical features of the brigade is the lightness of its 'tail'. On first deployment, the brigade HQ is only one fifth of the size of that of 3 Commando Brigade – which, in turn, is far smaller than anything else in the British Army. This facilitates flexibility in decision-making and provides comparatively high mobility. It works at several levels, the most basic being Para Tac 1 – a Land Rover and trailer that teams up with the brigade intelligence cell's Land Rover and trailer to comprise a unit similar to a light parachute battalion HQ. A satellite link is integral to Para Tac 1 for communications with higher formations or the UK

itself, though traditional high frequency communications have been used with a high degree of success. Para Tac 2 is a more substantial headquarters, and would go in with the follow-up forces after the airhead had been captured. Para Tac 3 is the full brigade HQ, and is broadly similar to that of 3 Commando Brigade in size and flexibility. The highly sophisticated communications equipment at the disposal of the brigade HQ enables it to support and control independent operations which may last for up to 72 hours.

5 Airborne Brigade provides the British Government with a military weapon that is as much a deterrent as a quick reaction force. Its ability to deploy rapidly and incisively to any part of the world where British interests are threatened makes the brigade unrivalled in its field. Unlike an embarked amphibious force, it cannot provide politicians with the opportunity to indulge in brinkmanship; but the brigade is not a tool for poker players – it is a weapon, pure and simple.

THE AUTHOR Gregor Ferguson is the former editor of *Defence Africa and the Middle East* and has contributed to a number of other military publications.

The current commander of 5 Airborne Brigade is Brigadier David Chaundler (above). As a lieutenant-colonel, Chaundler commanded the 2nd Battalion, The Parachute Regiment, during the Falklands campaign. At the battle for Wireless Ridge, he became the only British officer since Korea to command an all-arms (infantry, artillery and air) battle group in a conventional conflict. Far left: Crewed by airborne-qualified troops from The Life Guards, an FV 101 Scorpion armoured reconnaissance vehicle is driven down the ramp of a Hercules. Left: Royal Engineers attach specially shaped hollow demolition charges to the girders of a 'target' bridge. Below left: Major Batty (left of picture) directs members of 23 Para Field Ambulance during a mock field operation. Below: A mortar team from the 2nd Battalion, King Edward VII's Own Goorkha Rifles.

GLIDER PILOTS

In response to Churchill's airborne initiative of mid-1940, a major in the Royal Engineers, John Rock, was despatched to the Central Landing Establishment at Ringway on 24 June to gather the men who would become the nucleus of the Glider Pilot Regiment. Despite the Prime Minister's enthusiasm, progress was painfully slow; both gliders and the men to fly them were scarce, and it was not until the formation of the 1st Airborne Division in 1942 that the use of gliders was taken seriously.

It was during this revival of interest in the concept that the decisive move to Tilshead, an abandoned artillery range on Salisbury Plain, was made. Here, Rock was joined by Major George Chatterton and both men began to forge a formidable war machine.

Chatterton took charge of the recruits and set about turning each one into a 'Total Soldier' – a man capable of flying a glider into battle and then of fighting the enemy with any hardware that came to hand. After Rock's untimely death in a flying accident, Chatterton took over the regiment and oversaw the unit's first mission in November 1942. The glider pilots fought in most of the major paratrooper operations of the war.

Of the 3302 men who served in the unit, 551 were killed and 172 won awards. Above: The regiment's shoulder flash.

PEGASUS BRIDGE

The glider pilots who took in the British airborne forces during D-day, 1944, had to be 'Total Soldiers' – skilled in flying and fighting

AFTER MANY weeks of intensive training, there was a feeling of immense excitement and relief that the operation, code-named Deadstick, was about to begin. At Tarrant Rushton airfield, trucks taking 12 pilots and their passengers bounced to a halt beside the Horsa gliders that were to take them to France. The soldiers formed a queue, joking and shaking hands as they heaved themselves, weighed down by their equipment, through the small doors of the Horsas. Staff Sergeant Peter Boyle of the Glider Pilot Regiment walked around his glider doing the final checks. He looked down the long lines of aircraft on the runway. First were the six Horsas to be used in Deadstick; and stretching into the distance were the huge tank-carrying Hamilcar gliders, loaded and lined up on the runway ready to go the next day. Flanking the gliders were two lines of Halifax bombers, the tugs that would tow them into battle. It was an impressive sight and Boyle was excited that he and his fellow pilots were to lead this armada across the Channel and begin the liberation of Europe.

Moments later, the fading light was illuminated by flashes of flame from the exhausts of the Halifax tugs as their engines roared into life. Satisfied that all was stowed and ready, the glider pilots strapped in and completed their checks. The first Halifax lined up in front of Staff Sergeant Wallwork's Horsa, then the tow-rope and communications line were secured and Wallwork told the tug pilot that all was 'go'. The slack was taken up and, with a roar, the combination rolled down the runway and clawed into the air. In all six gliders were hauled aloft at one-minute intervals. The first three, piloted by Staff Sergeants Wallwork and Ainsworth, Boland and Hobbs, and Barkway and Boyle, were heading towards the Orne canal bridge. The others, piloted by Staff Sergeants Lawrence and Shorter, Pearson and Guthrie, and Howard and Baacke, headed for the Orne river bridge. The time

Below: Borne aloft by a Halifax bomber, a Horsa glider heads for Pegasus bridge on the eve of D-day. Above right: Three heavily armed members of the assault team. Above far right: Pre-invasion briefing for glider pilots.

303 hours on 5 June 1944 and the eve of D-day.

The flight was the beginning of a combined operation in which teamwork was essential. Crossing the Channel and navigating the gliders to their exact release point, 6000ft over the French coast, was the job of the RAF. Once released, the glider pilots had to navigate by dead reckoning to the objectives and land their Horsas at two landing zones (LZs). Known as 'X' and 'Y', the LZs' dimensions were approximately 200 by 500yds. Over France three Horsas would

THE HORSA

In December 1940 the British Ministry of Aircraft Production issued requirements for a new glider to Airspeed (1934) Ltd of Portsmouth. Although vague, the specifications demanded a light frame, seating for 26 men, exit doors at either side of the rear fuselage and a wide freight door at the front. Less than a year later, on 12 September 1941, the first prototype, the A. A. 51 Horsa, was pulled into the air by an Armstrong Whitworth Whitley bomber.

The Horsa's cylindrical fuselage and high wings were all-wooden with a plywood covering; the tail was covered in fabric. The undercarriage comprised a tricycle, and a skid, running along the base of the fuselage, for landing.

On landing, a section of the rear fuselage could be detached and the left cargo door opened for ease of exit. In the Mark II version, the nose, containing the cockpit for the two-man crew, could be opened for the removal of heavy equipment.

Although both pilots were often needed to control the glider, it handled well and was capable of flying through turbulence. The large flaps, fitted to the Horsa's wing, allowed steep descents at speeds of up to 180mph. Maximum towing speed was 160mph.

The Horsa's design was basically sound and during World War II a total of 3655 Horsas were built, taking part in small and large scale assaults. On D-day, over 250 swooped down on Normandy to secure the flanks of the Allied beach-heads.

break away and approach LZ 'Y' from the seaward side, while the other three made a wide right-hand semi-circle to approach LZ 'X' from the opposite direction; all six landing at the same moment. Once on the ground, it was the mission of D Company, 2nd Battalion, Oxfordshire and Buckinghamshire Light Infantry (2 Oxf and Bucks), commanded by Major John Howard, to seize intact the bridges over the Orne river and canal.

For the glider pilots' mission to succeed, they had been given all the help and assistance available. Glider pilot training was tough, disciplined and thorough. The commander of the Glider Pilot Regiment, Colonel George Chatterton, had tried to create what he called the 'Total Soldier'. This was a soldier who could master all infantry weapons, drive tanks, jeeps and trucks; fire field guns and use wireless sets – in short, operate in battle any load he was likely to fly in his glider. However, the shortage of tug aircraft for training meant that the glider pilots had much less flying experience than Chatterton would have liked.

Major Howard had received his orders on 2 May and immediately started his own planning and training. Only he knew the target. Although he placed great faith in the skills of the glider pilots, he had to assume that at least half his force might not arrive at the bridges. Therefore, he planned to put one platoon and five engineers of his enlarged company into each of the six gliders, training the teams to perform the tasks of all the other platoons as well as their own.

The briefing for the operation was also being prepared in great secrecy. Flight Lieutenant Lawrence Wright, attached to the Glider Pilot Regiment, had been given the task. A talented artist and keen photographer, he was to prepare a series of briefings which would have a lasting impression on all the glider pilots. Wright got permission to make a film using the sandtable models specially made for the planning of D-day. He set up a device using levers, pullies and cranks weighted with scrap iron, which ensured a steady 'flight' for a 16mm

Main picture: Enemy coast in sight. A Horsa pilot prepares to make the final approach to the target. Trained to the peak of fitness, every member of the Glider Pilot Regiment was expected to be a 'Total Soldier', able to fly to the target and then fight the enemy. A tough selection course weeded out all but the most ideal recruits. Above left: The Horsa prototype. Designed to carry 26 men, it became the mainstay of the British air-landing units. Top: Framed by the wreckage of their transport, troops race for their objective.

camera, above the models. With a rare colour film he simulated the exact flight paths of both groups of gliders, from cast-off right into their LZs by the bridges. It was a masterpiece of improvisation.

On 28 May, their flying training almost complete, the glider pilots walked down to a hutted camp where they met the Oxf and Bucks. The briefings began. Major Howard used a Nissen hut, its walls covered in photographs and with a model of the bridges in the middle. The pilots now realised how small their LZs were, but their confidence was supreme. They also understood the importance of landing as close to the bridges as possible to achieve surprise. Howard was impressed.

By the end of May flying training was completed and the loading and modifying of the gliders started. Modifications included fitting an extra perspex panel, to give the pilots better vision, a giro compass and an arrester parachute, to help slow the gliders during landing. Each glider carried an assault boat, a large number of PIAT anti-tank rounds, ammunition boxes and 30 troops. The glider pilots themselves had been given specialist equipment, including small hand-lights and special maps for night navigation. All was ready, the waiting began. At midday on 4 June, high winds and heavy rain cancelled the operation; more waiting. But 24 hours later the break in the weather came – it was on.

In Wallwork's glider, the co-pilot, Ainsworth, could not see the wood but they stuck to their pre-set course

After leaving the airfield, the tug pilots set a course of 062 degrees for Worthy Down and the Halifax-Horsa combinations climbed to 6000ft. Patchy clouds darkened the evening sky. As they crossed the coast over Worthing, Boyle peered down to see if he could find the invasion fleet. But, by then, it was too dark and the Royal Navy's blackout was complete. For everyone, the Channel crossing was the final proof that this was no ordinary training flight. In the gliders the soldiers were singing, joking and smoking. About 40 minutes after the take-off, Wallwork saw the white lines of surf on the French coast; he was two minutes from casting off. The tug pilot then gave him the windspeed, height and heading, and, after they had wished each other good luck, Wallwork released the Horsa. He ordered the doors to be opened. The other gliders started separating in the night sky.

Barkway and Boyle settled down after their release and started their flight drills. Boyle, using his hand-light, called out the first heading. Remembering the film, he looked for the black mass of the Bois de Bavent, a large wood that should appear on their port side. He saw it and told Barkway to start a turn to starboard; Barkway responded by heaving over the large wooden steering wheel – all was going well. Looking down, Boyle saw the bridge and shouted excitedly, 'There it is!' 'I got it,' Barkway replied calmly. In Wallwork's glider the co-pilot, Ainsworth, could not see the wood, but they stuck to their pre-set course.

Behind them, heading for the other bridge, Staff Sergeant Roy Howard was having difficulties. Immediately after release, he realised his glider was overloaded. With the trim right back and full flap, he could not reduce speed below 90 knots, which would be catastrophic at the other end of the glide path. He turned round to Lieutenant Fox, the platoon commander and yelled, 'Two men to the back – on the double.' Two soldiers scrambled up the fuselage and Howard regained control. Baacke, his co-pilot, gave him a course of 268 degrees for 80 seconds and then a turn to port onto 212 degrees for the final run-in – a distance of only 1200yds. At 1000ft, to their immense relief, they picked out in the moonlight the river, the bridge with its distinctive buttress in the middle, and the small rectangular field that was their LZ.

Wallwork and Ainsworth, also peering through the darkness, saw the unmistakeable lines of the river and canal shining out like two lines of silver thread in the moonlight. Wright's training film had made it seem so familiar that they knew exactly where to look. Then, they too experienced the exhilaration of seeing their objective, the bulbous structure of the canal bridge. Behind the pilots, the troops linked arms and lifted their feet off the floor, bracing themselves for the crash. Pointing the glider as far up the LZ as possible, Wallwork steered it for the ground. Ainsworth released the parachute as the wheels touched the grass. Then came three large crashes as the glider bounded across the field. Major Howard saw sparks flashing past the open door as the glider skidded along the ground, its undercarriage having been torn away on the initial impact. Wallwork fought to keep the Horsa straight until the cockpit disintegrated as the glider's nose tore through the barbed-wire defences surrounding the bridge. A few seconds of stunned silence followed before the troops piled out and went into action.

By the time Major Howard had disentangled himself from the wreckage, he realised that Lieutenant Den Brotheridge and the leading section were already walking quietly past the glider towards the bridge. There was no shooting. Then he saw the dark structure of the bridge not more than 50yds away. He realised that they had achieved total surprise and had landed so close to the bridge that the nose of the glider had breached the wire defences. The only noise at that moment was the moaning of the two pilots, lying injured and stunned in the wreckage of

Above right: Aerial view of Landing Zone 'X', the Caen canal bridge. **Right:** Two of the assault gliders. Flown by Barkway and Wallwork, they landed within a few yards of the bridge. **Below, left and right:** Two views of the Horsa flown by Pearson and Guthrie that landed just north of the Orne bridge.

their cockpit. The short period of calm ended with the explosion of a phosphorus grenade, which lit the scene as the first platoon went into action attacking the pillbox near to the bridge.

Boland and Hobbs had also seen the bridge and were lining themselves up on the final approach. Suddenly, slightly behind and to the right, Boland saw the huge shape of another glider bearing down on him. It was Barkway and Boyle. Boland flashed his landing light and banked to starboard to avoid a collision. In front of them, both crews saw the sparks off Wallwork's glider plummeting across the LZ. Boland rounded out, hit the ground and also lost his undercarriage. The glider careered across the field, halting almost intact. Both the pilots and their passengers were slightly shaken but quite conscious, and the platoon, commanded by Lieutenant David Wood, was in action almost immediately.

Simultaneously, the third glider hurtled in to land between the two gliders already down. Possibly because of sideslip during the approach, Barkway's glider hit the ground hard and at an angle. Quickly, it began to break up, leaving a trail of debris as it tore across the ground. Finally, its back broken, it stopped on the edge of a pond. Both pilots were thrown out of their cockpit into the water. Barkway, stunned by the crash, later remembered fighting for air, reaching for the surface and then crawling to the bank. Soaked to the skin and in a state of shock, both groped their way back to the remains of their glider to start unloading valuable ammunition. The platoon, with several injured and one killed, had to regroup and was the last to arrive on the bridge.

The double thump of two Mills grenades confirmed the destruction of the pillbox, and Lieutenant Brotheridge immediately headed across the bridge with his lead section. Woods' platoon, now at the bridge, was ordered by Howard to clear the trenches around the pillbox. By now, the defenders were resisting fiercely. Firing started from the other side of the bridge, knocking Brotheridge to the ground with a fatal wound in the neck. At that moment, Lieutenant Sandy Smith, with a broken arm, struggled up with the survivors of his platoon from the wreckage of Barkway's glider. Howard told him to move his men across the bridge to help Brotheridge's platoon and take the far bank. With Smith's platoon across, the bridge was captured. It had taken about 15 minutes.

Meanwhile, Staff Sergeant Roy Howard

Pegasus Bridge
The Glider Pilot Regiment
5/6 June 1944

At 2256 on 5 June 1944 — only hours before the beginning of the D-Day landings in Normandy — the first of six Horsa gliders, piloted by members of The Glider Pilot Regiment and towed by Halifax bombers, took off from Tarrant Rushton airfield in Dorset. Their mission was to land D Company of the 2nd Ox and Bucks Light Infantry at the vital Orne bridges.

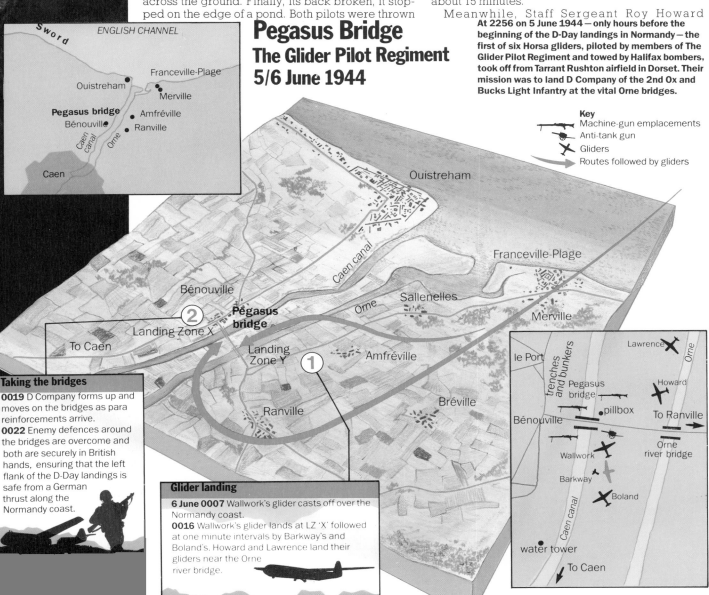

Key
Machine-gun emplacements
Anti-tank gun
Gliders
Routes followed by gliders

ENGLISH CHANNEL
Sword
Ouistreham
Franceville-Plage
Merville
Pegasus bridge
Amfréville
Bénouville
Ranville
Caen canal
Orne
Caen

Ouistreham
Caen canal
Franceville-Plage
Bénouville
Pegasus bridge
2
Landing Zone X
To Caen
Orne
Sallenelles
Merville
Landing Zone Y
1
Amfréville
Ranville
Bréville
le Port
trenches and bunkers
Pegasus bridge
Lawrence
Howard
Orne
pillbox
To Ranville
Bénouville
Orne river bridge
Wallwork
Barkway
Boland
Caen canal
water tower
To Caen

Taking the bridges

0019 D Company forms up and moves on the bridges as para reinforcements arrive.

0022 Enemy defences around the bridges are overcome and both are securely in British hands, ensuring that the left flank of the D-Day landings is safe from a German thrust along the Normandy coast.

Glider landing

6 June 0007 Wallwork's glider casts off over the Normandy coast.

0016 Wallwork's glider lands at LZ 'X' followed at one minute intervals by Barkway's and Boland's. Howard and Lawrence land their gliders near the Orne river bridge.

approached the trees at the beginning of his run to the river bridge. He took off some flap to flatten the glide and maintain more height to get into the LZ. Over the trees, Baacke deployed the parachute, which pulled the glider up sharply, and the Horsa rolled into the field. A herd of cows stampeded across their front. Either a cow or a bump took away the nose wheel but the glider skidded to a halt within six yards of the appointed place. To their horror, the pilots realised that they were alone. Of the other two gliders, one had landed two fields away and the third, piloted by Lawrence and Shorter, had landed at a bridge on the river Dives, some 10 miles to the west. However, there was no resistance at the river bridge, and the platoon took their objective without firing a shot.

Throughout the night and into the following day, they beat off repeated counter-attacks

The glider pilots had done more than enough. Five out of the six platoons had arrived on target and Major Howard's company had captured both bridges intact. After securing the bridges, the pilots unloaded their gliders and helped in the defence of the crossings. While unloading his glider, Barkway was hit in the wrist, an injury that resulted in the loss of his left arm. Throughout the night and into the following day, they beat off repeated counter-attacks by enemy tanks, infantry, and even a patrol boat sent down from Caen. However, by mid-day on 6 June Lord Lovat's Commandos had fought their way to the bridges from the invasion beaches to relieve Howard and his company.

Within two days, the glider pilots had been with-

Below: Courtesy of the Glider Pilot Regiment, a group of Allied soldiers cross Pegasus bridge, over the Caen canal, a few days after the Normandy landings. Bottom: Smiles all round as the regiment's commander, Colonel Chatterton (far right), congratulates his men at Fargo camp on 8 June. From left to right: Staff Sergeants Lawrence, Howard, Baacke, Shorter, Boyle and Pearson.

drawn to Fargo Camp in Wiltshire; Lawrence a Shorter having fought their way through enemy lin with their platoon from the Dives. At Fargo they m Colonel Chatterton who had already studied t aerial photographs showing the brilliant success the operation. It had exceeded all expectations a was later described by Air Chief Marshal Lei Mallory as: 'The greatest feat of flying in the Seco World War.' The pilots were all granted leave. T next day, Staff Sergeant Boyle caught a train ba home. On the station he was accosted by an irate la asking him why he was not in France with the othe 'I've been and come back,' he replied. She looked him in disbelief and turned away.

THE AUTHOR Captain Richard Folkes joined the Ar Air Corps after completing a degree in philosop at Exeter University. He now lectures at the Ro Military Academy, Sandhurst and is a member of Royal United Services Institute.

PATHFINDERS

The Pathfinder Platoon has the exacting and dangerous tasks of reconnoitring, securing and marking 5 Airborne Brigade's drop zones

THE SKY WAS OVERCAST with more than a hint of rain as the four-man patrol approached a stream that cut across its line of advance. Shallow, with a stone bed, the stream presented little problem to the paratroopers. Nevertheless, the patrol's commander decided to treat it as a serious obstacle. The lead scout moved across first, keeping an eye on the far bank and paying particular attention to a small copse 100m to the left – it could contain an enemy position. So far so good. As the lead scout started cautiously up the gully opposite the crossing point, the patrol commander began to cross the stream, covered by the remaining two men on the near bank.

Once across, the patrol slowed up slightly to regroup, then continued to move up the gully until the scout signalled the commander forward. Still silent, except for the sound of boots being lifted from the ankle-deep mud, the patrol covered their arcs of fire as the commander looked at the ground in front over the lip of the gully. No way around this one, he thought: flat open ground to the front, a rise to the right and ground levelling out down on the stream on the left – no cover.

The shout 'contact front' and the first two rounds fired by the lead scout seemed simultaneous

With little option open to him, the commander decided to move his patrol across the 500m gap between its present position and the nearest good cover. The patrol moved off, evenly spaced to reduce the likelihood of being caught in the open with one burst. The lead scout scoured the area for signs of any threat in the line of advance, while 'tail-end Charlie' covered the rear.

Half-way across, it happened. One round, fired from the right, landed in front of the lead scout. A split-second later, three electronically-controlled figure targets leapt up from the undergrowth 30m ahead. The shout 'contact front' and the first two rounds fired by the lead scout seemed simultaneous. Weapons were raised onto their targets, aimed, fired and fired again. The patrol broke left and right, and, having briefly engaged his target, the lead scout turned and raced down the 'funnel' created by the rest of the patrol. After running the gauntlet of live rounds being fired on either side of him, the lead scout ran beyond the last man before swinging out and around. 'Break,' he screamed over the crack and thud of rounds being fired and hitting the target. As the lead scout began putting down covering fire, the patrol commander leapt up and went through the same motions as the first man. This process was repeated again and again until the patrol reached the cover of the stream and gully. Three men

PATHFINDER PLATOON

The Pathfinder Platoon, 5 Airborne Brigade, was formed in 1984. Accorded the status of an independent unit within the brigade's headquarters and signals squadron, the platoon is based in Aldershot and has been given two distinct roles.

The first of these is the selection and marking of drop zones for the brigade's airborne assets. The second is to provide the brigade with short- to medium-range reconnaissance. These missions would take place after the main drop and would include close-target recces of both brigade and battalion objectives. In addition to reconnaissance missions, the Pathfinder Platoon is capable of setting up ambushes on enemy lines of communication, and carrying out small-scale raids and demolition tasks. The members of the platoon are drawn mainly from The Parachute Regiment's three regular battalions, supplemented by a small intake from The Household Division. At present, the Pathfinders are divided into one six-man patrol and four four-man patrols. The six-man headquarters patrol comprises a platoon commander (an experienced captain), a colour sergeant, two signallers and two paratroopers (one of whom is a medic). Each of the four-man patrols includes a signaller, medic and demolitions expert. With the exception of one patrol that is commanded by a lieutenant (the platoon's second-in-command), each four-man patrol is commanded by an experienced corporal.

Previous page: A trainee pathfinder's reflexes are tested with live firing at electronically-controlled targets. The Pathfinders expect each man to hold his own in the unit's four-man patrols. The exercises involve concealment (above left), cross-country movement with a 55lb bergen (above right) and live firing (left). Below, left and right: On tactical exercises, instructors (in red berets) are ready to exploit any faults in the trainees tactical approach with instant 'capture'.

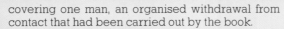

covering one man, an organised withdrawal from contact that had been carried out by the book.

The patrol was made up of four men from Britain's Parachute Regiment, and the risk of casualties had been a real one. These men had come from their various units and were attempting the gruelling selection process which, if they succeeded in passing, would allow them to become members of one of Britain's finest small units – the 'Pathfinders'.

The pathfinder is the first to parachute in before the main force: to reconnoitre, secure and mark out the drop zone for those who follow

The Pathfinder Platoon is the spearhead of 5 Airborne Brigade, Britain's rapid deployment force, and the platoon's training is both tough and realistic. It has to be. The Parachute Regiment has, since its formation during World War II, recognised the need for maintaining the highest standards in both the selection and the training of its paratroops. These high standards have stood the paras in good stead throughout the post-war conflicts in which they have been involved.

Britain's airborne forces experienced a major set-back with the disbandment of 16 Parachute Brigade in 1974, when the three parachute battalions lost their supporting elements. With the loss of para artillery and engineers went Britain's capability to mount large-scale airborne operations. This situation continued until October 1983 when, as a direct result of British experience in the Falklands, 5 Airborne Brigade was formed. From the outset, it was realised that the brigade required its own, independent unit capable of conducting reconnaissance, surveillance and other special-purpose missions.

The responsibility for the creation of this new unit fell to certain members of 5 Airborne Brigade's staff who, in true British tradition, had to scrounge, convince, cajole and connive, using much goodwill and occasionally the back-door, until they had amassed the men and material necessary to form this new unit – the Pathfinder Platoon.

The role of the pathfinder is one that is well known within the airborne fraternity. The pathfinder is the first to parachute in before the main force: to reconnoitre, secure and mark out the drop zone (DZ) for those who follow. This dangerous and exacting task became the primary mission of the new platoon. However, no elite unit is created by personnel and equipment alone, and the first and most important consideration had to be the selection and training of the men volunteering for inclusion in the Pathfinder Platoon. These volunteers, posted on attachment from the parachute battalions, and to a lesser extent various supporting units such as para signals, had already undergone the rigorous selection and training required by all those who aspire to be part of Britain's airborne forces. In spite of this, and because of the individual qualities and specialist skills demanded of a pathfinder paratrooper, the volunteers are required to undergo further tests and training before being allowed to join one of the platoon's four-man patrols.

Initially, the Pathfinders were fortunate to have on their strength an experienced Parachute Regiment NCO who had served with the 22nd Special Air Service (22 SAS) Regiment, and had been involved in running their selection and continuation courses. This provided the platoon with a concept on which they could base the pathfinders' selection and training. Although the roles of the two units are different, they do share a number of specialist skills. Indeed, since its formation the Pathfinder Platoon has built up a special rapport with the SAS.

INDEPENDENT PARACHUTE COMPANIES

Britain's first Pathfinders were formed during World War II as the brain-child of Lieutenant-General Sir Frederick Browning. The first platoon was raised in 1942 and underwent a rigorous selection process that included physical fitness, signalling, weapons handling and map reading. Following selection and tactical training, the first 20 men completed their parachute instruction in September 1942 and formed the nucleus of the 21st Independent Parachute Company. In common with the 22nd Independent Parachute Company (formed in early 1943), the 21st had a strength of around 200 men.

Both companies consisted of three platoons, each divided into two teams, and the paras were trained to fight both in small groups and as individuals. The initial task of these pathfinder platoons was to carry out sabotage behind enemy lines. It was not until the role of the independent companies was extended to include the laying out and marking of drop zones (DZs), however, that the units became officially known as 'Pathfinders'.

The 21st and 22nd Independent Parachute Companies distinguished themselves in action during World War II. The 21st served with the 1st Airborne Division in North Africa, while the 22nd, as part of the 6th Airborne Division, landed in Europe during the early stages of the Normandy invasion.

After both units were disbanded in 1946, the pathfinder role went to the Guards Independent Brigade. When the latter was disbanded to form the nucleus of G Squadron, 22nd Special Air Service Regiment, the pathfinder role remained unfulfilled until the formation of 5 Airborne Brigade's Pathfinder Platoon in 1984.

Although a great many recruits of the Pathfinders Platoon will have already completed the gruelling selection course of The Parachute Regiment, they must prove themselves all over again before being accepted into the Pathfinders. Top: Trainees surmount a wall obstacle, while others cross a river (above left) and scramble under barbed wire (above right). Right: Soaked through, would-be pathfinders emerge from a culvert.

The Pathfinder Platoon selection course is divided into three separate phases, and runs over a three-week period. Phase One/Military Skills begins with a battle fitness test (BFT), a three-mile road run that must be completed within 16 minutes. This is followed by the platoon commander's introductory briefing, in which he outlines the course. The combination of strenuous physical activity (each morning begins with a BFT at 0530), briefings and lectures is an important aspect of Phase One. It is designed to build up the volunteer's fitness and stamina, and give him the opportunity to recover from the exertion while he assimilates information vital to his successful completion of the course. Map reading and navigational exercises play an important part in the overall course, and during the first week each volunteer must successfully complete four navigational exercises, one of them at night, to reach the second phase. All these exercises are carried out on an individual basis, each man having his own route to follow around a series of check-points. The volunteer is also introduced to signalling, especially morse code. This is a skill each man must master before joining one of the platoon's patrols. Another aspect covered during the first week is 'resistance to interrogation'. Known in military parlance as RTI, the ability to resist interrogation is considered vital for men operating in small units behind enemy lines. Should a man be captured prior to a large parachute operation, he must be capable of denying the enemy information that could jeopardise the entire mission. The military skills phase ends with a morning on the range, followed by a briefing on the second phase.

They are confronted by a 30-mile march that must be completed in under 14 hours

Phase Two/Endurance is designed to test the individual's fitness and stamina, while at the same time testing his ability to navigate across inhospitable terrain. The preferred location for this phase is South Wales, and it consists of a series of timed navigation marches. The times allowed for these vary slightly according to local weather conditions, but each man starts off the week with a bergen rucksack weighing 40lb, plus his rifle. This weight is gradually increased until the man is carrying 55lb, which is considered the optimum operational weight. The introductory march is about 30 miles long which, taking into consideration the gradients encountered in this part of the country and the physical stress experienced by the volunteer during the previous week, makes this first march a severe test of both stamina and mental endurance. With little time for the volunteer to recover, this march is followed the next morning by a point-to-point march of between 10-15 miles. The volunteer must pass through a series of check-points manned by instructors who give him the grid reference of the next point he must pass through. This timed exercise is a test of the individual's map-reading ability, and it is a test that for some proves too difficult – it is usual to lose a number of volunteers at this stage. Those who survive the point-to-point are rewarded with a final endurance march the following day. By this time, the men are carrying a 55lb bergen. As they set off at first light, they are confronted by a 30-mile march that must be completed in under 14 hours. Again, the strain proves too much for some, and men fall by the wayside to join others who, for various reasons, have been unable to make the grade.

Those who successfully complete the final march find themselves through to the last stage of the pathfinder selection. Phase Three/Tactics starts with an introduction to the tactics employed by four-man patrols, and for most men this will involve a radical change from the way they have previously approached the tactics of reconnaissance. Before volunteering to join the Pathfinders, most of the men will have served at least three years with one of the rifle companies in The Parachute Regiment, where the smallest sub-unit is an eight-man section.

The candidates spend a day on the ranges, practising instinctive or reflex shooting

They soon learn, however, that there is a great difference between fighting in a section and operating as a four-man patrol. New tactics and techniques must be learnt and mastered. One of the first lessons concentrates on patrol movement, where the men are taught the usual patrol formations, primary arcs of fire, and how to judge the appropriate spacing for the terrain while keeping good command and control. No verbal orders are issued and each man must therefore be fully aware of his responsibilities within the patrol. This instruction continues throughout the third phase, much of it practical, and the men are taught such skills as obstacle crossing, how to establish lying-up positions (LUPs) and how to carry out close-target recces.

After two days of lectures and practical lessons, the candidates spend a day on the ranges, practising instinctive or reflex shooting. Known as 'snap-shooting', this is a necessary technique for men operating in four-man patrols; they will undoubtedly be outnumbered by enemy forces and will need to react very quickly to extract themselves unscathed. After leaving the ranges, the men divide into four-man patrols and deploy into the field where they spend two days practising their newly acquired skills under the watchful eye of an instructor. Each man gets the opportunity to take on the role of the lead scout and the commander in these exercises. For the final exercise of the selection course, however, one of the more experienced volunteers (there is usually at least one junior NCO per patrol) is chosen to command. The volunteers are watched closely during these two days and their progress is constantly assessed. It is still possible to fail the course, one of the reasons being a low score in fieldcraft. After the field-training exercise (FTX), the men must each pass a close-quarter battle (CQB) test. This is a live-firing exercise in which an individual must successfully negotiate various obstacles and engage (and hit) a number of targets. Each man is marked on his fieldcraft, camouflage, stealth and shooting ability. The range itself is up to 1000m long and can contain up to a dozen different targets, some of which are electronically controlled, while others are well hidden, making them difficult to spot.

If the men pass this stage of the selection process they spend the following day on the ranges. Now reorganised back into the four-man patrols, the candidates must practise their contact drills. This is one of the most dangerous parts of the course and involves anti-ambush procedures. These four-man patrol contact drills, conducted with live ammunition, are not usually practised in the British Army, except in such units as the SAS and Special Boat Squadron. They involve engaging a target, and then retiring under covering fire. The exercises involve a high degree of skill and competence on the part of both instructor and trainee, and to date there have been no problems. The day usually culminates with a period of strenuous physical exercise to alleviate the tension that has built up during the live-firing exercise.

The last, and in many ways the most exacting, stage of the pathfinder selection is the final FTX. During this exercise the patrols are given a number of tasks that will test their new skills, both as individuals and as part of a team. Over a period of between two and three days, each patrol must carry out a mission that involves an infiltration into a target area, establishing an observation position, conducting a close-target reconnaissance and, finally, successfully exfiltrating to a safe rendezvous. This part of the course is run in Wales during the winter months; weather conditions are virtually guaranteed to be severe. During their two nights out in the open, each patrol will spend up to 24 hours on 'hard routine'. This means no smoking, no lights, no fires and no cooking. Cold, tired and hungry, each patrol has to avoid 'enemy' mobile patrols and ambushes to reach its target area. It must then get past sentries in order to conduct close-target reconnaissance. In the past, when patrols have been caught out in the open, the men have been forced to dump their bergens and rely on the contents of their belt kit to carry out their task.

On completion of the final exercise the men are transported back to Aldershot, the base of the Pathfinder Platoon. Candidates are now individually assessed on their overall performance, and each NCO instructor involved in the selection course puts forward his own views as to the men's performance. By this time it is usually clear to the instructors which of the candidates are capable of becoming useful members of the platoon. In certain circumstances, however, a borderline candidate may be considered for further training on a provisional basis.

This assessment marks the end of the pathfinder selection course and for those on it a welcome weekend break – the first in three solid weeks of training and testing. Those who have passed will return the following Monday, ready to begin the two-week signals cadre and the first phase of their continuation training. Many, however, do not make it this far. In the early part of 1987, a total of 35 men, including two officers, began the three-week selection course. Only 12 men and one officer actually got through to the continuation phase. After the men have mastered the basics of CW (continuous wave/morse) signalling, the continuation phase continues with four to six weeks of jungle-warfare training in the Far East. Here the trainees become acquainted with the low-level tactics and techniques used in jungle warfare and learn how to survive and operate in this difficult environment.

On their return to Aldershot, the pathfinder trainees have one more skill to master before they can pass the continuation phase and become fully-fledged members of the platoon. The military freefall parachute course lasts a total of six weeks. The technique, known as HALO (high-altitude/low-opening) is taught to the trainees at RAF Brize

Right: A pathfinder drifts down on the new GQ 360 parachute. Below: This close-quarter night training area is designed to test trainees' responses in the dark. Feeling their way in the simple maze, the sudden appearance of dummy targets (and the occasional dead sheep) quickly puts the men on their mettle.

Far left: A four-man patrol deploys on an exercise. While the patrol commander and lead scout consult the map, one man maintains a constant watch, allowing the fourth patrol member to reach for his water bottle. Below: Two men carry out a Close Target Recon (CTR), familiarising themselves with the nightscope.

Norton. Here, the men come under the instruction of highly qualified NCOs belonging to No.1 PTS Freefall Training Flight. Beginning with a 45-second-delay jump from 12,000ft, the students progress to a freefall night jump from 25,000ft. Military freefall parachuting is a skill which could prove vital to the success of pathfinder operations. In order to perform their mission of marking out the DZ, the pathfinders must be able to freefall into the target area up to 72 hours prior to the main drop. The HALO course marks the end of the volunteer's continuation training and he now becomes a member of one of the Pathfinder Platoon's four-man patrols.

Britain's airborne units are renowned for their esprit de corps and individualism, and the Pathfinders are no exception. Other units, those not para-qualified, are generally referred to as 'crap-hats'. Indeed, for all Britain's airborne forces the non-maroon colour of other units' headgear denotes a distinct lack of status. During an exercise involving both the Pathfinder Platoon and members from the SAS Regiment, an NCO of the latter pointed out the similarities between the two units with respect to training, organisation and the level of individual skill. He concluded by commenting that the Pathfinders might just as well be part of the SAS. With characteristic good humour, one of the pathfinders quipped: 'What, and become a crap-hat?'

The men of the Pathfinder Platoon are a highly motivated and extremely efficient group of professional paratroop soldiers, skilled in a variety of specialised techniques. They are among the forerunners of the world's special operations units, and their motto – 'First In' – means just that.

THE AUTHOR Peter Macdonald is a freelance defence photo-journalist and author. He served with the British Army and Rhodesian Security Forces between 1974 and 1980.

REVOLUTION ON GRENADA

A British colony for 200 years, Grenada had received its independence in 1974. Until 1979 the island had been ruled by Prime Minister Eric Gairy who, though nominally accountable to a British-appointed governor-general, had created an increasingly authoritarian regime with the aid of his private army, known as the Mongoose Gang. Gairy was deposed in March 1979 in a coup led by the New Jewel Movement (NJM).

The new Prime Minister was Maurice Bishop, a charismatic barrister with strong ties with the Grenadan people. His deputy, Bernard Coard, was a doctrinaire Marxist who did much to organise the NJM into a coherent political party.

Although Bishop and Coard began as an excellent team in the leadership of Grenada, a deep division opened between them. It was Coard's fervent belief that Grenada should become fully aligned with the aims and principles of the Soviet Union, and he accused Bishop of seeking a position of compromise in Grenada's relations with America.

Bishop had developed a close relationship with Cuba and its revolutionary leader, Fidel Castro, but he was nevertheless ordered by the NJM to share the leadership of Grenada with Coard on an equal basis in September 1983.

The Grenadan joint leadership soon came to an abrupt end, however. On 13 October Bishop was placed under house arrest.

There was widespread popular anger at this, and on 19 October a large crowd freed Bishop and carried him triumphantly into Grenada's capital of St George's. At this point, units of the People's Revolutionary Army (PRA) seized Bishop and five supporters and they were summarily shot. The deterioration of public order after this was swift, and Grenada's neighbours viewed events there with increasing concern.

URGENT FURY

The US used its elite air and seaborne forces when it moved against the island of Grenada in 1983

OPERATION URGENT Fury, as President Ronald Reagan named his intervention in the Caribbean island of Grenada, began with clandestine landings on the island by men of the US Navy SEALs. Their mission was to reconnoitre and select landing sites for the main force due to arrive in 48 hours. Another 11-man SEAL team parachuted into the residence of the governor-general, Sir Paul Scoon, in order to bring him away to safety. However, no sooner had they landed at Government House than three BTR-60 armoured personnel carriers (APCs) rushed to block their exits. Without anti-tank weapons, the SEALs had no option but to lie low in the residency and await reinforcement. An operation had begun that was to use the resources of crack US units – the marines, the rangers, paratroopers and, of course, the SEALs who were already in action.

The decision taken by President Reagan to intervene in the internal politics of one of his Caribbean neighbours was greeted with horror by a great many nations, both Western and of the communist bloc. However, a number of factors which had developed over the preceding years had culminated in a political situation on Grenada which the Reagan administration chose to regard as an imminent threat to American security. By deploying military force to

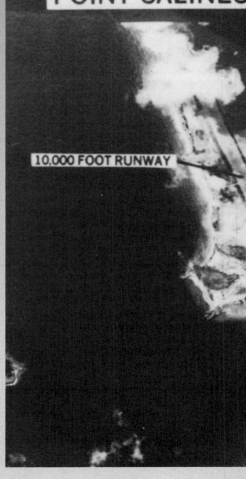

POINT SALINES

10,000 FOOT RUNWAY

Below: This aerial photograph of the Point Salines airfield, purporting to show Soviet-style military installations on the island, was used in testimony by US Defense Department officials before a Senate Foreign Relations subcommittee as the US considered armed intervention in Grenada. Right and bottom: US airborne troops deploy from Blackhawk helicopters on Point Salines airfield. Right centre: Well camouflaged and heavily armed, members of the 82nd Airborne pose for the camera.

ELD, GRENADA

POL STORAGE AREA

SUPPORT AREA

BARRACKS AREA

a meeting was held by Grenada's neighbouring islands in the Caribbean.

The Organisation of Eastern Caribbean States (OECS), together with Jamaica and Barbados, called upon President Reagan to provide military intervention. Reagan was not slow to comply, for here was a chance to restore American influence in an area increasingly dominated by the ideas and resources of Cuba, both of which had been welcomed by a left-wing regime which was now in a shambles. A successful military operation in Grenada would serve as a telling reminder that any communist expansion in the Caribbean would be met with powerful opposition. On another level, Reagan argued that an operation was vital in order to rescue several hundred American medical students who were unable to leave Grenada and would pose a very serious problem if used as hostages by the PRA. The authorisation for military action finally was given and a combined force of elite strike units was assigned the mission of securing Grenada and evacuating the students back to the US.

The Delta anti-terrorist unit was standing by to rescue any students who may have been taken hostage

The units selected were US Army rangers of the 75th Infantry (Ranger) Regiment, US Army paratroopers of the 82nd Airborne Division, and marines of the 22nd Marine Amphibious Unit (MAU), who were diverted on their way to Lebanon to take part in the Caribbean operation. Small contingents also came from such special operations units as the US Navy SEALs, the US Army Special Forces, the USAF Combat Control Teams (CCTs), and the Delta anti-terrorist unit, which was standing by in case its special skills were needed to rescue any students who had been taken hostage. Finally, a force of 400 police and military personnel supplied by Grenada's Caribbean neighbours was to move in to act as a garrison after the island had been secured.

Following on the landing of the SEAL teams, at 0536 hours on 25 October, 400 marines from the assault ship *Guam* landed by helicopter at Pearls Airport on the east tip of the island, meeting only light

eliminate the threat before it became fully developed, Reagan hoped simultaneously to restore a pro-American government in a strategic location and also to present the communist regimes of the world with hard proof that the USA was prepared to use arms in order to preserve the status quo in the Caribbean.

A coup in 1979 had brought to power on Grenada Maurice Bishop, a popular radical nationalist. He, in turn, was deposed in October 1983 by his former deputy, the hard-line Marxist Bernard Coard. This coup was unpopular; public order deteriorated, and

Above: Members of a US Air Force Combat Control Team, who are trained as pathfinders and airborne air traffic controllers, consult with rangers over a map of Grenada. Below: A US 105mm gun crew receives orders before going into action. Right: Equipment and supplies are unloaded from a C-130 transport at Point Salines.

Grenada
US Airborne Forces, October 1983

On the morning of 25 October 1983 the United States launched Operation Urgent Fury with an airborne assault on the airstrip at Point Salines and a heliborne landing near Pearls airport. As a second Marine task force worked its way down from Grand Mal Bay, the airborne forces at Point Salines overcame Cuban and Grenadan resistance and pushed northwards. St George's fell late on 26 October and mopping up operations began.

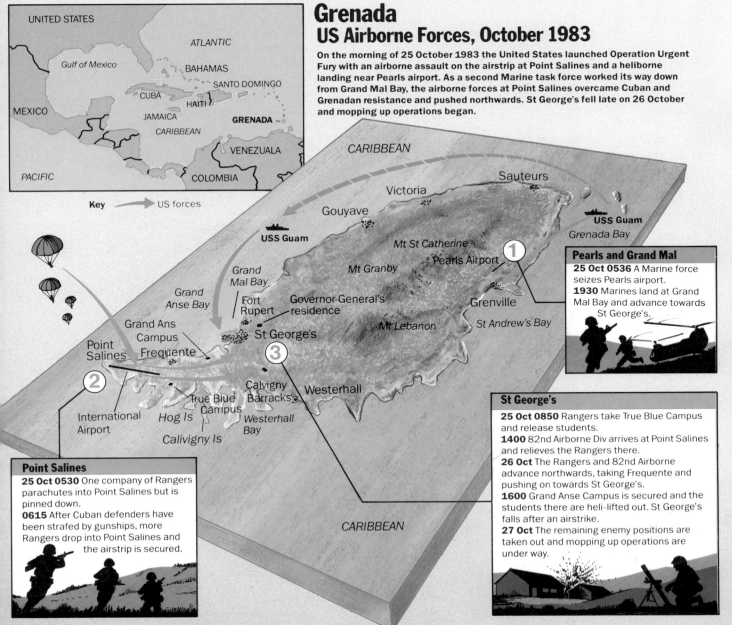

Key → US forces

Pearls and Grand Mal

25 Oct 0536 A Marine force seizes Pearls airport.
1930 Marines land at Grand Mal Bay and advance towards St George's.

Point Salines

25 Oct 0530 One company of Rangers parachutes into Point Salines but is pinned down.
0615 After Cuban defenders have been strafed by gunships, more Rangers drop into Point Salines and the airstrip is secured.

St George's

25 Oct 0850 Rangers take True Blue Campus and release students.
1400 82nd Airborne Div arrives at Point Salines and relieves the Rangers there.
26 Oct The Rangers and 82nd Airborne advance northwards, taking Frequente and pushing on towards St George's.
1600 Grand Anse Campus is secured and the students there are heli-lifted out. St George's falls after an airstrike.
27 Oct The remaining enemy positions are taken out and mopping up operations are under way.

THE SPECTRE GUNSHIP

'There goes Spectre, taking out some guys again.' So exulted one embattled young GI during Operation Urgent Fury, paying tribute to the devastating suppressive fire provided by the gunships circling overhead.

The Lockheed AC-130E Spectre gunship is but one member of a large family of specialised aircraft deriving from the outstanding C-130 Hercules transport. An aircraft with a long career of distinguished service, the Hercules first flew as prototype YC-130A in August 1954. Production began the following year, and in April 1962 the C-130E, the basic form of the Spectre, was introduced. It was powered by four 4050hp engines turning four-blade propellers, and new underwing fuel tanks had increased its range to 2420 miles.

The Spectre's predecessor as a Hercules-based gunship, the AC-130A, was armed with eight multi-barrel weapons, four of them 7.62mm and four 20mm. The AC-130E sported two 40mm guns, two 20mm, and two 7.62mm. A later development, the AC-130H, replaced one of the 40mm guns with a 105mm howitzer, mounted in the rear of the fuselage, greatly increasing its capacity against tanks and fortified installations. The howitzer first saw action in 1972 in Vietnam.

Designed for night operations, the Spectre carries light-intensifying devices, radar and forward-looking infra-red sensors, a laser designator and low-light-level television. One method of operation involved locking a computer onto a designated target; the pilot would then align his fixed guns, all firing from the port side, according to instructions issued by the computer. This innovation greatly increased the fire effectiveness of the circling Spectre.

opposition. As the marines were landing at Pearls, C-130 transports carrying 550 airborne rangers from the 1st and 2nd Battalions, 75th Infantry (Ranger) Regiment were approaching the Point Salines airstrip in the west. The original plan called for one company of rangers to parachute onto the airstrip and secure it so that the other rangers could be airlanded. During the flight, however, new orders were issued, based on intelligence gained by AC-130E Spectre gunships using their low-light TV cameras and infra-red sensors. All the rangers were now to make a combat parachute assault from 500ft, as their transport aircraft would be approaching at a level beneath the effective field of fire of the Cuban anti-aircraft guns surrounding the airstrip. Although members of the Rhodesian Light Infantry, the Rhodesian SAS and the Selous Scouts had carried out combat jumps from even lower altitudes during the anti-guerrilla war in Rhodesia, no US paratrooper had jumped from such a low level since World War II. A second reason for the low-level jump was that it would cut down the time the men would be in the air to 19 seconds, reducing their vulnerability to small-arms fire from the ground. As it was, many arrived on the ground to find their chutes riddled with holes from the defenders' fire.

Deploying the older T10 parachute, which is less sensitive to the effects of a heavy ground wind over the drop zone, and carrying extra ammunition instead of a reserve chute (which would have been worthless at the low altitude), rangers of A Company, 1st Battalion, 75th Rangers 'shotgunned' from both sides of the C-130. They came under so much gunfire, however, that the aircraft following did not drop their sticks of rangers. Instead, they veered off while Spectre gunships homed in to suppress the anti-aircraft weapons with their 20mm, 40mm and 7.62mm armament. At 0615 the jump was resumed, with the remainder of Lieutenant-Colonel Wes Taylor's 1st Battalion and Lieutenant-Colonel Ralph Hagler's 2nd Battalion, 75th Rangers quickly clearing their aircraft at 500ft. About 550 rangers who had been selected from the two battalions made the jump, earning a combat jump star for their parachute wings. A few members of the 82nd Airborne Division (including one heavy equipment operator who was to help clear the runway) and a few USAF CCT members also jumped over Point Salines.

The rangers immediately set up drop zones and began to bombard the Cuban positions on the bluff

Once the rangers were on the ground they moved out to secure the airstrip and to clear the runways of oil drums and other debris which had been strewn over them to prevent landings. The rangers' first priority was to take the bluff overlooking the airstrip and suppress the considerable fire from the defending forces which was pouring from it. After clearing the drop zone, the rangers immediately set up their mortars and began to bombard the positions on the bluff. Spectre gunships and carrier-based A-6 Intruder and A-7 Corsair fighters supported the rangers and they moved out to take the bluffs, knocking out machine-gun and mortar positions as they surged forward.

By 0715 the heights were secured, and the rangers

Left and above: 82nd Airborne gunners set up a heavy bombardment against Cuban positions on the third day of Operation Urgent Fury.

THE RANGERS

The first rangers in American history were formed by Major Robert Rogers in the mid-18th century to wage an anti-guerrilla war for the British against American Indian and French forces. When, in 1942 and 1943, the United States began to form commando-style units of volunteers for war in Europe the name was adopted, and eventually six ranger battalions were organised. The responsibility for selection fell to Colonel William Darby, and many now remember the formation as 'Darby's Rangers'.

The rangers remained a part of the US Army until their disbandment following the Korean War. No ranger force then existed until the US Army, anxious to 'start afresh' after the disappointments of the Vietnam War, began recruiting two battalions of rangers in 1975. They were designated the 1st and 2nd Battalions of the 75th Infantry Regiment, and were based respectively at Fort Stewart, Georgia, and Fort Lewis, Washington State.

With a total strength of 606 men, the two battalions came under the 1st Special Operations Command in October 1982. The men are equipped as light infantry battalions, and each must be airborne-qualified before he volunteers for service. The usual route is through the Ranger School, an establishment which survived the dismantling of the rangers after Korea by continuing as an officer and NCO training school. All the arts associated with elite, self-dependent units are now taught, including survival in the wild and close-quarters combat. The shoulder flash of the rangers is shown above.

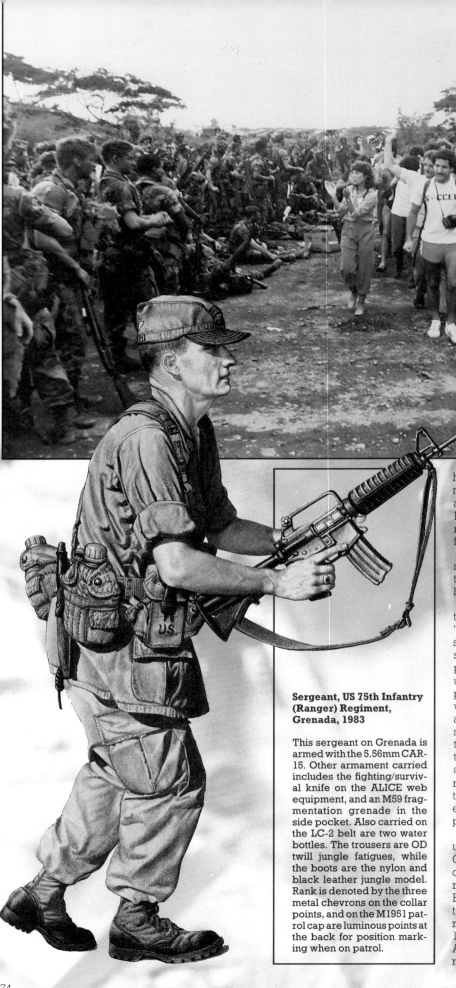

Sergeant, US 75th Infantry (Ranger) Regiment, Grenada, 1983

This sergeant on Grenada is armed with the 5.56mm CAR-15. Other armament carried includes the fighting/survival knife on the ALICE web equipment, and an M59 fragmentation grenade in the side pocket. Also carried on the LC-2 belt are two water bottles. The trousers are OD twill jungle fatigues, while the boots are the nylon and black leather jungle model. Rank is denoted by the three metal chevrons on the collar points, and on the M1951 patrol cap are luminous points at the back for position marking when on patrol.

had begun clearing the airstrip, using heavy equip ment which they had seized. Two Cuban counter attacks were beaten back, including one by thre BTR-60 APCs. Using recoilless rifles and LAWs, th rangers stopped the APCs, which were then drille full of holes by 20mm fire from a Spectre overhead.

Meanwhile, on the other side of Grenada, th marines at Pearls Airport had met only light oppos tion from smallarms, and by 0700 the leatherneck had secured their objective.

The rangers at Point Salines were soon moving ou to rescue the 130 American students holed up on th 'True Blue' campus of St George's Medical College situated near the end of the runway. The rangers too some casualties while breaking through to the cam pus, but by 0850 it was secured and the students wer under the rangers' protection. For the students th past few hours had been harrowing. Without fore warning of the intended rescue, they had heard th anti-aircraft guns battling it out with the gunships an seen the sky scored with red tracer bullets. Whe the first soldiers appeared on the campus perimete they had no way of knowing whether it was a friend c a foe who was coming for them. Reassuring them. th rangers learned that another group of students wa trapped on Grand Anse campus, some miles to th east and in an area surrounded by Cuban strong points.

Although Point Salines runway was still comin under sporadic sniper fire during the morning of 2 October, it was declared secure and transport air craft began bringing in supplies and evacuating th ranger casualties. Meanwhile, the Division Read Brigade of the 82nd Airborne had received notifica tion that the runway was operable, and the firs reinforcements took off for Grenada. By a little afte 1400 on 25 October, two battalions of the 82n Airborne were landing at Point Salines to relieve th rangers and free them for other operations. A

Cuban resistance had been proving stiffer than anticipated, additional 82nd Airborne paratroopers were organised to follow them to the island. Eventually 5000 members of the divison were on Grenada.

As all this was going on, the small team of SEALs holding Government House was withstanding a determined siege, and most were now wounded by the heavy enemy fire. The Cubans had also shot down two gunships which had attempted to give suppressive fire in support of the SEALs, although Spectres were still able to give suppressive fire when things got too hot. Finally, to relieve the SEALs and to begin the approach to Richmond Hill Prison and Fort Frederick, the *Guam* moved around the island and, at 1930, it landed 250 marines, with five tanks and 13 LVTP-7 amphibious assault vehicles near Grand Mal, not far from the island's capital of St George's.

The locals were impressed to see black officers and NCOs commanding white troops in the rangers

The marines moved southwest along the coast towards Government House and by 0700 the next morning the SEALs had been relieved. While the marines pressed forward, rangers and paratroopers of the 82nd Airborne were advancing north from Point Salines towards St George's and the Grand Anse medical campus. Although the soldiers encountered scattered opposition from Cubans and PRA members, most of the population welcomed them and gave information on the whereabouts of PRA personnel and Cubans who had gone into hiding. The locals were especially impressed to see black officers and NCOs commanding white troops in the rangers, para units and marines, a fact which demonstrated to them that much Cuban propaganda about life in the USA had been false.

The top priority now remaining was the rescue of the students held up at the Grand Anse campus. Men of the 2nd Battalion, 75th Rangers (2/75th) were assigned to this mission on the afternoon of 26 October, though, had the students appeared to be in imminent danger, an assault would have been carried out sooner. Using marine helicopters for their lift, the rangers landed on the north side of the campus at 1600 hours. One chopper was shot down

Left: Jubilant medical students cheer the rangers who have just rescued them. One of the rangers in the left foreground is armed with a 12-gauge shotgun. Known as a 'trench gun', this weapon is devastatingly effective in close-quarters combat and is also useful for blowing doors off their hinges during rescue operations. Below left: Members of the 82nd Airborne take away a bound and blindfolded Cuban prisoner for interrogation. Below right: US troops deliver the interventionary message, 'Communism stops here'.

during the operation, but the rangers it was carrying suffered only minor injuries and they continued on foot. After landing on the campus the men of the 2/75th quickly set up a defensive perimeter, enabling the 224 students to be heli-lifted to safety. Students living off campus in villages near St George's and in the town itself also had to be taken to safe areas as soon as possible. Throughout the remainder of 26 October, members of the 22nd MAU and the 82nd Airborne swept the island looking for Cubans and the PRA: a curfew was then enforced during the hours of darkness. Any resistance encountered was dealt with promptly.

As the third day of the invasion of Grenada dawned, the US task force was left with just one concentration of enemy troops before their mission was completed. The Cuban barracks at Edgmont was believed to contain up to 400 Cubans and it was expected that this site would see some of the heaviest fighting of the entire operation. Troops from the 82nd Airborne surrounded the barracks complex, while 105mm howitzers, naval guns, and carrier-based aircraft set up a heavy bombardment. Men of the 2/75th then spearheaded the assault on the barracks in Blackhawk helicopters, losing three rangers killed and 15 injured, most of the casualties occurring when three choppers crashed. As it turned out, however, the barracks complex was virtually deserted, its defenders having fled. By the evening of 27 October resistance had just about ceased, though patrols from the 22nd MAU and 82nd Airborne continued to search for enemy troops who remained at large, and they continued to enforce the curfew.

When the units of the American force searched the positions wrested from their Cuban and Grenadan defenders, caches of light and heavy weapons were unearthed, including AK-47 assault rifles, 120mm mortars, machine guns, anti-aircraft weapons and rocket launchers. Documents were also located which indicated that Cuba's interest in Grenada lay beyond the island itself, seeing it as part of a plan for the control of the Caribbean as a whole. The caches and the documents were re-

garded in Washington as a final vindication of Operation Urgent Fury, and the low casualties of the operation were deemed an acceptable price for what they believed had been achieved in the discouragement of communist expansionism in the area. It was confidently assumed that wavering Caribbean nations such as Surinam would now act to distance themselves from Castro, knowing that he had no answer to American military superiority. More than 1100 Cubans and Grenadans had been taken prisoner during the operation, and Cuban casualties were considerable. The US casualties finally totalled 18 dead and 113 injured.

The effect of Operation Urgent Fury on the voting public of the USA was similar to that caused by the Falklands campaign in Britain. The majority of voters experienced a resurgence of patriotism, accompanied by a renewed pride in the efficacy of their nation's armed forces. In the USA, the black beret of the rangers and the maroon beret of the 82nd Airborne suddenly became status symbols. The marines have no beret, and for them Grenada became just one more example of their corps' traditional role as a troubleshooter.

Within a few days the rangers were back at Fort Lewis and Fort Stewart, and the marines were continuing their journey to take up their peacekeeping role in Lebanon. Some of the 82nd Airborne paratroopers returned to Fort Bragg, though units such as the 508th Airborne Infantry Regiment remained in Grenada as a security force, operating with the multi-national force from Grenada's neighbouring islands. Other US troops, including army engineers, stayed on to help complete the airport at Point Salines and to clean up after the invasion.

Operation Urgent Fury, apart from successfully

Below: The end of the day. US troops take it easy as the Stars and Stripes flies triumphantly over Grenada after the successful conclusion of the Urgent Fury operation.

restoring order in Grenada, also served to test t rapid deployment capability of the American un: The rangers fulfilled their traditional role spearheaders admirably, carrying out a com parachute jump at very low altitude. The rang motto is 'Rangers lead the way!' and they did just th They hit hard and fast as they were trained to do. T 82nd Airborne also proved its ability to live up to goal of deployment from Fort Bragg in under hours. In fact, the first paratroopers were arriving Point Salines within 17 hours of being alerted. T marines carried out their amphibious operation i highly professional manner. Some new equipme was also tested in combat for the first time, includi the Blackhawk UH-60 helicopter and the 82nd A borne's Kevlar 'Fritz' helmet.

As military operations go, Urgent Fury was especially large-scale, though more than 6000 troops eventually became involved. However, d ing the three days of the campaign many you rangers, marines, and paratroopers – those m most likely to see combat in the near future – we able to adjust themselves to the realities of arm warfare. It showed them why the hard training th have to endure is necessary if they are to survive a give of their best, and demonstrated to them the vi role of gunship firepower in modern US comb tactics. Having faced the fire of a determined enem the soldiers who were involved in Operation Urge Fury are ready for further tests in the future.

THE AUTHOR Leroy Thompson served in Vietnam a member of the USAF Combat Security Police. has published several books including *Uniforms the Elite Forces* and *Uniforms of the Indochina a Vietnam Wars*.

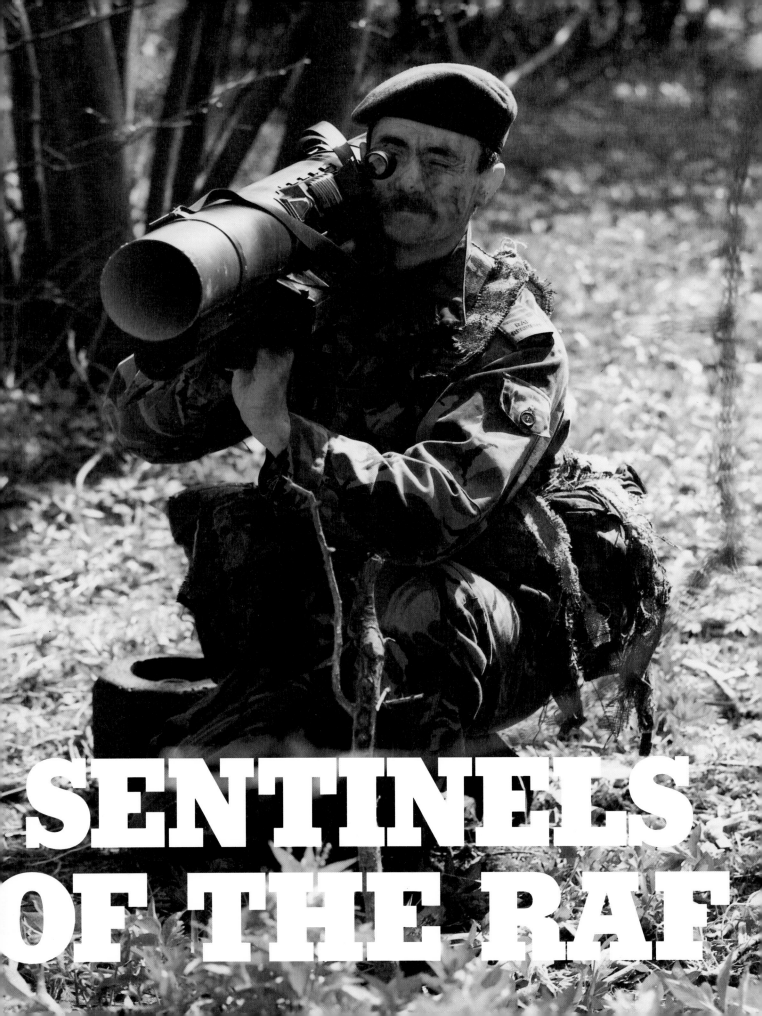

SENTINELS
OF THE RAF

The Royal Air Force Regiment owes its genesis directly and indirectly to two factors that exercised the minds of defence planners between the wars. One was a growth in the capability of airpower, which meant that even airfields in mainland Britain were highly vulnerable. The other was the colonial doctrine of 'air control' of dissident tribesmen. Operating in such places as Mesopotamia (Iraq), Transjordan, Kuwait and Aden, the RAF found itself not only responsible for carrying out air strikes, but also for defending its own airfields against ground assaults. In addition, policing units were required to back up squadrons in colonial areas. The result was the formation of armoured car companies (ACCs), eventually six in number.

In Iraq, the RAF raised a force of levies based around the airfields at Shaibah and Habbaniya. They fought with considerable gallantry in the Iraq Campaign of 1941, eventually replacing British troops in critical security roles throughout the Middle East. At their height the Iraq Levies, known from 1943 onwards as the RAF Levies (Iraq), numbered some 11,000 men under both British and Arab officers.

Another force was raised in Aden, known as the Aden Protectorate Levies (APL). The APL force saw continuous action against rebellious tribesmen from 1928 until 1961, when it became the Federal Regular Army (FRA) of South Arabia. As the FRA it continued to carry out anti-guerrilla operations under the direction of both RAF Regiment and British Army officers and NCOs, right up to the British withdrawal from Aden in 1967.

At its formation in 1942, the RAF Regiment inherited the anti-aircraft and anti-guerrilla roles of these earlier units, and a great part of the early success of the RAF ACCs in the North African campaign was due to experience gained with the colonial ACCs and RAF Levies before the war.

The men of the RAF Regiment are ready to stand firm against all comers as the last line of defence for Britain's vital airbases

THE ROLE FORCED on the RAF Regiment by its membership of the Royal Air Force is an unusual one. Ships and aircraft are inherently mobile and capable of running away to fight another day. Most armies accept that sometimes it is necessary to withdraw, trading space for time. But the RAF Regiment can do none of these things. The regiment's role, in the most brutally simple terms, is to stand and fight for as long as possible. For as long as British troops and ships require air cover and air support, the RAF Regiment will defend RAF airfields against every conceivable form of attack. Because an airfield cannot move, the RAF Regiment will not move.

When the RAF was first formed in 1918, the new service adopted the well established doctrine that local defence was the responsibility of the unit concerned. But during the early part of World War I

when the air threat began to grow with the evolving capabilities of new generations of fighters and bombers, this tidy arrangement began to fall apart.

After Dunkirk, the situation was complicated still further. On RAF stations at that time light anti-aircraft (LAA) defence was the responsibility of the Royal Artillery. RAF ground defences, consisting of machine guns for both air and area defence, were under the command of the local air force commanders, while infantry for ground defence was commanded by an army infantry officer. With the threat of invasion many of the LAA and infantry troops were withdrawn for urgent tasks elsewhere, leaving the RAF stations feeling uncomfortably naked.

The Battle of Britain and the Luftwaffe's ferocious attacks on Fighter Command airfields showed how vital the whole question of airfield defence was, and how good the RAF were at doing some of this work for themselves. A re-organisation of the RAF ground defences raised the number of RAF gunners from 45,000 to 72,000 and the first UK-based RAF armoured car companies (ACCs) were formed in the United Kingdom in 1941. The British Army withdrew from the problem of airfield defence to prepare for the fighting in North Africa.

The German parachute assault on Crete in May 1941 seriously frightened the Air Staff yet again. The threat of paratroops and glider-borne troops overrunning airfields had to be dealt with. This process led directly to the formation of the Royal Air Force Regiment by Royal Warrant on 1 February 1942.

The new force consisted of 79,000 men and was an integral part of the Royal Air Force. It immediately released 92,000 valuable army troops from airfield defence duties. Progress was rapid, with the regiment being organised into anti-aircraft flights and field squadrons. Training was provided by the Brigade of Guards and the Royal Marines, and RAF Regiment units sprang up all over the world, from West Africa to Burma.

The ACCs were usually right behind the first echelon in any advance, ready to seize enemy airfields

It was the war in North Africa, however, that showed the worth of the new regiment. The RAF ACCs performed sterling work in the periodic retreats and advances between Cairo and Tunis. The great value of tactical air support was being demonstrated in this campaign, but for support to be effective and quick to react it was necessary for aircraft to be sited close to the front line. The ACCs were usually right behind the first echelon in any advance, ready to seize enemy airfields as soon as possible – preferably with enemy aircraft still in place. The crews earned special praise for their stout defence of these same airfields when the army retreated, leaving Hurricanes and Spitfires exposed to the enemy advance.

On the other side of North Africa, the first properly constituted regimental squadrons to see action went in with the spearhead of Operation Torch, the amphibious invasion of Northwest Africa. Five squadrons and five independent AA flights landed at Algiers in November 1942. They kept up with the British and American armoured and airborne spearhead throughout the campaign, seizing airfields from the retreating Germans or reinforcing fields taken by

the British 1st Parachute Brigade during their three major drops. In mid-1943, the five squadrons were the first British troops into Bizerta and Tunis, where they went straight for the airfields and Luftwaffe installations.

A career in the regiment was becoming no sinecure by this stage. Two field squadrons went in with the amphibious spearhead during the invasion of Sicily and had to contest occupation of the Luftwaffe airfields at Catania and Palermo with the outgoing aircraft, who bombed and strafed them mercilessly. Elsewhere, special elements of the regiment were parachuted into Yugoslavia to assist Tito's partisans in anti-aircraft operations. The first British troops to land in Greece were from No.2908 Squadron, RAF Regiment, and they liberated the country's third-largest port at Patras in the Peloponnese, fighting alongside the Long Range Desert Group.

The Battle of the Ardennes saw the regiment fighting a desperate but successful rearguard action

Over airfields in the south of England, detachments of 'flak wagons' armed with multiple Browning 0.5in and 0.3in machine guns, or twin Vickers 'K' machine guns, enjoyed good sport against Luftwaffe marauders. The field squadrons and anti-aircraft flights, meanwhile, were preparing for the invasion of Europe, Operation Overlord. One of the vital tasks given to the regiment was to get ahead of friendly forces during their advance into Germany and capture airfields and aircraft, radar and radio installations, and any Luftwaffe personnel whose interrogation could prove worthwhile. Two complete wings of the regiment landed with the first wave on D-day.

Two and a half months later, on 26 August 1944, a flight from No.2728 Squadron was one of the first Allied units to reach Paris, in advance of General de Gaulle himself. The Battle of the Ardennes, during that winter, saw the regiment fighting a desperate but successful rearguard action to prevent the highly secret mobile air defence radars now employed by the RAF from falling into enemy hands. The rest of the Allied army seemed to have withdrawn with remarkable speed, but once again the regiment's field squadrons fought with stubborn courage to ensure that a vital feature of Allied air supremacy remained unharmed.

Like the rest of the British armed forces, the RAF Regiment went into a decline when peace broke out. Nevertheless there was still a role for the regiment. A highly capable force soon found itself operating against terrorists in Palestine and in the Malayan jungle. During the Suez Crisis of 1956, No.48 Squadron landed at El Gamil airfield just after 3 Para had secured it. Their intended role was to protect the aircraft at El Gamil before they flew on from there to support planned operations down the Suez canal towards Cairo.

Operations in Borneo during the Confrontation of 1963-1966 showed the direction the regiment was now taking. The British Army relied on RAF and Royal Navy helicopters operating from dispersed sites, often in dense jungle. The regiment supplied the machine-gun crews for the helicopters and provided an apparently seamless air and ground defence against the Indonesian commandos and guerrillas who were infiltrating the British-dominated area close to the Kalimantan border. The regiment was fully prepared to carry out all the elements of the modern RAF Regiment's role: air

defence against enemy bombers, local area defence against guerrilla forces and conventional defence against regular army units.

The grudging respect accorded to the RAF Regiment by its green-uniformed British Army counterparts is manifest in the regiment's partly affectionate nickname 'Rock Apes'. In fact, the regiment fills a number of critical roles both in the UK and in RAF Germany (RAFG). One of the most vital is that of the air defence of both RAF and US Air Force (USAF) airfields and aircraft. It is a fundamental fact of military life today that air power is absolutely indispensable. But with the exception of the RAF Harrier force, modern tactical combat aircraft rely on long, smooth, immobile runways. The rough fields used by the RAF Hurricanes and Typhoons in Normandy are no longer adequate.

Just as important as air defence is the area defence role. In the context of the RAF Regiment's normal operating areas, the UK and West Germany, the main threat comes from two main sources: first, from Soviet special forces, the Spetznaz, who would in wartime try to sabotage airfields, aircraft and nuclear installations, and second, from Soviet airborne forces, who would be dropped by parachute or helicopter deep in NATO's rear to create diversions and overrun airfields, logistics depots and headquarters facilities in order to weaken NATO.

The third major threat facing the RAF is Nuclear, Biological and Chemical (NBC) warfare. It is generally assumed that a major Soviet attack would be preceded by a massive chemical bombardment aimed at catching airfield and nuclear weapons crews unprotected.

It uses a battery of captured Argentinian Oerlikon 35mm guns with their associated Contraves Skyguard fire control radars

None of these threats can be seen in isolation from another, and the RAF Regiment deals with each one. The air defence role is perhaps the most critical as, no matter how effective the joint RAF/USAF combat air patrols over the North Sea, a number of Soviet attack aircraft would be almost certain to get through. If they breached the RAF long-range Bloodhound missile belt and the AIM-9L Sidewinder-armed Hawk T.1A fighters, then the last line of defence would be the RAF Regiment's Rapier SAMs and Oerlikon guns.

Five regular UK-based squadrons operate Rapier in its most advanced Blindfire mode. They are based at West Rainham (No.66 Squadron, covering the USAF bases at Mildenhall and Lakenheath), at Brize Norton (No.19 Squadron, covering Fairford and Upper Heyford, again USAF bases) and at Honington (No.20 Squadron, covering the bases at Bentwaters, Alconbury and Woodbridge). No.27 Squadron is based at RAF Leuchars in Fife and No.48 covers RAF Lossiemouth.

One reserve (Royal Auxiliary Air Force (RAuxAF) Regiment) squadron, No.2729, is based at RAF Waddington, where it uses a battery of captured Argentinian Oerlikon 35mm guns with their associated Contraves Skyguard fire control radars. Although these guns have a far shorter range than the seven kilometres of Rapier, they certainly proved their worth against the RAF and Fleet Air Arm in the Falklands. It was a stroke of genius not to consign them to some museum, and the officer who brought them into UK service, setting up a cost-effective

Below: Men of No.48 Squadron, RAF Regiment, man a Rapier unit in Belize. Left: The radar mounted on the missile fire unit alerts the operator of the optical tracking unit (below, on left) to the approach of an intruder. The missile is guided to its target either by radar or by the tracker operator using a control joystick. Centre left: Men clad in full NBC (Nuclear, Biological, Chemical) kit operate the Rapier tracking unit in the field. Bottom left: An ex-Argentinian Oerlikon anti-aircraft gun of the RAF Regiment.

RAuxAF Regiment squadron to use them, made a major contribution to the UK's air defence.

There are, in fact, six other RAuxAF Regiment field squadrons based around the country and these carry out area defence duties around the airfields and the air defence installations dotting the North Sea coast of Britain.

In West Germany the four RAF bases are protected by No.63 Squadron, based at Gutersloh; No.37 Squadron, based at Bruggen; No.16 Squadron,

NBC TRAINING AND PROTECTION

Training and protection against Nuclear, Biological and Chemical (NBC) warfare is perhaps the most critical of all the airfield defence roles that fall to the RAF Regiment.

The effect of a chemical attack on an RAF base is easily imagined. The regiment's tasks lie in active defence, preventing chemically-armed bombers and cruise missiles getting through, and in passive defence, making sure that chemical weapons cause the minimum of disruption. Finally, the regiment is responsible for recuperation and decontamination. In the field of passive defence the RAF Regiment and USAF have unrivalled knowledge and experience within NATO of NBC warfare, and RAF Regiment officers are based as advisers on NBC problems at every major NATO headquarters as well as every RAF base.

Several functions fall to these officers. The first is to train everyone in the proper use of NBC equipment, and the second is to advise on the design of everything from personal equipment to airfield buildings. This involves taking into account the problems of absorption of chemical agents or nuclear fallout by brickwork or tent canvas and the time and effort required to decontaminate.

The third function is to ensure that all procedures for sealing off buildings would be observed and carried out with lightning speed. Finally, the regiment's advisers must ensure that, even in the aftermath of a chemical attack, RAF or USAF aircraft and their weapons can still be serviced, refuelled and turned around for the next sortie as soon as possible.

based at Wildenrath, and No.26 Squadron, based at Laarbruch. Elements of No.63 Squadron deployed to the Falklands during the 1982 conflict.

The Rapiers represent one of the regiment's areas of excellence. The other is covered by the six regular light armoured squadrons (LAS), Nos.1, 2, 15, 34, 51 and 58, and by six RAuxAF Regiment field squadrons. To these 12 squadrons falls the task of protecting airfields in the UK and West Germany. One of their most important roles is protecting the RAF's dispersed Harrier and helicopter hides in the NATO area.

It is a measure of just how important their job is that these squadrons are, with the exception of a few UK-based army units, the only British ground forces trained specifically to take on Soviet airborne and special forces. A further measure is the secrecy in which the entire subject is shrouded.

The main element of the regiment's area defence role is its range of CVR(T) armoured vehicles, which includes the Scorpion, Spartan, Sultan and Samson.

The regiment originally wanted to get its hands on the Scimitar and its 30mm Rarden gun, but ended up with the Scorpion and its 76mm gun instead. This was no handicap as it turned out, because it provided a wickedly effective anti-personnel capability that was lacking with the smaller Rarden, and it also made up for the regiment's 81mm mortars that were sacrificed in favour of the CVR(T).

The basic tactical unit is the four-man 'brick' carried in the Spartan; this, with its three-man crew and the excellent image intensifiers that it shares with the Scorpion, provides collective NBC protection, protection against artillery and bomb fragments, and very high mobility to get out to the scene of the action in quick time. The Scorpion's main gun is of no use against modern Main Battle Tanks, of course, but it will deal very nicely with the Soviet ASU-85 airborne assault gun and the six-man BMD armoured infantry fighting vehicle. Anyway, if any Soviet T-64, T-72 or T-80 tanks are in the area, it is generally reckoned that the majority of British aircraft will have vacated the airfields in any case.

The regiment has had a parachute capability since the early part of the Mediterranean war. Today it resides in No.2 Squadron, based at RAF Hullavington. No.2 is a light armoured squadron like all the others, but it is a direct descendant of the squadron that formed the spearhead of General Montgomery's armies in North Africa and in Northwest Europe. Its primary role is area defence of the RAFG Harrier sites but it is also earmarked to be first, or very nearly first, into any attack within NATO or outside it where the objective is to capture or recapture an RAF

Background: An RAF
Regiment anti-aircraft team
salutes a Hurricane as it
swoops low over their gun
position on the Arakan front,
Burma, in 1945. The modern
role of the regiment includes
the capability to provide
effective counter-measures
against infiltration by enemy
paratroopers or special
forces. Officers and men
undergo training in the
techniques of field and urban
combat. Centre left: A team
engaged in a house clearance
operation radioes its position.
Below left: RAF Regiment
personnel on field exercises
in Germany work out their
next move. Below right: Men
on an exercise board a
Westland Wessex helicopter.

airfield. The airfield itself could be almost anywhere.
No. 2 Squadron has the normal complement of six
Scorpions, 15 Spartans, one Sultan and one Samson,
but each man is additionally a trained parachutist.
The squadron has another role as well: when the RAF
introduces a new paratrooping aircraft, parachute,
or some other item of airborne equipment, the
regiment tries it first before the paras are turned
loose on it.

The regiment's infantry skills are put to good use when the missile convoys disperse to their secret launching sites

No. 2 Squadron's parachute capability is one way of
keeping the RAF's finger on the army's tactical
requirements and tactical thinking, but the unit is not
earmarked specifically for out-of-area operations.
Instead, it is intended primarily for the anti-Spetznaz,
anti-airborne role, and also to lead the counter-
attack that will bring RAF tactical aircraft and their
protective Rapiers back within range of a retreating
enemy. However, while the CVR(T)s are parachute-
capable, it is usually more tactically desirable nowa-
days for troops and vehicles to be landed together in
good order, either off the ramp of a Hercules following a steep night approach, or by helicopter.

The other feature of regimental operations that
receives little publicity is its role in the defence of the
USAF cruise missile sites at RAF Greenham Common and Molesworth. Here, the Spetznaz threat is at
its greatest and some 45 RAF Regiment troops are
assigned to each base to train the Field Security
Police and support them on duty. The regiment's
infantry skills are put to good use when the missile
convoys disperse to their secret launching sites
during exercises. The skills of camouflage and concealment employed by the regiment's detachments,
perfected over years of practice with RAFG's Har-

rier and helicopter units, have meant that anti-cruise
protesters have so far only ever been able to intercept the convoys as they leave the bases or during
their return journeys. Nobody has ever ambushed a
convoy at its exercise area.

The RAF Regiment is one of those organisations of
which one hears little. This is perhaps understandable as it is the far more glamorous RAF strike
aircraft and fighters that really catch the eye. Yet in
the age of the Harrier, the helicopter and long-range
strike aircraft, the men on the ground matter. The
RAF Regiment has one of the trickiest roles in NATO
– the more so because its field squadrons cannot
trade space for time in protecting RAF bases. Its men
must stand and fight. They must face not only air
attack but also the finest troops that the Soviet Union
can throw at them – at a time and in a place of the
Soviets' choosing. Not many people in NATO can say
that, and not many people are trained and paid
specifically to do that either.

THE AUTHOR Gregor Ferguson is a writer and journal-
ist specialising in defence and military affairs. He
has written a short history of The Parachute Regiment, in which he served himself as a Territorial. His
latest book, *Coup d'État – A Practical Manual* is
published this year by Arms and Armour Press.

AIRBORNE

MARKET GARDEN

In mid-August 1944, the German front in France had collapsed. The forces in Normandy were destroyed by the Allied breakout, and the landing of French and American troops in the south of the country (Operation Dragoon) had liberated vast areas.

Allied advance was swift: Paris was liberated on 25 August, and by 3 September British forces had arrived in Brussels. The main block on the Allies was now the limitations of their logistics. The opportunity to finish off the Germans once and for all seemed to be there for the taking – if the momentum of the advance could be kept up.

It was Field Marshal Montgomery's intention that the Second British Army should drive through Holland to attack Germany from the northwest. His plan, later codenamed Operation Market Garden, demanded that a 60-mile salient be opened up between the front of XXX Corps on the Maas-Scheldt Canal and the town of Arnhem. This stretch of road crossed numerous water obstacles, including two canals north of Eindhoven, and the Maas, Waal and Neder Rijn rivers. Montgomery's operation involved large-scale drops by the First Airborne Army on three major zones along the salient. The 101st US Airborne Division were to take the southernmost sector around Eindhoven, and the US 82nd Airborne Division was to gain control in the Grave and Nijmegen area. The toughest task, that of seizing the bridgeheads in Arnhem, fell to the 1st British Airborne Division with the Polish Parachute The British Airborne Forces' insignia is shown above.

HEROES OF ARNHEM

The men of the 1st Airborne Division little knew what awaited them at Arnhem in September, 1944

AFTER THE ROAR of the Stirling's engines and the tension of the flight from England, it was a relief to jump out of the aircraft into the skies over Holland. Major 'Boy' Wilson, commander of the 21st Independent Parachute Company, looked down onto a calm and seemingly empty panorama of patchwork fields and isolated houses: 'Everything looked so peaceful. Not a sign of fighting or war. Not a glimpse of the enemy.' It was 1315 hours on Sunday, 17 September 1944, and the air assault on Arnhem had begun.

Wilson's unit was acting as spearhead of the British 1st Airborne Division, tasked to capture bridges across the Neder Rijn at Arnhem as the most northerly part of Field Marshal Bernard Law Montgomery's 'Market Garden' operation. Simultaneously, paratroops and glider-borne units of the US 82nd and 101st Airborne Divisions were landing around Eindhoven and Nijmegen, aiming to seize similar bridges across the myriad of canals and rivers of southern Holland, and the British XXX Corps, part of Montgomery's 21st Army Group, was preparing to push north from the Belgian frontier to link up. Once XXX Corps reached Arnhem, the Allies would be ideally placed to strike onto the North German Plain and to swing east to squeeze out the industrial centre of the Ruhr, dealing the Germans a mortal blow that would significantly shorten the war in Europe.

Commanded by Major-General Robert 'Roy' Urquhart, 1st Airborne Division was a superbly trained elite, raring to go, but the men were frustrated. Three months earlier they had watched their 'rivals' in 6th Airborne Division fly off to participate in the D-Day assault, and since then they had prepared for 1 operations, each one of which had been cancelled. They were beginning to think that the war would be over before they could prove their worth, and for this reason accepted with enthusiasm a plan which contained a number of basic flaws. When Urquhart was briefed on 10 September, being told in essence 'Arnhem bridge, and hold it', he faced two immediate problems: on the one hand a shortage of available transport aircraft; on the other persistent claims by the RAF that Arnhem was heavily defended by anti-aircraft guns. He had only six days in which to finalise his arrangements and this forced him to accept compromise solutions. Sacrificing the principle of concentration, it was decided to commit the division in three separate 'lifts', spread over three days, and in an effort to avoid the flak it was planned to land the troops on open ground to the west of Arnhem, between five and eight miles from their objectives. The latter intention could only be contemplated because of an intelligence assessment that Arnhem itself was poorly protected by enemy ground forces. Too much was being left to chance.

Even so, the final plan was kept fairly simple – on

aper, at least. Once on the ground, the paras of the rst lift – 1st, 2nd and 3rd Parachute Battalions of rigadier G.W. Lathbury's 1st Airborne Brigade – rould march into Arnhem to seize a railway bridge, a erry site and a road bridge across the Neder Rijn. his left the 1st Battalion Border Regiment (1 Border), th Battalion King's Own Scottish Borderers (7 KOSB) nd part of 2nd Battalion, South Staffordshire Regi- ıent (2 South Stafford) of Brigadier P.H.W. Hicks' 1st irlanding (that is, glider-borne) Brigade to secure ıe landing zones for the second lift, scheduled to rrive after 24 hours. This would comprise the rest of st Airlanding Brigade and the whole of Brigadier .W. Hackett's 4th Airborne Brigade (10th, 11th and 56th Parachute Battalions), which would then move

Background: Most of the British gliders and paratroopers made safe landings to the west of Arnhem, but the landing zones were far from the objective. Inset below left: Field Marshal Montgomery inspects troops with Brigadier Hackett and Major-General Urquhart. Inset below right: Paratroopers take cover on the debris-strewn landing zone after their glider's crash landing.

Paratrooper, 1st Airborne Division, Arnhem 1944

Like other men of the airborne forces this soldier wears the famous 'Denison' camouflage smock, a popular item of clothing that remained in service use long after World War II. Other airborne features include adapted battledress trousers (with large map pocket) and the 'cut-down' steel helmet, worn here with camouflage net and scrim 'foliage'. Web equip- ment is 1937-pattern, worn with a small pack with enamel mug attached. Armament comprises the .303in SMLE Rifle No. 4, a reliable bolt-action weapon that was the standard rifle of British troops during World War II.

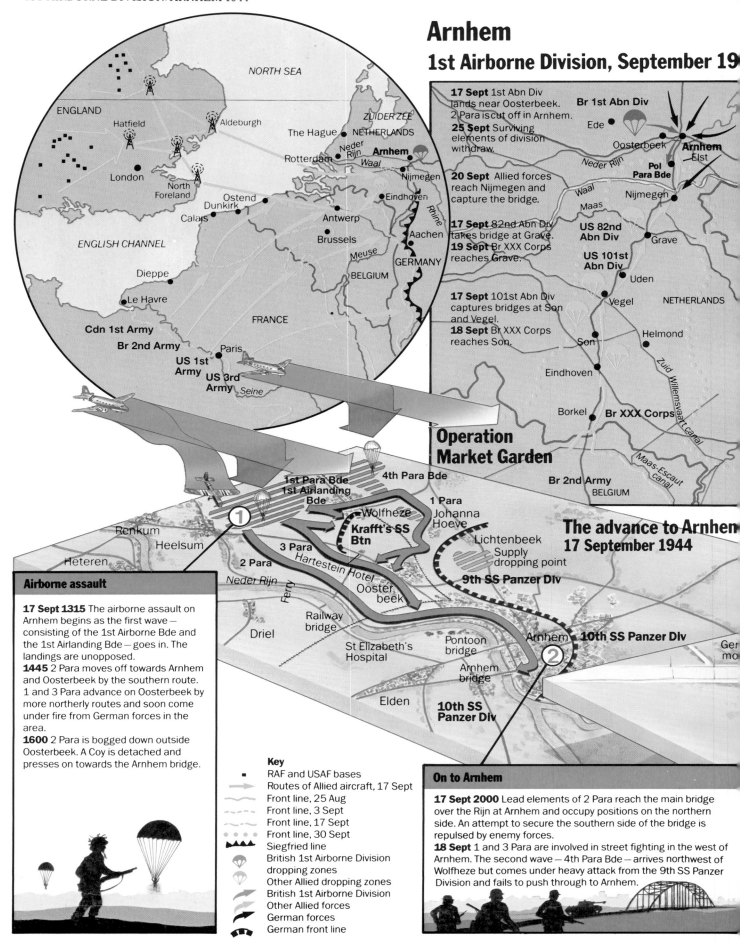

Arnhem
1st Airborne Division, September 19⸺

17 Sept 1st Abn Div lands near Oosterbeek. 2 Para is cut off in Arnhem.
25 Sept Surviving elements of division withdraw.

20 Sept Allied forces reach Nijmegen and capture the bridge.

17 Sept 82nd Abn Div takes bridge at Grave.
19 Sept Br XXX Corps reaches Grave.

17 Sept 101st Abn Div captures bridges at Son and Vegel.
18 Sept Br XXX Corps reaches Son.

Br 1st Abn Div

Ede
Oosterbeek
Arnhem
Elst
Neder Rijn
Pol Para Bde
Waal
Nijmegen
Maas
US 82nd Abn Div
Grave
US 101st Abn Div
Uden
Vegel
NETHERLANDS
Helmond
Son
Eindhoven
Borkel
Zuid Willemsvaart canal
Maas-Escaut canal
Br 2nd Army
BELGIUM

Operation Market Garden

The advance to Arnhem
17 September 1944

NORTH SEA
ENGLAND
Hatfield
Aldeburgh
The Hague
NETHERLANDS
ZUIDER ZEE
London
North Foreland
Rotterdam
Neder Rijn
Arnhem
Waal
Nijmegen
Ostend
Dunkirk
Calais
Antwerp
Eindhoven
Rhine
ENGLISH CHANNEL
Brussels
Aachen
Meuse
GERMANY
BELGIUM
Dieppe
FRANCE
Le Havre
Cdn 1st Army
Br 2nd Army
US 1st Army
Paris
US 3rd Army
Seine

1st Para Bde
1st Airlanding Bde
4th Para Bde
1 Para
Johanna Hoeve
Wolfheze
Krafft's SS Btn
Lichtenbeek
Supply dropping point
9th SS Panzer Div
Renkum
Heelsum
3 Para
Hartestein Hotel
Ooster beek
2 Para
Neder Rijn
Heteren
Ferry
Railway bridge
Driel
St Elizabeth's Hospital
Pontoon bridge
Arnhem
Arnhem bridge
Elden
10th SS Panzer Div
10th SS Panzer Div

Airborne assault

17 Sept 1315 The airborne assault on Arnhem begins as the first wave — consisting of the 1st Airborne Bde and the 1st Airlanding Bde — goes in. The landings are unopposed.
1445 2 Para moves off towards Arnhem and Oosterbeek by the southern route. 1 and 3 Para advance on Oosterbeek by more northerly routes and soon come under fire from German forces in the area.
1600 2 Para is bogged down outside Oosterbeek. A Coy is detached and presses on towards the Arnhem bridge.

Key
- RAF and USAF bases
- Routes of Allied aircraft, 17 Sept
- Front line, 25 Aug
- Front line, 3 Sept
- Front line, 17 Sept
- Front line, 30 Sept
- Siegfried line
- British 1st Airborne Division dropping zones
- Other Allied dropping zones
- British 1st Airborne Division
- Other Allied forces
- German forces
- German front line

On to Arnhem

17 Sept 2000 Lead elements of 2 Para reach the main bridge over the Rijn at Arnhem and occupy positions on the northern side. An attempt to secure the southern side of the bridge is repulsed by enemy forces.
18 Sept 1 and 3 Para are involved in street fighting in the west of Arnhem. The second wave — 4th Para Bde — arrives northwest of Wolfheze but comes under heavy attack from the 9th SS Panzer Division and fails to push through to Arnhem.

ut to set up a defensive perimeter to the north of the aptured bridge sites. After another 24 hours, the division would be completed with the arrival of Major-General S. Sosabowski's 1st Polish Parachute Brigade, which would land to the south of the river, acting as a link between the Arnhem defenders and the forward elements of XXX Corps. The operation, it was envisaged, would be over in four days.

Things began to go wrong even before the assault went in. Reports that German forces in Holland were weak and demoralised were patently incorrect: despite the rapid withdrawal of units from northern France and Belgium in late August and early September, General Kurt Student's First Parachute Army had retained coherence and was being constantly reinforced by elements of the Fifteenth Army, retreating from the Scheldt estuary. More importantly, Arnhem itself was far from undefended, for General Willi Bittrich's II SS Panzer Corps, comprising the 9th (Hohenstaufen) and 10th (Frundsberg) SS Panzer Divisions, was deployed close to the town, and although it was by no means at full strength, it was still capable of providing formidable opposition, especially against lightly-armed airborne troops. Furthermore, Field Marshal Walter Model, commanding Army Group B, had his headquarters at Oosterbeek, on the western approaches to Arnhem, and so was ideally placed to co-ordinate a swift response. All the ingredients for a full-scale disaster existed, made more potent by the early capture by the enemy of a complete set of orders for the air assault, found in the wreckage of a crashed glider on 17 September, and by the fact that despite promises of good flying weather, the clear skies of the first day soon gave way to high winds, cloud and rain, denying the paras the air support they so desperately needed.

None of this was apparent to the British on 17 September, however, and, as Wilson's men hurried to lay out recognition strips on the landing zones, a vast armada of Stirlings and Dakotas approached the target. By 1400 a total of 319 Horsa and Hamilcar gliders had landed, delivering most of 1st Airlanding Brigade together with Divisional HQ under Urquhart, while Lathbury's three battalions had jumped according to plan. The landings were virtually unopposed, but as soon as Lathbury's men started to prepare for their march into Arnhem, problems arose. Crowds of Dutch civilians – 'excited, friendly, talkative and pressing'–poured out to greet the 'liberators', only to create confusion and impose delays. Nor was the situation helped by the fact that Major C.F.H. Gough's 1st Parachute Reconnaissance Squadron, tasked to move rapidly to seize the bridge sites in a *coup de main*, discovered that 22 of its jeeps had failed to arrive, and although the unit rushed off as soon as possible, few felt that its depleted strength would be sufficient.

Lathbury's battalions were therefore on their own, following a series of pre-arranged routes into Arnhem that would lead, it was hoped, to the capture of the bridges and the creation of a strong defensive perimeter. 2 Para, commanded by Lieutenant-Colonel J.D. Frost, led the way, taking a southerly route (codenamed 'Lion') to the east of Heelsum, along the

On 17 September 1944 the Allied plan to outflank the Siegfried Line – Operation Market Garden – was put into effect. As the British XXX Corps prepared to push through from the Maas-Escaut canal to Arnhem, spearheading an Allied drive into the German industrial heartland of the Ruhr, a massive airborne assault was launched to secure the line of XXX Corps' advance. The US 101st Airborne Division seized the canal bridges at Son and Vegel, and the 82nd Airborne Division took the Maas bridge at Grave. The British 1st Airborne Division landed near Arnhem and forward elements pushed through to the road bridge over the Neder Rijn. But by 20 September, as the British paras were coming under increasingly heavy attack from German forces in the area, the XXX Corps and US paras had only advanced as far as the Waal bridge at Nijmegen. The column pushed forward, but for the paras that were gallantly holding on to the bridgehead at Arnhem against heavy odds, time was running out.

Holding the bridgehead

18 Sept 2 Para is cut off in Arnhem as the 9th and 10th SS Panzer Divisions launch fierce attacks on the bridgehead, and the expected reinforcements fail to break through.

19 Sept The remainder of the 1st Airborne Division concentrate around Oosterbeek, leaving 2 Para isolated and unable to break out. Enemy forces attack the paras from the north and from across the river.

21 Sept 0900 After holding on without reinforcements or resupply against overwhelming odds, the remnants of 2 Para finally surrender.

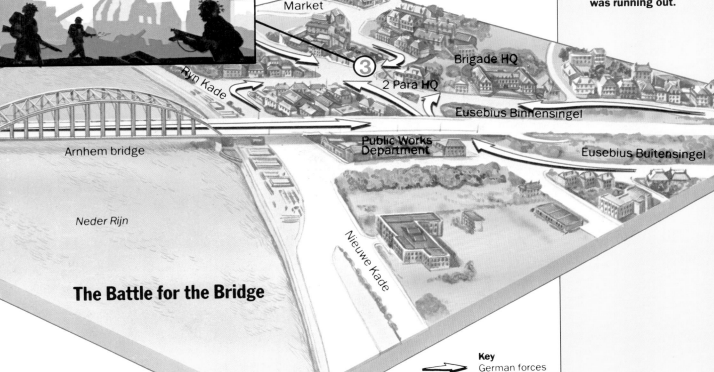

Market

Brigade HQ

2 Para HQ

Ryn Kade

③

Eusebius Binnensingel

Arnhem bridge

Public Works Department

Eusebius Buitensingel

Neder Rijn

Nieuwe Kade

The Battle for the Bridge

Key
→ German forces
⅄ German mortars
⚲ British 6-pdrs
⅄ British mortars

LIEUTENANT-COLONEL JOHN FROST

Of the many heroic actions by units of the 1st British Airborne Division and its Polish support at Arnhem, none is as well remembered as the epic stand by the 1st Parachute Brigade at Arnhem bridge. Equipped to hold the position for 24 hours, the men battled for three days and four nights before finally succumbing to overwhelming armoured and infantry assaults. In command of the 2nd Battalion of The Parachute Regiment was Lieutenant-Colonel John Frost, who was to be wounded in both legs and finally taken prisoner at the close of the action.

John Dutton Frost, the son of Brigadier-General F.D. Frost of the Indian Army, was gazetted to the Cameronians (Scottish Rifles), and served in England, Palestine and Iraq. He became one of Britain's first parachutists in 1940 and remained with the 2nd Battalion of The Parachute Regiment for the duration of World War II. After the war he became commandant of the Support Weapons Wing of the School of Infantry. He commanded the 44th Parachute Brigade TA before becoming GOC of the 52nd Lowland Division District. Then, as GOC Malta and Libya, he formed and commanded the Malta Land Force.

John Frost retired from the army as a major-general in 1968. He holds the MC, DSO and Bar, and is a Companion of the Bath and a Grand Officer of the Sovereign Military Order of Malta.

river to the railway bridge, the ferry site and, eventually, the road bridge in the centre of Arnhem. Frost set out at 1445, but progress was slow, initially because of the hordes of civilians and then, after about half-a-mile, because of sniper fire. The paras deployed to deal with the problem, only to be halted again at 1600 just outside Oosterbeek. Under pressure from Urquhart, who realised the need for a rapid advance to prevent a hardening of enemy defences, Frost split his force. B Company was left to contain German units between Oosterbeek and Arnhem, while C Company struck south to seize the railway bridge and A Company, with Frost in attendance, pressed on to the main objective – the road bridge – a few miles to the east.

The results were mixed. Although B Company fought well, allowing the rest of the battalion to bypass enemy snipers, it soon became bogged down, and when C Company reached the railway bridge, the paras were just in time to see the structure destroyed by its defenders. Meanwhile, Frost and A Company, joined by a group of engineers under Lieutenant E.M. Mackay and, surprisingly, by Gough's Reconnaissance Squadron, found the going hard, moving through streets that bore little resemblance to the maps issued in England, and it was not until 2000 that the lead sections saw the road bridge looming before them. Approaching it with caution, the paras occupied high buildings overlooking the northern ramp before sending patrols onto the structure itself, hoping to seize the southern end before the Germans could react. But they were out of luck. As Lieutenant McDermot led his section onto the ramp, a Spandau machine gun opened up from a pill-box on the bridge and he was forced to withdraw. Without reinforcement, Frost could not risk a frontal assault – when he tried to open the way by sending engineers with flame-throwers to destroy the pill-box, 'all hell seemed to be let loose' from enemy positions on the other side – and all he could do was to consolidate his hold on the northern approaches. As darkness fell, both sides took the opportunity to rest and prepare for what promised to be a bloody battle.

'Shells began to burst among us. Yells and whistles filled the air and machine guns opened fire.'

Frost should have been reinforced by 3 Para, following 'Tiger' route from the landing zones through Oosterbeek into Arnhem, but the battalion never arrived. At first they had made good progress, marching confidently towards their objectives, but after 'about one-and-a-half miles under sniper fire' they could go no further. As German opposition increased, with mortars and self-propelled guns zeroing in on the paras, the battalion commander, Lieutenant-Colonel F.A. Fitch, halted for the night. Patrols managed to capture the Hartenstein Hotel in Oosterbeek, soon to be Urquhart's HQ, and part of C Company made it through to the bridge, but the momentum had been lost. A similar pattern of events affected 1 Para on 'Leopard' route to the north, where elements of 9th SS Panzer were encountered. According to Private Andrew Milbourne, 1 Para's advance had been straightforward until they approached the village of Wolfheze, when, 'suddenly the scene changed. Shells began to burst among us. Yells and whistles filled the air and machine guns opened fire.' By nightfall, 1 Para too were bogged down in bitter fighting:

Above: Troops moving in orderly and painfully slow files to Arnhem with their glider-borne jeeps and anti-tank guns. Top: A paratrooper defends Urquhart's Divisional Headquarters at the Hartenstein hotel, with his M1 carbine. Above right: Snipers are hunted out in an Oosterbeek school. Right: House-to-house fighting in Oosterbeek.

'Everywhere we turned or moved, we were swept with a withering fire. Dead lay all around, wounded were crying for water. Groans and shrieks of pain filled the air...Time and again they overran our positions and had to be driven out with the bayonet.'

Under such pressure, and aware that Frost required assistance, the commander of 1 Para, Lieutenant-Colonel D. Dobie, decided to disengage, swing south and try to break through to the bridge.

A further problem immediately arose, for although Dobie had heard of Frost's dilemma over the brigade radio net, he found that he could not contact either Urquhart or Lathbury to confirm his decision. In fact, few of the radios were working properly, lacking the power to cope with the wooded areas of the landing zones or the buildings of an urban centre, and Urquhart, involved with Lathbury in 3 Para's street-fighting, was totally out of touch with the battle as a whole. To make matters worse, early on 18 September he found himself cut off by a German counter-attack and forced to take shelter in an attic from which he could not escape for 24 hours. During that period Hicks assumed command of the division, but there was little he could do to prevent deterioration. Early on 18 September, 3 Para managed to push into the western suburbs of Arnhem, only to encounter mounting opposition in the streets around the St Elizabeth Hospital, and when 1 Para moved down from the north, they too became embroiled in savage house-to-house fighting in the same area. Hicks had few options open to him, for until Hackett's brigade arrived later in the day, he had to keep his own Airlanding Brigade on the landing zones. All he felt he could spare were B and D Companies of the South Staffords, but when they advanced along 'Tiger' route to reinforce 3 Para, they were too weak to have a decisive effect. Indeed, their removal from the landing zones was potentially disastrous, for the Germans, aware from the captured plans that 4th Airborne Brigade was about to arrive, infiltrated the thin defensive screen provided by 7 KOSB and 1 Border and stationed snipers in key positions. Hackett's brigade had a hot reception when they flew in during the early afternoon: Dakotas and gliders were shot down, paras were picked off as they dangled helplessly during their descent and, to top it all, the heather on the landing zones caught fire. It was, as one of the paras remarked, 'a bit of a shambles'.

Hackett was not well pleased, and his anger grew when he learnt that Hicks had already decided to detach 11 Para from his brigade to act as yet another reinforcement around the St Elizabeth Hospital. Receiving 7 KOSB in compensation, Hackett gathered his men together and tried to carry out his original orders, advancing through Wolfheze to take up positions in the north, astride the roads from Apeldoorn and Zutphen. Almost immediately, he encountered strong enemy forces, drawn principally from 9th SS Panzer: by the end of the day, Hackett's men were occupying a straggling line between Johanna Hoeve and Lichtenbeek on the northern outskirts of Arnhem, and although they were preparing to mount further attacks, they were to all intents and purposes stalled. A similar fate had befallen 11 Para and 2 South Stafford (by now complete), for they had made little headway along 'Tiger' route, mounting attacks that were poorly co-ordinated against tough opposition. Small pockets of men found themselves cut off by superior enemy forces equipped with tanks, self-propelled guns, armoured

cars and mortars, and despite heavy fighting, n
contact was made with the embattled remnants of
or 3 Para by nightfall. As one of the soldiers said, 'W
did all we could to get through, but it wasn't blood
well possible.'

Meanwhile, 2 Para had faced an entire day withou
the expected relief, fighting a bitter defensive battl
against 9th SS Panzer units determined to wipe then
out. At first, the German attacks were relativel
unsophisticated, comprising lorry-loads of panze
grenadiers who fell prey to well-directed smallarm
fire from the paras, but as the day progressed th
assaults grew stronger. By far the worst occurre
during mid-morning, when 16 armoured cars and
half-tracks, supported by panzer grenadiers, tried t
race across the bridge into the British positions. The
paras kept their nerve – 'We just sat there waiting.
had my Piat aimed smack at the leading car. My
fingers were trembling', recalled one of Frost's mei
in the aftermath – and when they did open fire, the
results were impressive. In what Frost called 'the
most lovely action you ever saw', six vehicles were
destroyed, several set on fire and the remainde
forced to withdraw. But it was a hollow victory
draining the ammunition stocks of the paras and
wearing down their resolve. Reinforcement wa:
imperative.

When Urquhart resumed command of the divisior
early on 19 September, therefore, the battle wa:

Below: Signallers occupy defensive positions in the area of Brigade Headquarters. In an airborne operation, where the surrounding territory is enemy-occupied, most personnel double as combat troops. These men are equipped with the Mark V Sten sub-machine gun, a model which was first used in combat at Arnhem. Left: One of the best-known photographs of Arnhem: a 1 Para 3in-mortar crew fighting only yards from II SS Panzer Corps in Oosterbeek. The mortar's high angle of fire is a clear indication of the short range.

already out of control. Elements of four battalions – 1, 3 and 11 Para and 2 South Stafford – were firmly bogged down in the vicinity of the St Elizabeth Hospital, 2 Para was cut off and running short of supplies, 1 Border was under pressure in the west and Hackett's brigade (7 KOSB, 10 and 156 Para) was caught up in fighting to the north. In essence, three separate actions were being fought simultaneously, with no co-ordination between them. The weather had deteriorated and, because of communications' problems, there was no way of stopping the RAF delivering supplies onto pre-arranged drop zones that were still in enemy hands. It was, as Hackett said, a 'grossly untidy situation' that had to be rationalised as quickly as possible.

Urquhart's response was to order Hackett to disengage and move south to join in the fight to relieve 2 Para at the bridge. It was a logical rearrangement but fraught with danger: as a member of 10 Para pointed out, 'you can't just get up and rush away from the enemy in daylight.... You just can't bloody well do it.' At first, the withdrawal was orderly, but as the enemy realised what was happening they tried to cut off Hackett's men by seizing the railway crossing at Wolfheze. Under artillery, mortar and smallarms fire, the paras soon became disorganised, with small pockets of men left on the wrong side of the railway line to fight hopeless battles for survival. To add to the chaos, a Polish glider unit suddenly decided to land in the midst of the battle: fired on by both sides, the newcomers understandably panicked. It was, as one of the few survivors of 10 Para remarked, 'a real cock-up'. 'But then,' he added ruefully, 'it was a real cock-up everywhere that day.'

In fact, the only piece of good news, relayed to Urquhart by members of the Dutch Resistance, was that XXX Corps had at last begun to advance. US paras had captured the bridges at Eindhoven and Grave and, in company with Guards Armoured Division from XXX Corps, were approaching Nijmegen, only 10 miles from Arnhem. From his HQ at the Hartenstein Hotel, Urquhart drew his remaining forces into a tight defensive ring, aiming to maintain at least a foothold on the northern side of the Neder Rijn for XXX Corps to exploit. In the process, his units suffered yet more casualties: by the end of 19 September 10 Para had virtually ceased to exist, joining 1 and 3 Para as little more than nominal entries in the divisional order of battle; 11 and 156 Para, together with the South Staffords, were struggling to retain their viability, and both 7 KOSB and 1 Border were under pressure from recently-reinforced German units intent on squeezing out the British bridgehead. Another re-supply failure only added to the gloom.

Urquhart's decision to concentrate on the divisional area around Oosterbeek, understandable as it was, unavoidably left 2 Para in a desperate situation. By now Frost's men had been fighting for over 48 hours without relief and were running short of ammunition,

Below: Arnhem bridge on the second day of the battle. At this stage the paras were destroying everything thrown at them by the Germans, as the debris between their positions on the north bank testifies. Bottom: The bridge after the British surrender. Right: German Stug IIIs manoeuvre into position at Arnhem.

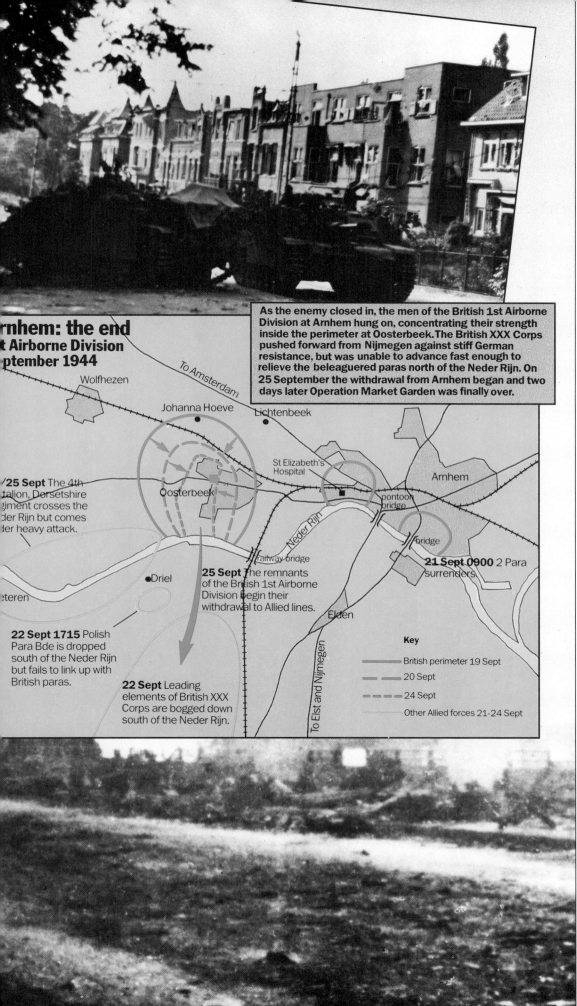

'A BRIDGE TOO FAR'

When General Browning uttered the line subsequently made famous by the writer Cornelius Ryan, '…but I think we might be going a bridge too far', he was expressing a view that ran counter to a powerful optimism which was sweeping through the staff and the men of the 1st British Airborne Division. Pent up by a series of aborted operations, the division was battle-hungry and aching to play its part in finishing the war. Few believed that the German Army would recover from the devastating blows landed by the Allies in France, and this attitude was to have a fatal influence on British intelligence appraisals of the situation in Arnhem.

The Arnhem operation suffered from misleading intelligence reports in three major aspects. Firstly, the polderland south of Arnhem bridge, which would have been an invaluable landing zone hard by the target, was wrongly judged to be swampy and therefore unusable. Secondly, the danger of flak installations in central Arnhem was seriously over-estimated, resulting in the RAF's adamant veto of landings in the immediate area of the bridge-head. Thirdly, the appraisal of German strength in Arnhem took little account of reports from the Dutch Resistance of the presence of armoured units in the vicinity, and even a specific identification of the crack 9th SS Panzer Division 'Hohenstaufen' was discounted.

General Browning was not the only man who felt that the British optimism was misplaced. Major Brian Urquhart, the Chief Intelligence Officer at Corps HQ, was shown photographs which clearly indicated tanks in the Arnhem area, yet his representations at HQ were over-ruled, and it was only after the division's costly action that his fears were proved justified.

As the enemy closed in, the men of the British 1st Airborne Division at Arnhem hung on, concentrating their strength inside the perimeter at Oosterbeek. The British XXX Corps pushed forward from Nijmegen against stiff German resistance, but was unable to advance fast enough to relieve the beleaguered paras north of the Neder Rijn. On 25 September the withdrawal from Arnhem began and two days later Operation Market Garden was finally over.

rnhem: the end
t Airborne Division
ptember 1944

Wolfhezen

To Amsterdam

Johanna Hoeve

Lichtenbeek

St Elizabeth's Hospital

Arnhem

Oosterbeek

pontoon bridge

Neder Rijn

bridge

railway bridge

Driel

21 Sept 0900 2 Para surrenders

eteren

25 Sept The remnants of the British 1st Airborne Division begin their withdrawal to Allied lines.

Elden

/25 Sept The 4th talion, Dorsetshire giment crosses the der Rijn but comes der heavy attack.

22 Sept 1715 Polish Para Bde is dropped south of the Neder Rijn but fails to link up with British paras.

22 Sept Leading elements of British XXX Corps are bogged down south of the Neder Rijn.

To Elst and Nijmegen

Key

— British perimeter 19 Sept
– – 20 Sept
- - - 24 Sept
— Other Allied forces 21-24 Sept

93

food and water. The original force of nearly 500 had been whittled down to about 150, clinging tenaciously to a small group of shell-battered buildings close to the northern ramp. The wounded (among whom was Frost) suffered particularly hard, being packed into cellars with no hope of evacuation. Enemy pressure increased inexorably and by 20 September the paras were being hit by artillery, mortars, tanks, self-propelled guns and phosphorus shells, and their posts were being attacked by panzer grenadiers who were proving adept at urban warfare. Lieutenant Mackay and his dwindling band of engineers came under sustained fire in the school they had occupied, until the building:

> 'was like a sieve. Wherever you looked you could see daylight....Splattered everywhere was blood; it lay in pools in the rooms, it covered the smocks of the defenders and ran in small rivulets down the stairs....The only clean things in the school were the weapons.'

Hardly surprisingly, despite remarkable displays of courage, the defensive perimeter around the bridge gradually crumbled. It was only a matter of time before 2 Para would be wiped out, although their resolve was boosted late on the 20th by news that XXX Corps and the Americans had seized the Nijmegen bridge. There was still a faint flicker of hope.

But this was soon snuffed out. When the tanks of Guards Armoured Division moved out at dawn on 21 September, aiming to push through to the Neder Rijn, they experienced unforeseen problems. By now they were acting as the tip of an Allied spear that had thrust deep into enemy lines, and the shaft – a single road back to the Belgian frontier along which all supplies and reinforcements had to travel – was dangerously weak. As elements of 10th SS Panzer set up defensive lines around Elst, to the south of the river, the advance ground rapidly to a halt. Reinforcements, comprising the three infantry battalions of 43rd (Wessex) Division, were ordered forward, but their trucks could not move through a traffic jam

Above: Field Marshal Walter Model, commander of Germany's Army Group B, was based at Oosterbeek and his rapid and decisive response to the airborne raid was to spell disaster for the British. Below: Germans move up to the front. Above right: German prisoners under guard. They are probably members of the 9th SS Panzer Division 'Hohenstaufen'. Right: The staff car of General Kussin, ambushed by 3 Para.

that worsened as the day progressed. Enemy attack on the road only added to the chaos, and by nightfall XXX Corps was no nearer to Arnhem than it had been 24 hours before. Moreover, during that period, the Germans had concentrated on destroying the remains of 2 Para at the bridge – the last pockets of gallant resistance surrendered at 0900 – and had moved additional forces to probe the Oosterbeek perimeter. Conditions among Urquhart's men deteriorated as supplies gradually ran out, isolated incidents of panic occurred, and everyone faced the physical and mental drain of savage and seemingly endless house-to-house fighting.

This was not perhaps the ideal moment for the Poles to arrive, but at 1715 on 21 September Dakotas droned over landing zones to the south of the river and disgorged two battalions under the personal command of Sosabowski. He was shocked by what he found, for although his arrival caught the Germans off-balance, he could do little to help his divisional commander. That night he tried to push supplies and reinforcements across the river, only to find the task impossible without specialised equipment, and it was not until lead elements of XXX Corps finally made contact on 22 September that DUKW amphibious carriers could be brought forward. Even these vehicles found the going hard across flooded and swampy ground. As late as the night of 24/25 September, when men of 4th Battalion, Dorsetshire Regi

RADIO COMMUNICATIONS

Of the various circumstances which led to the British failure to secure the bridge-heads at Arnhem, perhaps the most exasperating to officers and men alike was the almost complete breakdown in radio links.

The inadequacy of the 1st British Airborne Division's radio equipment was noted in England before the operation. Most of the sets had an effective range of three miles, yet Divisional Headquarters was sited eight miles from Arnhem bridge and more than 15 miles from Corps HQ at Nijmegen. The option of heavy, high-powered sets was rejected, however, as transport would have to be re-allocated for them and expert operators were not available. In addition to these problems, interference from a powerful German station severely disrupted the division's long-distance transmissions.

The force's radios were also almost useless on a local level. General Urquhart, trying to raise his operational units, could get no intelligible response over the extended range, and his chances of success were further reduced by the sandy soil and tall trees and buildings of the area. When he finally drove into the town with a Rover radio operator his vehicle fell victim to a mortar bomb and the radio was put out of action.

Another serious problem was the division's inability to call on the RAF. For this it had been relying on two 'Veeps' (jeeps with VHF trans-receivers) transmitting on a special network. On landing, neither proved serviceable and it was not until the very last day that the RAF was able to give close air support.

ment (part of 43rd Division) attempted yet another crossing, the results were catastrophic. As Sosabowski recalled:

'the whole world seemed to be exploding around us. Hour by hour all through the night I received messages of boats being sunk. Every time I went out to have a look around, files of stretcher bearers trudged past, bringing back the wounded.'

In the circumstances, Urquhart's shattered units stood little chance of holding out, particularly as the pressure on their thinly-held perimeter mounted as each day went by. The defenders could no longer 'even think straight' and were now having to sustain the undivided attention of German forces that included the formidable King Tiger tanks of *Panzerabteilung* 503. Airborne troops, already short of supplies, had no answer to these monsters – Piat shells, even if they had been available in sufficient numbers, merely bounced off the thick armour plate – and it required a special type of courage to survive. Some men, such as Major R. H. Cain and Sergeant J. D. Baskeyfield (both of the South Staffords) responded with awesome displays of bravery that won welldeserved VCs, but the majority adopted the grim fatalism described by an anonymous para caught up in the fighting around Oosterbeek Laag church:

'I didn't care by then if I never saw the bloody bridge at all; and I don't think many of us did neither. But we dug in and held on. That's how you get. Fed up but flipping stubborn.'

Above: Happy to be alive! Survivors of the 1st British Airborne Division in Nijmegen pose for the camera after their evacuation from Arnhem. Many of their comrades did not share their fate – 1200 British soldiers were dead, and a great many more wounded or taken prisoner. One survivor was to comment later: 'The mistakes are not so important now, except when they provided lessons for the future. The important thing is not to forget the dead.'

Montgomery had no choice but to authorise a withdrawal, and on 25 September, after eight days of battle, Urquhart briefed his surviving commanders on Operation Berlin, scheduled for that night. Glider pilots, many of whom had fought with the para throughout, acted as guides and at 2200 hours phased withdrawal to the river began. British and Canadian engineers worked hard to provide the necessary boats, but the night was 'black and wet' and the enemy soon realised what was happening. Machine-gun and mortar fire swept the river, destroying boats and contributing to the confusion; the wounded had to be left behind and many men drowned as they attempted to swim across. By 26 September, when the operation was finally called off, only 2163 of the original 10,000 soldiers under Urquhart's command had reached the relative safety of Polish lines. With 1200 killed and 6642 wounded, missing or captured, a crack formation had ceased to exist. In the process, however, it had displayed a tenacity and depth of courage that remains an inspiration to The Parachute Regiment today.

THE AUTHOR John Pimlott is Senior Lecturer in War Studies and International Affairs at the Royal Military Academy, Sandhurst. He is author of *World War II in Photographs* and *Vietnam: the History and the Tactics*.

THE ANGELS IN KOREA

On 25 June 1950, seven divisions of the North Korean People's Army (NKPA) invaded the Republic of (South) Korea. Almost immediately, the United Nations committed an international force, with a large element from the USA, in support of the South Korean Army.

With few airborne troops available at the start of the Korean War, the US Army selected a depleted regiment of the 11th Airborne Division at Fort Campbell, Kentucky, and within two months raised it to full strength. Other units from the 11th Division were attached to the regiment, including a field artillery battalion, an anti-aircraft battery, an engineer company and two pathfinder teams.

Finally comprising some 4400 officers and men, the 187th Airborne Regimental Combat Team, known as the 'Angels from Hell', began the journey to Korea in September.

As the 187th arrived in Korea, allied forces of the United Nations were poised to cross the 38th Parallel, the border between North and South Korea. The communist invasion force had been almost destroyed, and on 9 October 1950 the US Eighth Army and the separate X Corps crossed the border into North Korea to finish off the NKPA. The Eighth Army's I Corps was ordered to advance 70 miles to Pyongyang, capital of North Korea. With this objective nearly secured, the Angels from Hell were to carry out their first mission of the Korean War, a jump north of the city to block the retreat of NKPA units from the capital.

Above: The shoulder insignia of the 'Angels from Hell'.

ANGELS FROM HELL

In October 1950, the crack paras of the 187th Airborne Regimental Combat Team jumped into North Korea to join battle with communist forces

KIMPO AIRFIELD, lying close to the South Korean capital of Seoul, was not a good place from which to stage an airborne operation. It possessed a hard-surfaced runway 6000ft long and 150ft wide, but little else. Its parking space was so limited that all the tactical aircraft normally based there had been moved to make way for 120 carrier planes arriving from US air bases in Japan. On the morning of 19 October 1950, a steady rain was falling over the airfield and riggers were working in the open to prepare cargo. Trucks and fork-lifts were in such

force completely.

The first UN troops had crossed the 38th Parallel on 9 October, and the Eighth Army's I Corps, led by the US 1st Cavalry Division and with the 27th British Commonwealth Brigade in support, had advanced 70 miles up the western side of the peninsula to the North Korean capital of Pyongyang, arriving there 10 days later. Meanwhile, seeing that the capture of the city was certain, General MacArthur had alerted his waiting airborne formation, the 187th Airborne Regimental Combat Team, to be ready for an air drop north of Pyongyang on 21 October to block enemy withdrawals, cut off enemy reinforcements and disrupt enemy communications. He shortly rescheduled the drop for the morning of 20 October after intelligence reports revealed that trains carrying North Korean political officials and American prisoners of war had begun to move out of Pyongyang, creeping north at night and staying concealed in tunnels during daylight. Though the information in the reports was almost a week old, MacArthur hoped that the airborne troops could intercept at least some of the trains.

Two railway lines, each with a highway alongside, ran northwest and northeast in a 'V'-shaped configuration out of Pyongyang. MacArthur instructed the commander of the 187th, Colonel Frank S Bowen, Jr, to block these routes about 30 miles north of Pyongyang, at the towns of Sukch'on on the western arm of the 'V' and Sunch'on on the eastern arm. Colonel Bowen was to land the bulk of the combat team at Sukch'on, since the rail line and the highway passing through that town were the main lines of communication. After establishing the blocks, Bowen was to send a battalion south from Sukch'on, in concert with a northward attack out of Pyongyang by I Corps, to trap North Korean forces in the area and destroy them.

The 187th Airborne Regimental Combat Team was to be carried to its drop zones by 120 aircraft brought from American bases in Japan. A third of the planes were C-47s of World War II vintage. The remainder were the newer C-119 type, known as the 'Flying Boxcar', and designed with a roomy, rear-loading cargo compartment, a high wing, two

short supply that paratroopers were doing much of the loading by hand. An important new phase of the Korean War was underway.

On 27 September 1950, US President Harry Truman had authorised the commander of the United Nations Command (UNC) in Korea, General of the Army Douglas MacArthur, to cross the 38th Parallel, the border set between North Korea and the Republic of (South) Korea (ROK). By this time the tide had turned for the North Korean People's Army (NKPA), which had invaded the southern republic in June, and much of the communist invasion force had been destroyed. Then, on 7 October, the UN General Assembly had confirmed Truman's authorisation by voting for the restoration of peace and security throughout Korea, thus giving tacit approval for the UNC's entry into North Korea. General MacArthur had already alerted his ground commanders on 2 October that a counter-invasion was imminent: its objective was the eradication of any chance of the NKPA mounting another invasion by wiping out the

187TH AIRBORNE REGIMENTAL COMBAT TEAM

The United States Army activated the 187th Infantry Regiment in February 1943 as a glider formation in the 11th Airborne Division. Shipped with the division to the Pacific theatre of operations in May 1944, the 187th saw action in New Guinea and on the islands of Leyte and Luzon in the Philippines. It received a Presidential Unit Citation for its operations on Luzon. When the 187th returned to the US in April 1949, the Army reorganised it as a parachute regiment. Following the outbreak of the Korean War in June 1950, the Army reinforced the 187th with artillery, engineer personnel and other forces to form the 187th Airborne Regimental Combat Team, and shipped it to the Far East in September. The team made two combat jumps in Korea, at Sukch'on and Sunch'on in October 1950 and at Munsan-ni in March 1951. Altogether, the 187th participated in six campaigns during the war. It was awarded a Presidential Unit Citation for its action at Sukch'on and Sunch'on. The regiment returned to the US in July 1955.

During the Vietnam War, the 3rd Battalion of the 187th served with the 101st Airborne Division from 1967 to 1971. The battalion participated in 12 campaigns during the war, including the battles at Trang Bang and Dong Ap Bia Mountain, for which it received Presidential Unit Citations.

Currently, the 187th Airborne Infantry is headquartered at Fort Campbell, Kentucky, where it serves under the army regimental system as a parent regiment for five battalions. Three of these battalions are stationed at Fort Campbell, and the other two are in Panama.

powerful engines and a twin-boom tail structure. The total number of aircraft was not sufficient to take all the combat team in one lift, however, and over 1000 of Colonel Bowen's men were obliged to wait for a second flight.

At 0230 hours on 20 October the airborne troopers turned out onto the rain-soaked airstrip at Kimpo. The rain was expected to cease at any time but it was not until noon, six hours after the planned time for take-off, that the weather improved sufficiently to allow the first of the transport aircraft to leave. Once all the planes were circling above the strip, the air armada headed northwest to the Yellow Sea, then directly northward over water for about 50 miles. The aircraft then split into two echelons, each group flying on a heading to the northeast towards its drop zone. Meanwhile, F-51 and F-80 fighters and B-26 bombers were rising from other airstrips in South Korea and heading directly for the drop zones at high speeds, rocketing and strafing the ground as the troop carriers approached. General MacArthur and members of his staff were also en route aboard MacArthur's personal plane, the 'Bataan', to observe the air drop.

Beginning at about 1400 hours, the bulk of the 187th, including the 1st and 3rd Battalions and Colonel Bowen himself, dropped at Sukch'on. There was no enemy anti-aircraft fire and only light rifle fire. One man dangling from his chute was killed by the rifle fire, and 25 other men sustained jump injuries. Other troopers appeared to be in danger when they landed on or near a high-tension electric power line that had not been spotted in aerial reconnaissance photographs of the drop zone. Fortunately, the line was dead. The heavy equipment drop included three-quarter ton trucks, jeeps, 105mm howitzers, and large pallets loaded with ammunition for the artillery pieces. Men launching the equipment from the aircraft – they were called 'kickers' – dropped several loads so close together that 100ft parachutes used to land some items stole air from smaller parachutes, causing the latter to stream. Other parachutes tore, and a few vehicles slipped their rigging and crashed. But almost all the equipment reached the ground in good condition.

Against light resistance, the 1st Battalion moved north, cleared Sukch'on, and set up road-blocks north and east of the town, capturing 15 North Koreans in the process. The 3rd Battalion turned south out of the drop zone and established road-blocks across the highway and rail line two miles below Sukch'on, killing five and capturing 42 North Koreans as it advanced. Neither battalion suffered any casualties. All captives taken by the airborne troops proved to be remnants of the North Korean 2nd Regiment, which, as part of the 1st Division, had played a large role in the North Korean invasion of South Korea.

Within minutes of the start of the Sukch'on jump, Colonel Bowen's 2nd Battalion began parachuting into its drop zone a short distance southwest of Sunch'on. The battalion was unharmed by enemy fire, but 20 men were injured in the jump. Against virtually no resistance, two rifle companies of the battalion organised road-blocks west of Sunch'on and across the road and railway south of town. The remaining rifle company moved without opposition northeast into the town, and there made contact with

a unit of the South Korean 6th Division, which reached Sunch'on from the southeast in the Eighth Army's general advance above the 38th Parallel.

After watching Colonel Bowen's forces land and assemble successfully, General MacArthur flew to Pyongyang. There, he told an assembly of reporters that perhaps 30,000 North Korean troops, half the number that remained in North Korea, were now caught between the 187th Airborne Regimental Combat Team in the north and I Corps in the south. But there was no such large number in the trap; the main body of North Korean forces had already withdrawn north of Sukch'on and Sunch'on by 17 October. Neither were there any trains carrying North Korean officials and American prisoners north out of Pyongyang. As learned from civilians in the capital, the principal North Korean government authorities had left the city on 12 October.

Two trains carrying prisoners had left Pyongyang on the night of 17 October, both of them moving

Suk'chon and Sun'chon
187th Regimental Combat Team
October 1950

By October 1950, the United Nations forces in Korea had pushed the invading North Korean People's Army back north of Seoul and reached the 38th Parallel. On 9 October, UN forces crossed the border, and 10 days later the North Korean capital, Pyongyang, was in UN hands. The following day, the 187th Regimental Combat Team jumped into action at Sun'chon and Suk'chon, some 30 miles further north.

Key

..... UN front line, 20 Oct

— UN front line, 24 Oct

⌇ North Korean People's Army concentration area

Sun'chon and Suk'chon

20 Oct 1200 187th RCT leaves Kimpo airfield near Seoul by C-47 and C-119 transport.

1400 Col. Bowen's 2nd Btn, 187th RCT secures Sun'chon and links up with the South Korean 6th Div. The 1st and 3rd Btns jump at Suk'chon. While the 1st Btn moves north, the 3rd Btn advances south.

The Battle of Yongyu

21 Oct As 3rd Btn nears Opa-ri, moving south along the road and railway line to Pyongyang, troops encounter forward elements of the North Korean 239th Regt.

22 Oct The North Koreans are trapped between British troops and the 187th RCT near Yongyu. After a fierce fight they are destroyed.

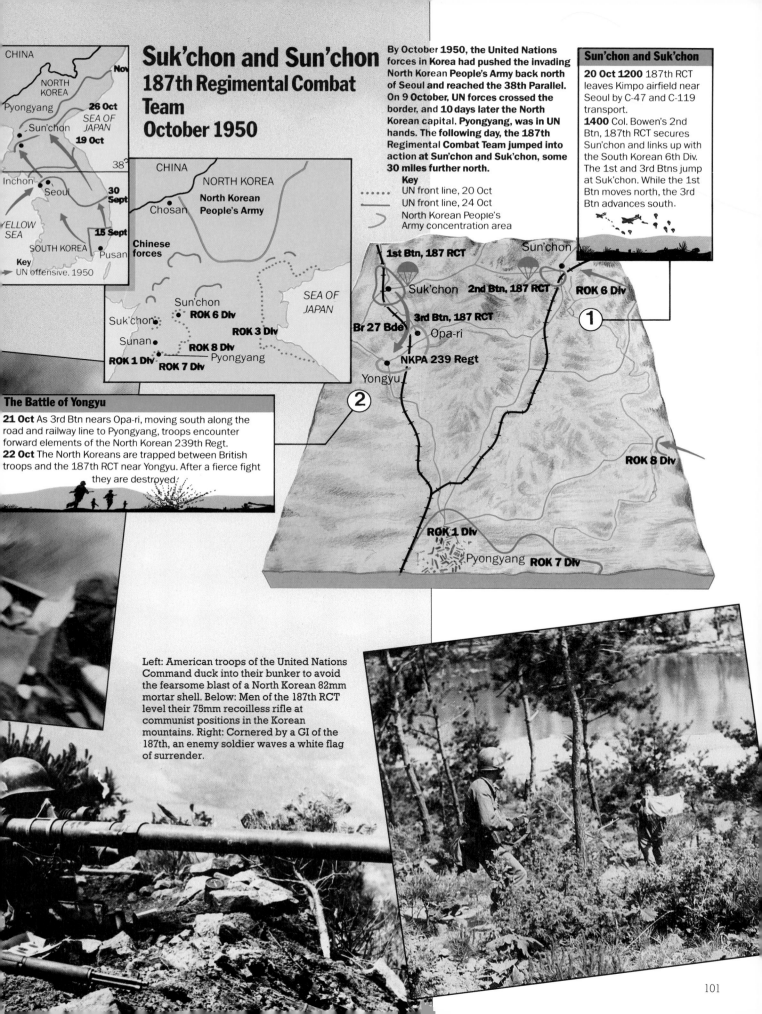

CHINA

NORTH KOREA

Pyongyang

Sun'chon
19 Oct
SEA OF JAPAN
26 Oct
Nov

38°

Inchon
Seoul
30 Sept

YELLOW SEA

15 Sept

SOUTH KOREA
Pusan

Key
→ UN offensive. 1950

CHINA

NORTH KOREA
North Korean People's Army

Chosan

Chinese forces

Sun'chon
ROK 6 Div

Suk'chon

ROK 3 Div

Sunan

ROK 8 Div

Pyongyang

ROK 1 Div
ROK 7 Div

SEA OF JAPAN

1st Btn, 187 RCT

Sun'chon

Suk'chon

2nd Btn, 187 RCT

ROK 6 Div

①

3rd Btn, 187 RCT

Br 27 Bde

Opa-ri

NKPA 239 Regt

Yongyu

②

ROK 8 Div

ROK 1 Div

Pyongyang ROK 7 Div

Left: American troops of the United Nations Command duck into their bunker to avoid the fearsome blast of a North Korean 82mm mortar shell. Below: Men of the 187th RCT level their 75mm recoilless rifle at communist positions in the Korean mountains. Right: Cornered by a GI of the 187th, an enemy soldier waves a white flag of surrender.

the Sunch'on rail line. By the 20th, both were above Sunch'on, the lead train well on the way north. During the air attacks and the landing of the airborne troops on the afternoon of the 20th, the second train, with about 100 American prisoners aboard, remained hidden in a tunnel five miles northwest of Sunch'on. That evening, North Korean guards took the prisoners from the train in three groups to receive their evening meal, then shot the Americans as they waited for food. The train and the guards continued north during the night. A Korean civilian brought word of the massacre to the 2nd Battalion's command post in Sunch'on at about noon on the 21st. Search parties going to the tunnel area discovered the bodies of 66 Americans who had been shot and of seven others who had died either of starvation or disease. They also located 23 survivors, men who either had feigned death after being shot or had managed to get away from the train before the massacre took place. Two of these died during the night. Their bodies and the remaining survivors were taken to Pyongyang and evacuated by air to Japan on 22 October.

While the majority of the North Korean troops had escaped the trap, one enemy group was sandwiched between the 187th Airborne Regimental Combat Team and I Corps. This was the independent North Korean 239th Regiment, which had been ordered to delay the United Nations Command's advance north of Pyongyang. The enemy regiment, with a strength of some 2500 men, had established defensive positions between the towns of Yongyu and Opa-ri, about eight miles south of Sukch'on. The troops were on a line of high hills cutting across both the main highway and rail line, which at that point were three miles apart.

On the morning of 21 October, while C-119s delivered those men of Colonel Bowen's forces who had been stranded at Kimpo airfield the day before by the lack of aircraft, the 3rd Battalion started south from its road-block below Sukch'on towards Pyongyang. Company I moved along the rail line, Company K along the highway. Company L and the battalion Headquarters Company followed Company K. Neither the 3rd Battalion nor the North Korean 239th Regiment was aware of the other until Company I, as it followed the rail line through a narrow valley just north of Opa-ri, encountered and drove back an enemy outpost. The engagement revealed the position of an entire enemy battalion, supported by 120mm mortars and 40mm artillery.

Recovering quickly from the surprise of being attacked from the rear, the North Korean battalion countered with a flanking attack, overrunning part of Company I and forcing it to withdraw onto high ground west of the rail line. But, having lost 200 men, the enemy battalion at that point broke contact and returned to its defensive position near Opa-ri. During Company I's withdrawal, Private First Class Richard G. Wilson, a medical-aid man, assisted wounded paratroopers to safety, scouting the battle area thoroughly to make sure that no casualties were left behind. Then, as the company reached its position on high ground, he was informed that one man previously thought dead had been seen attempting to crawl to safety. Wilson, despite the protests of his comrades, returned to the battle area in search of him. A patrol later found the

Left: General of the Army Douglas MacArthur, Commander-in-Chief UN Command in Korea, tours captured territory with Lieutenant-General Matthew Ridgway (left) and Lieutenant-Colonel Arthur Wilson, CO of the 187th's 1st Battalion. Below left: Paratroopers with camouflaged ox-carts laden with ammunition that were captured near Sukch'on. Below: Members of the 'Angels from Hell' mop up after a village used by North Koreans to store ammunition has been destroyed by fire.

bodies of both Wilson and the man he had gone to find. Wilson had been shot several times, obviously while trying to shield and administer aid to the wounded man. Wilson received a posthumous award of the Medal of Honor.

Company K, meanwhile, had engaged two enemy companies a mile north of Yongyu, killing 150 North Koreans and forcing the remainder to withdraw to well south of the town. By nightfall, Company K had organised defensive positions on high ground overlooking Yongyu from the north, and large quantities of enemy supplies had been captured in the town itself. The battalion Headquarters Company and Company L took position immediately to the rear of Company K.

After dark, the 239th Regiment regrouped for an attempt to break through Company K and escape north. Beginning at midnight, the North Koreans launched four separate assaults against Company K, but were repulsed each time after fierce fighting at close quarters. Attempting next to bypass Company K on its western flank, the North Koreans ran blindly into Company L and suffered high casualties from the company's fire. Persisting nevertheless, the North Koreans kept both Company L and the Headquarters Company under attack through the remainder of the night, but suffered heavy losses.

The 187th suffered 45 jump casualties and 66 battle casualties, small numbers indeed compared to the enemy losses

By dawn on 22 October, the 27th British Commonwealth Brigade was approaching on the main highway to join the airborne troops. Having moved north from Pyongyang the day before, the brigade had halted for the night within hearing-distance of the battle in the Yongyu area. At first light, the 1st Battalion, Argyll and Sutherland Highlanders, led the way into Yongyu without meeting resistance. The 3rd Battalion, Royal Australian Regiment, took the lead from there, and just north of Yongyu it came under rifle fire from apple orchards located on each side of the highway. The Australian battalion commander, Lieutenant-Colonel Charles H. Green, immediately deployed forces to attack on both sides of the road. In hand-to-hand fighting with rifles, grenades and bayonets, the Australians suffered only seven men wounded while killing 270 and capturing 200 North Koreans. The 1st Battalion, Middlesex Regiment, then took over the lead and, meeting no opposition, it reached the airborne troops before noon. It was found in the final count that the airborne battalion had killed 805 and captured 681 enemy troops in the Yongyu battle.

Caught between the 187th Airborne Regimental Combat Team and the 27th British Commonwealth Brigade, the North Korean 239th Regiment had been destroyed. In fulfilling its major role during the operation, the 187th suffered 45 jump casualties and 66 battle casualties, small numbers indeed compared to the enemy losses. The hundreds of North Koreans later hauled south to prisoner-of-war camps probably never learned the identity of their captors. Had they known, their enemy's name of the 'Angels from Hell' would have seemed particularly apt.

THE AUTHOR Billy C. Mossman is a well-known American writer and historian. He is currently working on a volume on the Korean War for the US Army Center of Military History.

1st CAVALRY DIVISION (AIRMOBILE) IA DRANG 1965

The early history of the 1st Cavalry Division (Airmobile) is a story of a dedicated few overcoming the prejudices of the many. Although the US armed forces had used helicopters for casualty evacuation in the Korean War (1950-1953) and the Marine Corps had carried out several pioneering airborne assault tests, the Pentagon remained lukewarm to the idea. The report of the Howse Board in August 1962 changed all that: 'Adoption by the Army of the airmobile concept,' it stated, 'is necessary and desirable'.

The 11th Air Assault Division (Test) was ordered to put theory into practice and a series of trials in early 1965 proved so successful that it was given the go-ahead to prepare for active service. Men of the 2nd Infantry Division joined the unit and on 1 July the 1st Cavalry Division (Airmobile) came into being.

A month later the division, 16,000 strong with 400 fixed-wing aircraft and helicopters and 1600 vehicles, sailed for Vietnam. After establishing a base at An Khe and conducting a few small-scale actions against local Viet Cong guerrillas, the formation got the chance to show its worth in the Ia Drang Valley in the autumn of 1965. Its performance heralded a new era in military thinking, and demonstrated that in creating a force in which technology was allied with skill and determination, the US Army had formed a battlefield elite.

GRUNTS AND GUNSHIPS

Swooping from the sky, the troopers of the US 1st Air Cavalry pitted their wits and their machines against the battle-hardened veterans of the North Vietnamese Army during a desperate battle for the Central Highlands in 1965

ON 22 OCTOBER 1965 Major-General Harry W.O. Kinnard, Commanding General of the 1st Cavalry Division (Airmobile), received the message he had been anxiously waiting for. Short and to the point it stated: 'Commencing first light 23 October First Air Cav deploys one Bn TF [Task Force] minimum 1 Inf Bn and 1 Arty Btry to PLEIKU, mission to assist in defense of key US/ARVN [Army of the Republic of Vietnam] installations at PLEIKU or reinforce II Corps operations to relieve PLEI ME CAMP.' Since the division's arrival in South Vietnam it had had a few brushes with small bands of local Viet Cong guerrillas and, although Kinnard knew his men had performed well, he remained aware that they had yet to face the cream of the North Vietnamese Army.

Kinnard was a great believer in the value of airmobility and had been involved with the division from its early days. Indeed, as a brigadier-general, he had led the 11th Air Assault Division, where his enthusiasm and firm but relaxed style made him popular with the men. Close attention had been paid to their training and he felt sure that the successful completion of an operation lasting more than a few days would silence those critics who complained at the cost of the division.

Kinnard knew the men of the 1st Cavalry were special. They had to be: helicopters were temperamental beasts. A large part of the division would be used to keep them in the air. Pilots needed the skill to fly at tree-top level at over 100mph. The division's strength was speed and firepower. Eagle Flights, the basic tactical unit, consisted of six UH-1C Hueys, armed with 2.75in rockets and a minigun capable of saturating an area the size of a football pitch in a few seconds, and seven UH-1Ds for carrying combat troops. Going into action they flew in a V-formation to give all-round vision and mutual protection. It worked in theory – would it work in practice?

Good up-to-the-minute intelligence on the strength and position of the enemy would be essential to the mission. A few days after the initial attack on the Plei Me Camp Captain William P. Gillette, the Air Cavalry Squadron intelligence officer, was able to give a full and remarkably accurate report. It was clear that the NVA assault on the camp, 40km

Left: An M60 machine gun slung over his back, an Air Cav trooper clambers down from a Chinook in the Ia Drang Valley. Above: A Huey door-gunner blasts away at enemy positions. Right: Deep in the jungle a radio operator scans the tree line for Viet Cong snipers during the battle for Ia Drang.

Left: A patrol of the 1st Air Cavalry wends its way through enemy territory around Ia Drang. Bottles of inspect repellent – known as bug juice – are carried in the troopers' helmet bands. Right: Air Cavalry troopers leap from a hovering Huey slick to reinforce a patrol under enemy attack. Below: The defenders of the Plei Me Special Forces Camp watch US fighter-bombers pound Viet Cong positions during the early stages of the battle for Ia Drang.

southwest of Pleiku, was meant to be the beginning o a full-scale offensive aiming to cut South Vietnam i two. Two enemy regiments were in the area: the 33rd around Plei Me and the 32nd, lying in ambush read to destroy any ground force attempting to relieve th camp. The month-long battle that was to follow became known as the Battle of the Ia Drang Valley. I was to be a major test for the 1st Cavalry Division and was the first time that regular NVA troops controlled by a divisional headquarters fought a conventiona battle against US forces.

Initially the 1st Cavalry Division acted in suppor of the South Vietnamese Army. The Cav's 1st Brigade ordered to secure Pleiku, to provide artillery back up and to furnish a reserve force, was soon in action At 1730 hours the NVA hit a relief column at two point and the air cavalry was called up. The brigade was quick to respond – its helicopters were in the air in 1 minutes – and the firepower it deployed was widely recognised as the decisive factor in the defeat of th enemy. Plei Me camp was relieved on 25 October.

With a deafening roar eight claymore mines were exploded and then the cavalrymen fired continuously

It soon became clear that a major opportunity for the full deployment of the air cavalry was unfolding. The NVA was pulling back after receiving a bloody nose and a quick response might give them a furthe mauling. General William C. Westmoreland, Com mander of the US Military Assistance Command Vietnam (MACV), flew up to the front and after a brie conference ordered the cavalry in pursuit. For Kin nard it was the chance he had long waited for. He was given a free hand and his job was no longer jus reinforcement and reaction but unlimited attack. A pattern for future actions was being born: the divi sion was to engage in hard-hitting search-and destroy missions against NVA forces operating in the difficult terrain of Vietnam's Central Highlands.

It was not just the enemy that caused problems Much of this part of South Vietnam consisted of dense vegetation, and jungle composed of 30m high trees

Rocks hidden by man-tall elephant grass could flip a helicopter on its side. Most clearings were too small for even a single Huey, but by using the tail-rotor as a chain-saw – strictly against regulations – pilots could hack a way to the ground. A slight error of judgement, all too easy after six hours in the saddle, would be costly, and maybe fatal.

For the next 12 days much of the 1st Brigade was deployed to the west of Pleiku. Most of their operations involved fierce fighting and most of them proved successful. On 1 November, for example, a routine reconnaissance patrol flying 12km west of Plei Me spotted some unusual ground activity beneath the jungle canopy and ordered in units of the 1st Brigade. The enemy had no time to melt back into the undergrowth. Seventy-eight were killed and 57 captured. More damaging was the capture of a complete field hospital – dozens of cases of essential medical supplies, including morphine and penicillin, were stacked to chest height over a large area.

The 1st Squadron, 9th Cavalry, again drew blood two days later in a perfectly executed ambush on an enemy unit of company strength moving along an east-west trail just north of the Chu Pong mountains. The troopers had to wait an agonising 90 minutes before the unit entered the ambush zone, but their training taught them to wait until the leading elements had gone by. With a deafening roar eight claymore mines were exploded and then the cavalrymen fired continuously for two minutes. There was no return fire. But the Cav did not have things entirely their own way this time. Back at base they came under sustained, almost fanatical, attacks from three companies of NVA regulars and by midnight their perimeter was in grave danger of being over-run. Now, however, the advantages of airmobility became apparent. Help was soon at hand, as Company A, 1st Battalion, 8th Cavalry, located 20km to the north, flew in. The first platoon was on the ground and in combat 40 minutes after midnight.

These first sustained combats by units of the 1st Brigade though small in scale were, for Kinnard, ample justification of the airmobile concept. Scout ships were regularly finding enemy forces. Highly

mobile rifle units were then being flown in to fix the enemy before massive air and ground firepower was used to inflict maximum damage. Many lessons were learnt through combat experience.

In their first skirmishes many cavalry troopers were disconcerted by the suicidally close ranges at which they came to grips with the enemy. Several units were almost dropped into the laps of the NVA and firefights often took place at ranges of less than 20m, where the firepower of Soviet and Chinese-built assault rifles could be devastating. It was often difficult to organise artillery support and the emergency medical evacuation of casualties was delayed because of the lack of equipment to clear landing zones. The early encounters of the Ia Drang campaign were also remarkable for the successful deployment of airborne units at night. The battle of 3 November, for example, was the first time a defensive perimeter under heavy fire was reinforced in

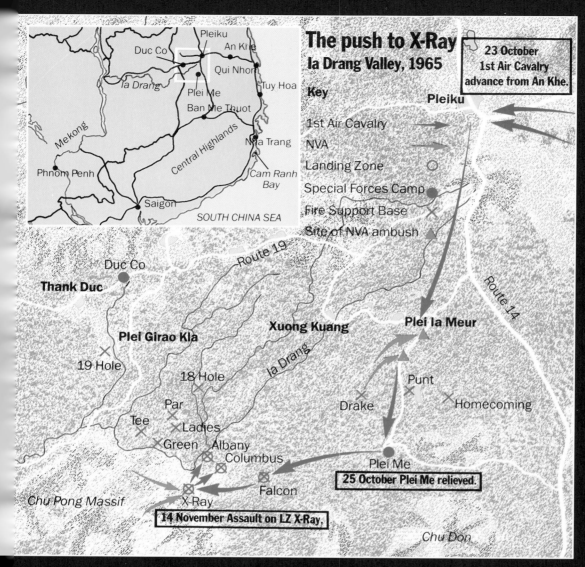

The push to X-Ray
Ia Drang Valley, 1965

23 October 1st Air Cavalry advance from An Khe.

Key

1st Air Cavalry →
NVA →
Landing Zone ○
Special Forces Camp ●
Fire Support Base ✕
Site of NVA ambush ▲

25 October Plei Me relieved.

14 November Assault on LZ X-Ray.

Map labels: Pleiku, Duc Co, An Khe, Qui Nhon, Ia Drang, Plei Me, Ban Me Thuot, Tuy Hoa, Nha Trang, Central Highlands, Mekong, Phnom Penh, Saigon, Cam Ranh Bay, SOUTH CHINA SEA, Route 19, Route 14, Thank Duc, Duc Co, Plei Girao Kla, Xuong Kuang, Plei Ia Meur, 19 Hole, 18 Hole, Ia Drang, Punt, Par, Tee, Ladies, Drake, Homecoming, Green, Albany, Columbus, Falcon, Plei Me, Chu Pong Massif, X-Ray, Chu Don

Above: Festooned with M60 ammunition belts, a patrol of the 1st Air Cavalry prepares to set out on a mission. Above right: M16 at the ready, an Air Cav trooper takes the surrender of an NVA soldier in the Ia Drang Valley. Right: After having rappeled (abseiled) down into the jungle from a helicopter this patrol prepares to hunt down Viet Cong and NVA regulars. The trooper in the foreground has an M148 grenade launcher fitted to his M16.

the dark by airborne troops flown into an unfamiliar landing zone. It was also the first time that aerial rocket artillery was used at night and as close as 50m to US troops.

Basic training taught the pilots to fly low and fast – they would be away before the enemy could get them in their sights. That was the official line, but most pilots took it as a sick joke. Fully-laden they had to fly low, but there was no way they could fly fast.

Flying at night or dropping into a vicious firefight from 500m was every pilot's nightmare. No amount of training could prepare them for it. The enemy always knew they were coming. Helicopter engines were noisy and in the jungle-quiet could be heard several miles away. Over the drop zone tracers would shoot up out of the undergrowth. Beautiful but deadly, a 0.5in calibre round would go through anything. If the enemy were lucky they might hit the 'Jesus nut' that held the rotor blades in place. There would be no survivors after a hit like that.

On 9 November the 1st Brigade was withdrawn from the Ia Drang battles. Its deployment had clearly been a major success: some 200 North Vietnamese soldiers were killed and an estimated 180 wounded. More importantly it had destroyed over 100,000 rounds of 7.62mm ammunition, two 82mm mortars and three 75mm recoilless rifles, and captured over $40,000 worth of medical supplies.

The 1st Brigade was replaced by the 3rd, consisting of the 1st and 2nd Battalions, 7th Cavalry. For the battles in the Ia Drang it was supported by the 2nd Battalion, 5th Cavalry. By this stage Kinnard's major concern was that the NVA might slip away and that the cavalry would fail to capitalise on its earlier successes. He ordered Colonel Thomas W. Brown, the 3rd Brigade commander, to initiate patrols south and southeast of Plei Me. Colonel Brown, well versed in airmobile techniques, started a vigorous hunt for the enemy. Intelligence reports suggested that the 33rd NVA Regiment was reorganising between the Ia Drang river and the Chu Pong mountains. It was also believed that the 32nd Regiment was nearby and that other reinforcements had arrived.

The LZ was saturated with fire – helicopter gunships fired 50 per cent of their rockets in 30 seconds

On 14 November the 1st Battalion, 7th Cavalry, commanded by Lieutenant-Colonel Harold G. Moore, began a sweep along the base of the Chu Pong range. The battalion was, however, short of helicopters. Only 16 UH-IDs were available. Fire support, the most essential part of any airborne assault, was to be provided by two 105mm batteries

ocated at Landing Zone (LZ) Falcon, 9km east of the
search area. Like the senior officers of the 1st
Brigade, Moore was conscious that his men had yet to
be tested against a large NVA force.

LZ X-Ray, 10km west of Plei Me, and capable of
taking up to 10 UH-IDs at one time, was chosen by
Moore as the best place for the opening air assault.
The co-ordination of all arms was of crucial importance in the early phases. At 1017 hours a preliminary
bombardment by 105s began and was quickly followed by an aerial attack. The LZ was saturated with
fire – helicopter gunships fired 50 per cent of their
rockets in 30 seconds. Company B of the 1st Battalion
was the first to drop. On landing the troops spread out
to secure a perimeter around the LZ, and Companies
A and C quickly followed.

By 1330, however, the North Vietnamese had
made further reinforcement extremely hazardous.
At ground level the LZ was ringed by sparse brush
which, with elephant grass and anthills, provided
ideal cover for the enemy who were able to pin down
the cavalrymen. Several Hueys carrying the leading
elements of D Company were hit and, though none
was shot down, Colonel Moore forbade a further
eight from landing. A and B Companies were
ordered to pull back and prepare a tight defensive
perimeter for the night. Of the two, Company B was in
the worse position. One of its platoons had become

2nd-Lieutenant Walter J. Marm was awarded the US Army's Congressional Medal of Honor for his part in the battle at Landing Zone X-Ray on 14 November 1965. Marm was ordered to lead his 2nd Platoon of Company A, 1st Battalion 7th Cavalry against an NVA machine-gun position that was holding up the relief of an isolated cavalry unit. Lieutenant Marm moved his men out of a dry river bed and raced ahead until machine-gun fire coming from behind a large anthill 30m in front stopped them dead. With no regard for his safety, Marm stood up to draw their fire. Having pinpointed the enemy position, he fired an M72 anti-tank round that inflicted some casualties but failed to silence the enemy. Realising that a well-placed grenade might do the trick, Marm ordered a trooper to use an M26 fragmentation bomb. It fell short of the target, but the lieutenant charged across a stretch of open ground and hurled it into the enemy position. Marm finished off the dazed survivors with his M16. Shortly afterwards he was hit in the face by a sniper's bullet and had to be evacuated from the battlefield. However, his brave action saved the lives of men in his own command and greatly contributed to the relief of the encircled platoon.

President Johnson presents a unit citation to the 1st Air Cavalry following the Ia Drang battle.

separated and could not be precisely located.

LZ X-Ray was hot. Sitting in a pilot's seat, the target of all surrounding hostile fire, the men who flew the helicopters were desperate for the troopers to get out of the craft as quickly as possible; and then there was the agonising wait as the wounded were loaded aboard. Crews counted themselves lucky if they got back into the air in under a minute. It was a hell of a long time to wait. A pilot who was present recalled the atmosphere of tension:

'"Orange One, abort your landing. Fire on the LZ is too heavy," a pathfinder called from X-Ray. Orange flight turned and we followed. There was a whole bunch of yelling on the radios. I heard two ships in the LZ call out they were hit badly. What a mess. Finally we heard Yellow One call to take off, and we saw them emerge from the smoke on the left of the LZ, shy two ships. They had waited in the heavy fire while the crews of the two downed ships got on to other Hueys. One crew chief stayed, dead. One pilot was wounded.'.

By mid-afternoon on 14 November Moore knew he was in a major battle and his men were fighting for their lives against the 66th and 33rd NVA regiments. It seemed obvious to Colonel Brown at Plei Me that the enemy were intent on destroying the 1st Battalion, 7th Cavalry. He prepared to send in reinforcements to strengthen the landing zone. Company B of the 2nd Battalion, 7th Cavalry, arrived at X-Ray by 1800 hours, and night landing facilities were set up.

The situation around the perimeter was by this stage less dangerous and it was only the isolated platoon of Company B that was causing concern. Although reports suggested it was holding its own with morale still high, eight men had been killed, 12 had been wounded in action and only seven remained unhurt. The platoon faced several attacks but all were beaten off by smallarms and artillery fire. Dawn revealed dozens of enemy dead around their position. Savage close fighting went on inside the perimeter. The 1st Platoon leader of C Company was found dead with the bodies of five NVA soldiers around his foxhole and one trooper was found with his hands locked around the throat of an adversary. By 1000 hours on 15 November air strikes and aerial rocket artillery units firing 2.75in rockets and miniguns had blasted the North Vietnamese out of their positions.

Moore was confident that the enemy was n longer capable of attacking the landing zone in an strength and at 1330 ordered his tired men to pull ou The troopers were quick to realise they had inflicte a heavy defeat on the enemy. Many bodies littere the battlefield, and heavily bloodstained bandage suggested that far more had been very badly wound ed. By noon a relief force, the 2nd Battalion, 5t Cavalry, reached Moore's position and the relief o the isolated platoon was little more than a formality The troops at LZ X-Ray were ordered to sit tight an await the arrival of the 2nd Battalion, 7th Cavalry, wh had been detailed to act as a relief force. By 093 hours on 16 November its leading elements began t arrive and Colonel Moore's men were airlifted out

The two-day battle around LZ X-Ray was th highpoint of the 1st Cavalry campaign in the Ia Dran Valley. Colonel Moore's men suffered nearly 20 casualties but the NVA lost many more: 634 know dead, 581 supposed dead and six taken prisone Large amounts of their equipment fell into the cava ry's hands. It was clear to both sides that there woul now be no full-scale offensive in South Vietnam Central Highlands. The 3rd Brigade continued t sweep the Chu Pong area until 20 November and th 2nd was withdrawn on the 26th.

The 1st Cavalry Division fought in the Ia Dran Valley for 35 days and during that time changed th nature of the war in Vietnam. No longer would U forces have to footslog through dense undergrowt in search of an elusive foe. Air cavalry units coul respond to any situation in a short time and maintai contact with the enemy for longer than was previous ly possible. Commander-in-chief General Wes moreland was full of praise: 'The ability of th Americans to meet and defeat the best troops th enemy could put into the field of battle was once an for all demonstrated beyond any possible doubt a was the validity of the Army's airmobile concept.'

THE AUTHOR Ian Westwell is a graduate of St. Cather ine's College, Oxford , has contributed articles o post-war conflicts to a number of magazines; he is a specialist on the 19th-century British Army.

ROCK FORCE

The air assault on Corregidor by the US 503rd Parachute Infantry Regiment on 16 February 1945 was one of the most spectacular airborne operations of World War II

503RD PARACHUTE INFANTRY REGIMENT

Activated at Fort Benning, Georgia, on 24 February 1942, the 503rd Parachute Infantry Regiment arrived in Australia that November, becoming the first US airborne regiment to enter the Pacific theatre in World War II. It fought in New Guinea, where it performed the first Allied combat jump in the Pacific at Nadzab airfield on 5 September 1943, as a preliminary to the capture of Lae on the Huon peninsula. Another combat jump was carried out on 3 July 1944 on the small island of Noemfoor in Geelvink Bay, which was being developed as an air base and troopship way-station by the Japanese. During the invasion of the island of Leyte in October 1944, which was the first stage of General Douglas MacArthur's campaign to retake the Philippines, the paratroopers of the 503rd acted as the tactical reserve. On 15 December they participated in the amphibious invasion of Mindoro island, lying to the northwest of Leyte. Then came the daring airborne assault on Corregidor of 16 February 1945 which was to earn the 503rd their title of 'The Rock Regiment'. Combat did not end with World War II. The 173rd Airborne Brigade, known as 'The Herd', included the 503rd's 1st and 2nd Battalions and was the first US ground combat unit to arrive in South Vietnam. All four battalions of the 503rd Infantry Regiment eventually saw combat with The Herd.
Below: The shoulder patch of the 11th Airborne Division, the 503rd's parent formation in World War II.

DEATH MARCH ON BATAAN

By January 1942, the American defence of the Philippines was concentrated on the Bataan peninsula, lying west of Manila on the island of Luzon. There, a force of 15,000 Americans and 65,000 Filipinos withstood for 98 days a determined siege by the Japanese 14th Army, finally surrendering on 10 April. The victorious Japanese found themselves in possession of a vast number of prisoners, 64,000 Filipinos and 12,000 Americans, most of whom were in very poor physical condition, due to long-standing shortages of food and medicine and the ravages of malaria and dysentery.

There followed one of the most notorious episodes of the Pacific War. The Japanese chose to transfer the men to Camp O'Donnell, a former US training area near Tarlac, which was accessible by rail from San Fernando. The 76,000 prisoners, many desperately ill, were forced to march 55 miles through jungle from Mariveles on the peninsula to the San Fernando railhead in terrible tropical heat, after which they were packed into boxcars to complete the journey. During the 'Death March', between 7000 and 10,000 Filipinos and 2330 Americans died, many the victims of abominable cruelties perpetrated by their Japanese guards.

The Japanese capture of the Bataan Peninsula in 1942 (bottom left) yielded thousands of Allied prisoners (below), many of whom were lost during the Bataan Death March (left). Below: Led by cigar-chewing First Sergeant Albert Baldwin, the men of the 503rd Parachute Infantry Regiment line up in their C-47 for the jump over Corregidor on 16 February 1945. Page 933: Paras of the 503rd survey the smoking, bomb-blasted island. The initial bombardment was very effective – well-aimed bombs detonated a large underground ammunition dump, and large areas of the island were in flames when the paras arrived.

AT 0830 HOURS on 16 February 1945, Japanese troops on the tiny, heavily fortified island of Corregidor were astonished to see American paratroopers jumping from C-47 transports directly overhead. One after the other, members of the 3rd Battalion, 503rd Parachute Infantry Regiment (PIR), flung themselves from the low-flying Skytrains. In support were Company C, 161st Airborne Engineer Battalion, and Battery D, 462nd Parachute Field Artillery Battalion (PFAB). Although they were unlikely to appreciate it at the time, the Japanese were witnessing one of the most difficult and courageous airborne operations of World War II.

The island fortress of Corregidor, part of a system of defences commanding the shipping entrance to Manila Bay in the Philippine island of Luzon, had fallen to the Japanese 61st Infantry Division on 6 May 1942. American and Philippine forces had held out since January on Corregidor and the Bataan peninsula to the north, and their heroic defence against a superior force had allowed the Americans valuable time to reorganise after the disaster at Pearl Harbor. Nevertheless, in the years following the forced unconditional surrender of all Allied forces in the Philippines, thousands of men were to die on their way to captivity and in the terrible conditions of the Japanese prison camps.

The Allied servicemen who suffered at the hands of the Japanese were never forgotten by the American people. General Douglas MacArthur, Commanding General, United States Army Forces in the Far East, when ordered out of Luzon by Washington in February 1942, had uttered his famous promise to journalists, 'I shall return!', but it was not until late 1944 that American soldiers were once again to set foot on Philippine soil. Then, as part of the campaign to regain Manila and the seaborne approaches in Manila Bay, Corregidor, known as 'The Rock' to the Americans, became the target for an assault from the air.

Caught wrong-footed by the air assault, the Japanese were nevertheless prepared to fight to the last man to defend Corregidor

What the US airborne force did not know as it leapt into battle over Corregidor was that the US Sixth Army intelligence estimates of enemy strength on the island were grossly inaccurate. Instead of 600 Japanese defenders, the island was garrisoned by between 5000 and 6000 well entrenched Japanese who included, apart from regular troops, tough 'marines' of the Special Naval Landing Force (SNLF) under the command of Captain Akira Itagaki of the Imperial Japanese Navy. Although the Japanese were well dug in and fully expecting an attack, they supposed that it would be an amphibious assault and the occupied positions were therefore facing the sea. Caught wrong-footed by the air assault, the Japanese were nevertheless prepared to fight to the last man to hold Corregidor.

That the Japanese did not expect paratroopers is hardly surprising. Corregidor, an island three and a half miles long and only 600 yards wide at its narrowest point, resembles a tadpole in outline, with a long 'tail' section of low ground lying to the east. The neck of land connecting the 'tail' with the 'head' was known as 'Bottomside', which was separated from the high land to the west by 'Middleside', a central plateau. The high land to the west, the most important area of the island, was called 'Topside'. The only

By the spring of 1943, the US Joint Chiefs of Staff were agreed that victory over Japan could not be achieved without an invasion of the Japanese mainland. They differed, however, on the correct approach to that end, and it was not until 3 October 1944 that they finally conceded to General Douglas MacArthur's view that conquest of the Philippines was vital to their ultimate success and ordered him to proceed. The first objective selected was the island of Leyte, capture of which would split the Japanese defence. Between 23 and 25 October MacArthur's vast armada of invasion transports was attacked by the Japanese Navy, and in the Battle for Leyte Gulf the entire Japanese aircraft carrier force was destroyed. The battle for Leyte itself cost the Americans 3504 killed, while a staggering total of 60,000 Japanese died. Organised resistance ended in February 1945 but, as was the case in most of the Philippine islands, groups of Japanese retreated into the mountains to harass the Americans until their nation's surrender in August. Meanwhile, from Leyte the Americans were moving north and south. In the north, air bases on Mindoro were captured in December, and on 9 January 1945 four divisions landed in northern Luzon. The capture of Corregidor and Manila opened the port to Allied shipping in mid-March.

In the south, troops landed on Palawan on 28 February, and landings followed in rapid succession on the islands of Mindanao, Panay, Cebu, Negros and Bohol, as well as the Sulu archipelago. Organised resistance ceased by June, by which time the Americans had taken Iwo Jima and were pressing home their campaign at Okinawa.

The American reconquest of the Philippines cost them 62,143 casualties. The Japanese lost 450,000 troops, their fleet was destroyed, and their air force decimated. It was the greatest battle of the war in the Pacific.

Corregidor
February 1945

By late 1944, the first US foothold in the Philippines — Leyte — was secure except for isolated Japanese forces in the mountains of northwest Leyte. Preparations for the Luzon campaign began with landings on Mindoro in mid-December to secure airbases.

On 9 January 1945, four divisions of the US Sixth Army went ashore at Lingayen Gulf in northwest Luzon. A second landing by the US XI Corps was followed by a drive southwards through the Bataan Peninsula. By 4 February, the Sixth Army had reached Manila.

Guarding the entrance to Manila Bay, Corregidor remained in Japanese hands — and on 16 February a force of US paras made a daring drop on the island.

Para drop on Corregidor

16 Feb 0830 The US 503rd Para Infantry Regiment drops on the heavily defended island of Corregidor.
0930 Topside is secured.
1030 The 34th Infantry lands on Black Beach.
1240 503rd Para Infantry reinforcements are dropped.

Invading Luzon
January — February 1945

Aparri
LINGAYEN GULF
Cordillera Central
Madre
Tuguegarao
US 6th Army 9 Jan
Ilagan
US I Corps
PHILIPPINES
Sierra
San Fernando
US XIV Corps
Baguio
LUZON
Jap 14th Area Army
Tarlac
21 Jan
Cabanatuan
San Fernando
US XI Corps 29 Jan
5 Feb
BATAAN
Manila
Lamon Bay
Corregidor
BICOL

Retaking Bataan
January — February 1945

29 Jan Layac
Olongapo
Subic Bay
5 Feb
15 Feb BATAAN
Manila Bay
Moron
Abucay
Mauban
Pilar
XI Corps
Orion
Bagac
Caibobo Point
Limay
Mariveles Mts
Quinauan Point
Limao
Mariveles
Longoskawayan Point
21 Feb
Cabcaber
CORREGIDOR

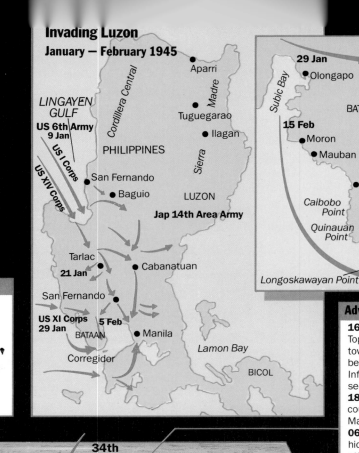

Advance to Kindley Field

16/17 Feb The paras on Topside begin to advance towards the 34th Infantry's beachhead. The 34th Infantry move out and secure Malinta Hill.
18 Feb 0300 A Japanese counter-attack against Malinta Hill is repulsed.
0600 Japanese defenders hiding on Topside launch an attack but are overcome.

CORREGIDOR
Rock Point
Battery Point
Hospital
Bottomside
Malinta Hill
34th Inf Regt 16 Feb 1030 ②
Kindley landing field
Cavalry Point
North Point
Topside
Middleside
Malinta tunnel
Monkey Point
27 Feb
Barracks
San Jose
①
Golf course
16 Feb 0830
③
Hooker Point
503rd Parachute Infantry Regiment
Geary Point

Key
→ US forces
▲ Batteries

Corregidor secure

24 Feb The advance east from Malinta Hill begins.
26 Feb Against tough opposition from the remaining Japanese defenders, US forces reach Kindley Field and Monkey Point.
27 Feb Corregidor is secure.

easonably good parachute drop zone (DZ) was Kindley Field, which was on the low, tail end of the island, but if the paratroopers had landed there the Japanese defenders on Topside would have had ample time to prepare for a slaughter of the paratroopers as they attempted to advance towards the high ground. It was thus essential to make the initial descent directly on Topside. The problem had been how to determine whether such a landing was possible.

The commanding officer of the 503rd PIR, Colonel George M. Jones, was able to work from excellent aerial photographs and a terrain model. After flying on a reconnaissance mission over the island himself he was satisfied that a jump on Topside was tactically imperative. Two possible drop zones were located on Topside. One was a tiny golf course, measuring only 500yds by 75yds, and the other was a former parade-ground of about 500yds by 150yds. These were chosen as the drop zones on the heights and planning proceeded accordingly. For his 'Rock Force' Jones had the three battalions of his own 503rd Parachute Infantry Regiment, with the 3rd Battalion, 34th Regiment (3/34th), 24th Infantry Division, to carry out an amphibious assault in conjunction with the airborne landing. Augmented by parachute artillery and parachute engineer units, Jones' force actually comprised a parachute combat team.

As a preliminary to the assault, Corregidor's defences were pounded by naval and aerial bombardment until virtually everything above ground was turned into rubble. The square mile of Topside was subjected to 3125 tons of high-explosive bombs dropped by the US Fifth and Eighteenth Air Forces, a very substantial bomb load for such a small area. The bombardment lifted only when the first paratrooper made his exit through the door of his C-47 over the island. Not only had it forced most of the defenders into underground caves and tunnels, but it also had the fortuitous effect of cutting most of Itagaki's phone lines, making centralised command of the Japanese garrison utterly impossible.

When Jones and his staff were planning the assault their biggest problem, other than the unsuitability of Corregidor itself for the jump, was the lack of transport aircraft. Only 51 C-47s were available from the 317th Troop Carrier Group for 'Rock Force'. The planners had great difficulty with the combination of so few aircraft and such small drop zones, and eventually decided to divide the airborne assault group into three parachute battalion assault teams, to be dropped in three waves. The first would drop at 0830 hours, the second at 1200, and the third at 0830 on the following day. Normally, the first wave would have jumped earlier, probably at first light, but it was considered essential that aircraft should complete the softening-up bombardment before the paratroopers went in.

Because of the tiny size of the drop zones, it was decided to insert the C-47s into the area flying two abreast. Thus, if things went perfectly, each plane would have about six seconds over the drop zone to drop a stick of six to eight paratroopers. Each transport would have to complete three runs over the DZ to drop its entire complement of men. The timing also had to be very precise, for a miss would land paratroopers in the sea. To allow for this contingency, PT boats were stationed offshore to pick up any drifters. The lack of transport also forced the men of the 503rd to jump with their mortars and heavy machine guns strapped to their bodies, rather than having them dropped separately.

Although he was aware of the difficulties of the jump, Colonel Jones had no doubt that his tough, confident paratroopers could cope with them. He admitted to his staff that he feared casualties might run as high as 50 per cent and that he had decided

Below left: Paratroopers sail down onto a scrub-covered section of one of the landing zones, while Private Lyle O. Slaught crouches to keep out of sniper fire (below). Inevitably, many members of 503rd narrowly missed the tiny landing zones on Topside, sustaining minor injuries as they landed on shattered concrete or became entangled in trees. Below, far left: To the south of the island's gutted garrison buildings, discarded parachutes lie clustered around the two landing zones. Some paratroopers were blown over the steep cliffs and had to haul themselves up under fire.

Right: A paratrooper maintains a watch on Japanese positions on Malinta Hill from a water tower on Topside. Below right: A 75mm pack howitzer of the 462nd Parachute Field Artillery Battalion is fired point-blank at Japanese gunners holed up in a cave. Determined to fight to the death, groups of Japanese refused to surrender even when their situation became hopeless. Bottom left: Paras comb the shattered hillsides in Corregidor, mopping up squads of Japanese suicide snipers. Bottom right: Two members of a bazooka section take on a Japanese pillbox.

that 20 per cent casualties would be acceptable. As it turned out, the biggest hazard was the jagged, broken concrete created by the initial bombardment, which took a toll when some of the early jumpers were dragged onto it by 25-knot winds. A few paratroopers were also shot by Japanese snipers as they descended, but fortunately most of the defenders had been caught completely by surprise.

Circling in his command plane above Corregidor, Colonel Jones observed the descent of the first sticks of men. He ordered the C-47s to release their sticks at a slightly lower altitude to allow for the wind, holding the men back for a few seconds before release. This solved most of the problems with drift and brought the paratroopers down near their objectives. Some of the first to land began clearing out the snipers to make the drop zones safer for their comrades following them in. One of the first groups, happening to land near Itagaki's command post, killed the Japanese commander with a grenade, thus leaving the Japanese without a leader very early in the battle.

It took an hour and 45 minutes for the initial parachute infantry battalion and the supporting artillery and engineer units to be dropped. Colonel Jones

Paratrooper, 503rd PIR, Corregidor 1945

This paratrooper is wearing a two-piece olive green jungle suit with the standard US M1 steel helmet and high-leg parachute boots. He carries a small pack, with two water canteens on his belt, and his weapon is a 0.45in Thompson sub-machine gun with a box magazine.

had jumped himself on his C-47's final pass, establishing his command post soon after landing. As it turned out, about 25 per cent of the paratroopers were injured or killed during the landings and early skirmishes, although this figure is misleading since many of the injuries were only minor scrapes incurred while touching down. As soon as possible, the initial sticks had moved to clear snipers out of the ruins of the Topside barracks, the old hospital and the quartermaster's store, and within an hour of the first paratrooper's landing the whole of Topside was under the control of the 503rd PIR.

Shortly after the landing of the last paratrooper, the amphibious assault began at Black Beach on Bottomside. Although the Japanese had been well dug in to oppose just such a landing, the airborne operation had diverted them from the beaches and the first four waves of infantry came ashore virtually unopposed. The fifth wave, however, met heavy Japanese fire which pinned them down until it was suppressed by the 503rd PIR's 0.5in machine guns on Topside and by 5in naval gunfire. The heavy firepower of 'Rock Force', the battery of 75mm pack howitzers from the parachute field artillery battalion, received a welcome addition when two tanks came ashore with the men of the 24th Infantry Division.

Although the combination of the wind and the broken concrete on the drop zones made parachuting hazardous, Jones was aware that he would need reinforcements if the Japanese were to counterattack. He therefore ordered the 2nd Battalion, 503rd PIR, with Battery B, 462nd PFAB and his 503rd PIR Service Company, to jump at 1240 hours. When these men were safely down, Jones had 3000 men on

Topside ready to repel the Japanese. Meanwhile, the men of the 3/34th, coming in over the beaches, had occupied Malinta Hill to the east of Bottomside and had begun to prepare defences against the expected Japanese counter-attack.

Once the 2nd Battalion of the 503rd had landed, it took over the responsibility of protecting the Topside drop zones, which were still vital for aerial re-supply and reinforcement. Moving also into the area directly to the south, the 2nd Battalion freed the 3rd Battalion to move north against the Japanese on Morrison Hill and to secure the ravines which afforded access to Topside. By sunset the two battalions of the 503rd had the high ground well secured and had pushed to within 250yds of the 3/34th Infantry's beach-head. Most importantly, the 503rd controlled the high ground from which the 75mm howitzers could deliver devastating fire. The 3/34th on the lower ground could also call on its tanks for heavy fire support. Jones was now in a strong position for, even though the Japanese outnumbered the Americans on the island, his forces occupied a commanding site and possessed artillery and tanks. In addition, aircraft and warships were available to provide bombardment.

Throughout the night of 16/17 February, there were sporadic Japanese attacks by small numbers of men sneaking out of their hiding places, and the fighting became hand-to-hand at some points. On the 17th, the 1st Battalion, 503rd PIR and Battery A of the 462nd PFAB were brought in by landing craft, Jones having decided against running the risk of further jumping casualties, and only their heavy equipment was dropped by parachute on Topside.

Landing at Black Beach, these units suffered only light casualties. The afternoon of the 17th also saw the final link-up of the 503rd PIR and the 3/34th.

At midnight on 17/18 February about 50 Japanese of the SNLF launched a 'banzai' attack on the lower part of the island and were wiped out. A larger banzai attack was launched against Malinta Hill at 0300 hours on 18 February and was repulsed with heavy losses on both sides. The largest counter-attack, however, came at 0600 on 18 February when up to 600 Japanese who had been hiding in caves charged the men of the 503rd PIR on Topside. More than 500 Japanese were killed in heavy fighting, much of it hand-to-hand, while the Americans lost 33 killed and 75 wounded. Private Lloyd McCarter won a Congressional Medal of Honor for his part in blunting the Japanese attack. During the banzai charge, McCarter had been in a foxhole near the Japanese starting point. He fired his sub-machine gun into the sea of Japanese charging towards him until the weapon overheated. Grabbing an automatic rifle from a dead paratrooper, he continued to lay down a hail of fire until the rifle overheated, whereupon he claimed another weapon and continued firing until his foxhole was surrounded by dead Japanese. As McCarter stood up to peer past the corpses for more of the enemy, he was hit by a bullet in the chest. Down but still conscious, he refused to let a medic drag him to safety until he passed out. Nevertheless, he did survive to receive his Congressional Medal of Honor.

For the next two days, the paratroopers scoured the island for the Japanese who had survived these engagements, finding that most of the ones they managed to corner committed suicide rather than surrender. What made the Americans' task especially difficult was that they had no firm idea of how many Japanese remained hidden in the warrens beneath the island. There were, for example, at least 2000 Japanese who had been trapped by the preliminary bombardment in the Malinta Tunnel, lying beneath Malinta Hill. Attempting to blast their way out on 20 February, up to 1500 of them were killed by underground explosions. The few hundred who

survived the explosion retreated to the narrow, eastward portion of the island, where they fired upon the advancing Americans.

On 24 February, Jones ordered the 1st Battalion, 503rd PIR, to begin clearing the 'tadpole's tail' of the island, and by the 26th the men had advanced to Monkey Point and Kindley Field, although the opposition had been fierce. At noon on the 26th another subterranean explosion shook the ground at Monkey Point where, attempting to blow up ammunition supplies, 150 Japanese were killed: the explosion also killed 52 Americans and wounded another 144.

By 27 February the island was finally secured. Over 4500 Japanese were known killed, and hundreds, if not thousands, more had been blown to pieces or buried in caves and tunnels which had been sealed by explosions. Of the handful of Japanese prisoners taken, a mere 20, most had been captured only because they had been knocked unconscious. The Americans had lost 225 killed or missing in the operation and 645 had been wounded or injured while landing.

Early in March 1945, General MacArthur returned to Corregidor to congratulate 'Rock Force' on a job well done. The reconquest of the island had been a remarkable tactical success: by following an airborne assault immediately with an amphibious landing, the well entrenched Japanese defenders had been surprised and disorientated. A member of the 503rd Parachute Infantry Regiment was later to redesign the unit's shoulder patch to incorporate the motif of 'The Rock', thus commemorating what many still consider one of the toughest airborne operations ever carried out.

THE AUTHOR Leroy Thompson served in Vietnam as a member of the USAF Combat Security Police.

Bottom: The Americans triumph at Corregidor. On 2 March 1945 the Stars and Stripes were raised once again over the island after nearly three years of Japanese occupation. Present at the ceremony were members of the 503rd Parachute Infantry and General Douglas MacArthur, who had earlier commented, 'I see that the old flagpole still stands. Have your troops hoist the colours to its peak and let no enemy ever haul them down.' Below: Powerful 12in mortar batteries, part of the defensive armament installed by the Americans before the island's capture by the Japanese, are still in place today, a reminder of the thousands who died in the battles for Corregidor.

MOUNTAIN WAR

The Soviet 105th Guards Airborne Division in Afghanistan, face an enemy that tests its mettle

THE YEAR 1979 was drawing to its close and, as the fourth week of December began, Afghan service personnel manning the airbase at Bagram, north of Kabul, paid little attention to several Russian transport aircraft which touched down. After all, large numbers of Soviet advisers were already helping the Afghan Army in its operations against dissident tribesmen, the Mujahidin, who were opposed to the policies of the Kremlin-backed government in Kabul. In recent weeks these instructors had persuaded one Afghan unit after another to hand in its weapons which, it was claimed, were to be replaced with modern equipment from the Soviet Union.

It was soon apparent, however, that there was something noticeably different about the new arrivals. They wore the light-blue berets and striped shirts of airborne troops, and they moved and acted with the consciousness that they were regarded as an elite within their own country. They had all undergone pre-service training, which in itself made them the pick of the twice-yearly conscript crop, and were not only jump-qualified but were also required to make a minimum of 10 jumps each year to retain their personal qualification as parachutists. It did not take long to establish that they belonged to

This page: A Mil Mi-24 Hind gunship swoops in low over a Soviet base near Kabul. Ideally suited to the cut and thrust of a counter-insurgency campaign, the heavily-armed and titanium-armoured Hind has proved to be the guerrillas' most deadly opponent. Working in conjunction with gunships, the crack paras of the 105th Guards Airborne Division are used to spearhead Soviet attempts to clear the valleys occupied by guerrillas, and also operate as a fire force, capable of reacting to any incident at a moment's notice.

the 105th Guards Airborne Division, a unit normally stationed in the Turkestan Military District of the USSR, and that the paratroopers had arrived to give orders rather than advice – at gunpoint if necessary. By the evening of 24 December the 105th's advance party was in complete control of the airbase.

Throughout the next few days a continuous stream of Il-76, An-12 and An-22 transport aircraft landed the main body of the division and its heavy equipment. On the 27th, long convoys of BMD armoured personnel carriers streamed south from Bagram into Kabul and occupied key positions around the capital, to the bewilderment of the inhabitants.

By this stage Soviet motor rifle divisions had already crossed the frontier and were advancing south with air support. Units of the 105th simultaneously pushed north and successfully secured the strategically vital Salang Tunnel through which the 201st and 360th Motor Rifle Divisions would have to pass. By the beginning of 1980 there were approximately 100,000 Russian troops in Afghanistan, controlling all the principal centres of population, and the headquarters of the Soviet Fortieth Army had been established with the 105th at Bagram.

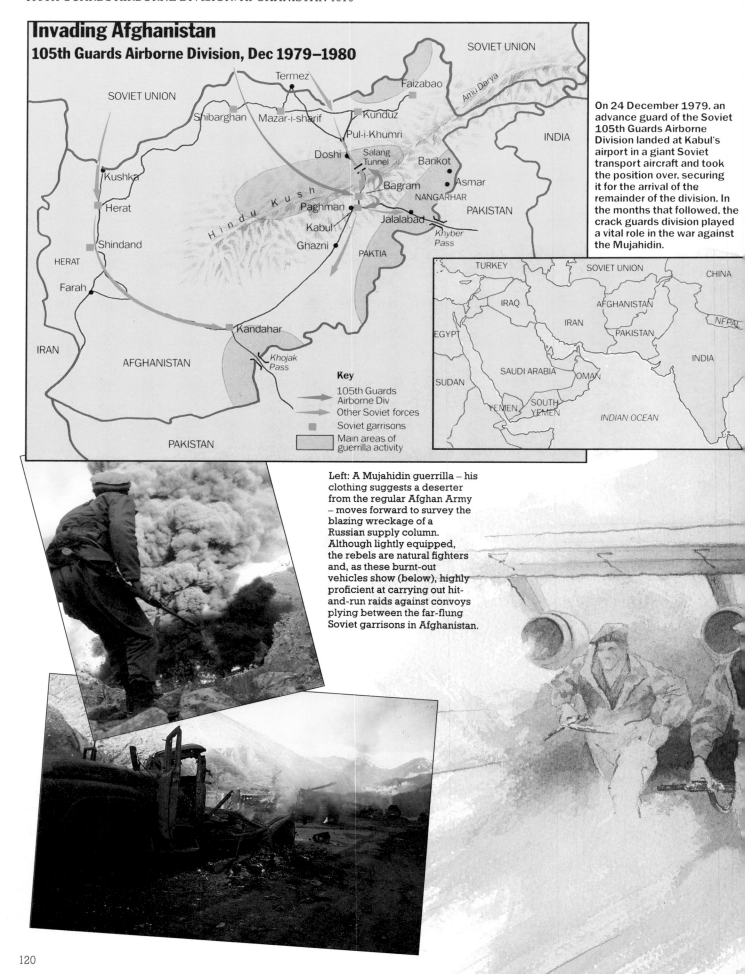

Invading Afghanistan
105th Guards Airborne Division, Dec 1979–1980

SOVIET UNION

Termez

Faizabao

Amu Darya

SOVIET UNION

INDIA

Shibarghan

Mazar-i-sharif

Kunduz

Pul-i-Khumri

Doshi

Salang Tunnel

Barikot

Bagram

Asmar

NANGARHAR

Kushka

Paghman

PAKISTAN

Herat

Kabul

Jalalabad

Hindu Kush

Khyber Pass

Shindand

Ghazni

HERAT

PAKTIA

Farah

IRAN

Kandahar

AFGHANISTAN

Khojak Pass

Key

→ 105th Guards Airborne Div

→ Other Soviet forces

■ Soviet garrisons

▨ Main areas of guerrilla activity

PAKISTAN

TURKEY

SOVIET UNION

CHINA

IRAQ

AFGHANISTAN

IRAN

NEPAL

EGYPT

PAKISTAN

SUDAN

SAUDI ARABIA

OMAN

INDIA

YEMEN

SOUTH YEMEN

INDIAN OCEAN

On 24 December 1979, an advance guard of the Soviet 105th Guards Airborne Division landed at Kabul's airport in a giant Soviet transport aircraft and took the position over, securing it for the arrival of the remainder of the division. In the months that followed, the crack guards division played a vital role in the war against the Mujahidin.

Left: A Mujahidin guerrilla – his clothing suggests a deserter from the regular Afghan Army – moves forward to survey the blazing wreckage of a Russian supply column. Although lightly equipped, the rebels are natural fighters and, as these burnt-out vehicles show (below), highly proficient at carrying out hit-and-run raids against convoys plying between the far-flung Soviet garrisons in Afghanistan.

At this point the Soviet Union's difficulties began. In some areas Afghan units had put up an unexpectedly fierce resistance, while in others they had accepted the situation passively – but, in the days following the invasion more than half the 80,000-strong Afghan Army deserted, many of its men joining the dissident Mujahidin groups, taking their modern weapons with them. The virtual disintegration of the Afghan Army brought the Soviets into direct contact with the dissidents who, now more than ever, were able to claim the status of freedom fighters. Worse still, many of the Soviet motor rifle troops were Moslems recruited in Turkestan and Uzbekistan and, since they sympathised with the religious aims of the Mujahidin and were clearly half-hearted in their attempts to deal with them, they had to be replaced with unaffected troops drawn from the Soviet central reserve.

The Soviets' regular motor rifle divisions had trained incessantly and repetitively to fight a mechanised war over the flat landscape of central Europe and had no experience whatsoever in the techniques of counter-insurgency or mountain warfare, both of which were in constant demand. Nor did they give the impression that they were capable of acquiring these skills quickly. The same was not true of the 105th Airborne which, by its very nature, maintained a far more flexible approach to the fighting in Afghanistan. It was soon apparent that the division

was the lynch-pin of Russian military efforts in Afghanistan. Much of its heavy equipment had little relevance to the prevailing circumstances and was dispensed with, but its rifle element was considerably reinforced with drafts from the 103rd and 104th Guards Airborne Divisions, together with the appropriate number of BMDs (armoured personnel carriers), thereby giving the division a much higher proportion of infantry to supporting arms than usual.

Soviet casualties in the year following the invasion may well have run into the thousands. Since then, there has been a slow but steady improvement in Russian tactical practice and it is probably fair to say that much of this stems from within the 105th Airborne. The way ahead, however, was a hard one. The Mujahidin quickly proved to be natural guerrilla fighters raised in a long tradition of blood feud, mountain ambush and raiding. Soviet officers on the spot who saw the need for a radical new approach to the problem faced opposition from superiors who tended to view any departure from established principles with great suspicion.

In essence, the situation reflected the traditional high command view that personal initiative is not required, and should even be discouraged, in the Soviet Army's tank and motor rifle divisions lest it interfere with the details of the master plan. However, change was eventually forced upon the Fortieth Army by its very public failure to bring the situation under control, by the rising toll of casualties and equipment losses, and by the realisation that the 105th Airborne was producing better results at lower cost. In turn, it was apparent that the 105th was itself willing to learn by studying the American experience in Vietnam.

Once the Soviets had settled in, it soon became clear that their writ extended only as far as the areas controlled by their garrisons. Beyond Soviet-domin-

AIRBORNE

The Soviet airborne division normally consists of three airborne regiments, an artillery regiment, anti-aircraft, engineer, signals, transport, maintenance and medical battalions, plus reconnaissance, NBC and parachute-rigging companies. Each airborne regiment contains three battalions plus an anti-tank battery, an anti-aircraft battery and a mortar battery, an engineer company, a signals company, a transport company, a maintenance company and a medical company, an NBC platoon and a pathfinder platoon. At the present time only one airborne regiment is fully equipped with BMDs, plus one battalion in each of the other airborne regiments. Each airborne battalion consists of three rifle companies, mortar, signals and engineering platoons and a medical section; rifle companies contain three platoons, each of three sections, and an anti-tank platoon. The divisional artillery regiment consists of a howitzer battalion with 18 122mm howitzers, a multi-barrel rocket-launcher battalion with 18 140mm MBRLs, an assault gun battalion with 18 ASU-85s, an ATGW battalion and a fire-control battery. The total strength of the division amounts to approximately 800 officers and 8000 men. Above: The Soviet airborne insignia.

AKM

stock

auxiliary sear

selector lever

receiver cover catch

recoil spring

bolt carrier

cable
(part of rate reducer)

grip

trigger

hammer

magazine
catch

safety sear

INTERVENTION

On 27 April 1978 the Afghan prime minister, Mohammed Daoud Khan was toppled from power by an army-led coup backed by two left-wing parties, the Parcham and Khalq. Nur Mohammad Taraki of the Khalq faction became president. Although Taraki included members of Parcham in his government, disagreements over policy led to the disintegration of the coalition.

In pursuit of Marxist goals, the government, supported by Soviet aid, tried, but failed, to convince the country's Moslem majority as to the benefits of modernisation.

By April 1979 open rebellion had broken out. In an attempt to stifle dissent a hardline member of the regime, Hafizullah Amin, was made prime minister.

The Soviet Union, fearful of the growing strength of Islamic fundamentalism, began providing advisers and equipment for the Afghan armed forces. Moscow also tried to get Taraki to remove the extremist Amin, but the latter got wind of the move and was involved in a palace coup that led to Taraki's death.

With the unpopular Amin in control, the options open to Moscow were limited, and in mid-December Red Army units began mobilising along Afghanistan's northern border. When Amin refused to make way for the moderate leader of Parcham, Babrak Kamal, and also refused to allow direct intervention, the Soviet Union began secretly airlifting troops into Bagram on 24 December.

Left: A rebel waits to unleash a lethal fusillade on a convoy as it moves into range. The Soviet's use of the BMP, an armoured personnel carrier fitted with a handy 73mm gun (below right), and the Hind helicopter gunship has forced the Mujahidin to take much greater care when laying ambushes.

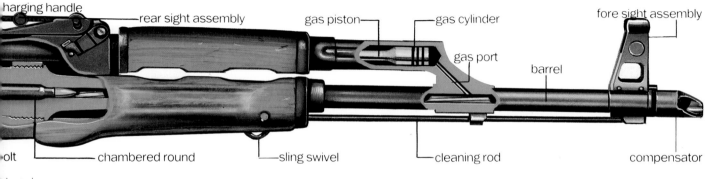

harging handle — rear sight assembly — gas piston — gas cylinder — fore sight assembly

gas port

barrel

olt — chambered round — sling swivel — cleaning rod — compensator

ring pin

nagazine

ollower

Calibre 7.62mm
Length 102cm
Weight (loaded) 3.76kg
Magazine 30-round box
System of operation gas
Rate of fire (cyclic) 600rpm
Muzzle velocity 715mps
Maximum effective range (semi-auto) 400m

ated areas, guerrillas operated at will. Convoys would suddenly find themselves brought to a standstill as a mine erupted beneath the leading vehicle or the rocks of a man-made avalanche thundered down onto the road, blocking the way ahead. Very quickly, the guerrillas would then knock out a vehicle near the convoy's tail, so trapping everything in between. On the heights to one side of the road there could usually be seen the tremendous muzzle-flash of a 12.7mm DShKM Russian-built heavy machine gun, a favourite weapon of the Mujahidin, its heavy slugs slamming into the trucks, perhaps causing a fuel tanker to disintegrate in a gigantic fireball.

Incoming smallarms fire might include everything from modern AK-47s and AKMs to elderly British Lee-Enfields that had last seen service on the Northwest Frontier, and be punctuated by the thump of mortars. Afghan conscripts would promptly desert or surrender when the Mujahidin came down to inspect the litter of wreckage and bodies, acquire weapons and replenish their ammunition.

Attempts to escort convoys with tanks proved worse than useless, and served only to emphasise how impotent the Soviet Army was in this style of warfare. The difficulty was that the main armament of most Russian tanks could not be elevated beyond +15 degrees, and the guerrillas soon learned to site

their own positions beyond the range of the tanks. Often the tanks were the only survivors of ambushes, having fought their way out covered with wounded, but sometimes they, too, fell victim to RPG-7 rocket launchers.

In this respect the 105th Airborne suffered less than the motor rifle divisions since it did not employ tanks, and its comparatively few (18) ASU-85 airborne assault guns possessed even less elevation and were clearly unsuited to mountain warfare. On the other hand, the 73mm smooth-bore gun of the division's BMDs possessed an elevation of +33 degrees and a range of 2200m which enabled it to search out the ambushers' positions with high explosive shells, and provide fire support for its six-strong paratroop section. The infantry section was usually deployed to make a dismounted reaction to the situation. This, as becomes a force noted for above-average fitness and aggression, was liable to be far more positive than that of the average motor rifle formation and would probably beat off the attackers, forcing them to abandon their ambush and disappear into the hills. It must soon have become apparent to the Mujahidin that there were no easy pickings to be had from the 105th Airborne.

Again, this sort of action convinced Fortieth Army headquarters that motor rifle divisions would obtain better results using their BMPs – which are similarly armed to the BMD – instead of tanks on convoy escort duties, and most of the latter were soon withdrawn to the Soviet Union. Some sources suggest that a proportion of the 105th's BMDs have been re-equipped with the 30mm AGS-17 automatic grenade launcher in place of the 73mm gun, confirming that consideration has also been given to the problems of close-quarter ambush.

Further anti-ambush techniques based on Vietnam and of necessity involving an improved communications network included artillery support from bases within range of the trapped column, the despatch of rapid-reaction groups to effect relief, and conventional air strikes directed onto the guerrillas' positions. The last mentioned was not without its difficulties, since flying high-performance jet aircraft in the mountains requires intense concentration, and the time available for precise target identification is very limited. This meant that much of the high-explosive payload was wasted, so recourse was made to napalm and, reportedly, chemical weapons which were intended to blanket the whole area occupied by the ambushers. Even so, inexperienced MiG and Sukhoi pilots would still fly their aircraft straight into the ground, to the delight of the dissidents.

It is galling for any elite to have to remain on the

Below: Heads held high, stern-faced members of an airborne division parade their colours. The blue berets and striped shirts are the hard-earned symbols of their elite status. After several years of frontline service in the wastes of Afghanistan, the battle-hardened warriors of the 105th Guards Airborne are probably the finest conventional troops in the Soviet armed forces.

defensive and the senior officers of the 105th Airborne, used to thinking in terms of a three-dimensional battle, were quick to accept that helicopter transports and gunships were the key to certain tactical situations and would enable them to get at the elusive Mujahidin. First, it was necessary to prevent the guerrillas getting at the road-bound convoys. This was achieved by instituting an airborne version of the tactics employed by British columns on the Northwest Frontier. When a Soviet force was ready to move along the floor of a valley, the heights on either side were occupied in advance by troops helilifted onto the summits. Once the convoy had passed, these picquets were lifted out and then re-inserted on hills further along the valley. If the Mujahidin tried to interfere, gunships were on hand to bomb, strafe and rocket them. Secondly, if a guerrilla group was located in the hills, gunships attempted to pin them down and soften them up. Simultaneously, some paratroop units were lifted into blocking positions to cut off their retreat while others were air-landed on carefully selected drop-ping zones from where they could converge on th dissidents. Thirdly, during large-scale cordon-and search operations in wild country, the use of helicopters as flying command posts enabled senior officer to co-ordinate the movements of their troops.

These measures certainly caused casualtie among the Mujahidin, although the guerrillas soo extended the scope of their operations and are nov in possession of sophisticated weapon systems. O the other hand, Russian casualties have almost ce: tainly been reduced by the measures pioneered b the 105th Airborne Division, which remains th Fortieth Army's principal offensive weapon.

THE AUTHOR Bryan Perrett served with the Roya Armoured Corps between 1952 and 1971. He ha written over 20 books on mechanised warfare and i a regular contributor to military publications.

STRIKE FROM THE SKY

The men of the German 7th Airborne Division landed on Crete in May 1941 – and swiftly found that they were fighting for their lives against strong Allied defences

AT APPROXIMATELY 0715 hours on 20 May 1941, the leading wave of the German XI Air Corps began to land by glider and parachute around the Cretan towns of Maleme and Canea. The Germans had been expecting light resistance, and their commander, General Kurt Student, had planned a quick seizure of the airfields after overwhelming the weak British, Dominion and Greek forces defending the northern coast. Instead, the Germans found themselves in the midst of a bloody, attritional battle.

At Maleme, two companies of Major Koch's 1st Parachute Battalion of the Assault Regiment had landed by glider near the beach at the mouth of the Tavronitis river and scattered inland towards the tactically crucial objective of Hill 107. The area was defended by New Zealand troops who had fired on the gliders as they came in. The rough ground forced many gliders to crash land and Koch, who had been wounded in the confusion and heavy fire of the New Zealanders, was forced to concentrate his paratroopers at the western end of Maleme airfield. His two companies had suffered over 100 casualties, half of their original strength. The 3rd Parachute Battalion of the Assault Regiment was dropped amongst the defending New Zealand troops to the east of Maleme. Massacre quickly followed as the New Zealanders directed all their firepower, and after 45 minutes, 400 of the original 600 paratroopers had become casualties. The battalion commander, Major Scherber, was among those killed. The 2nd and 4th Parachute Battalions of the Assault Regiment dropped without much opposition to the south and west of Maleme airfield. During their attempt to reinforce the remnants of the 1st Battalion, Major-General Meindl, the Assault Regiment commander who had landed with the last group, was severely wounded. By mid-morning, it appeared that the German paratroop attack on Maleme had ended in failure.

Further to the west, at Canea, the Germans were meeting similar resistance. Landing at the same time as Koch's paratroopers, the remaining two companies of the 1st Battalion attempted to eliminate an anti-aircraft battery and a heavy artillery battery. The glider landings were scattered, and the company attacking the anti-aircraft battery suffered heavy

HITLER STRIKES SOUTH

In the spring of 1941, just as the might of Germany was massing for the imminent invasion of Russia, Hitler had to deal with a new threat to his southern front.

There was a growing likelihood that Yugoslavia might be encouraged to join the Allies against Germany. Hitler determined to crush Yugoslavia to secure the southern front. After heavy fighting, Yugoslavia and Greece capitulated late in April and surviving British and Greek troops were withdrawn to Crete.

With Greece fallen, the island of Crete assumed a great strategic significance. It provided the only airfields available to Britain in the eastern Mediterranean, and her only hope of providing effective naval air cover in the area. In addition, only from Crete could Britain mount a bombing offensive on the Romanian oil fields that were vital to the German war effort. Again, without a British presence on Crete there was a strong possibility that Turkey would be tempted to side with Hitler in the war. It was evident that so valuable a base would soon be attacked.

Top: The cuffband that was awarded to the German units that participated in the invasion of Crete.

125

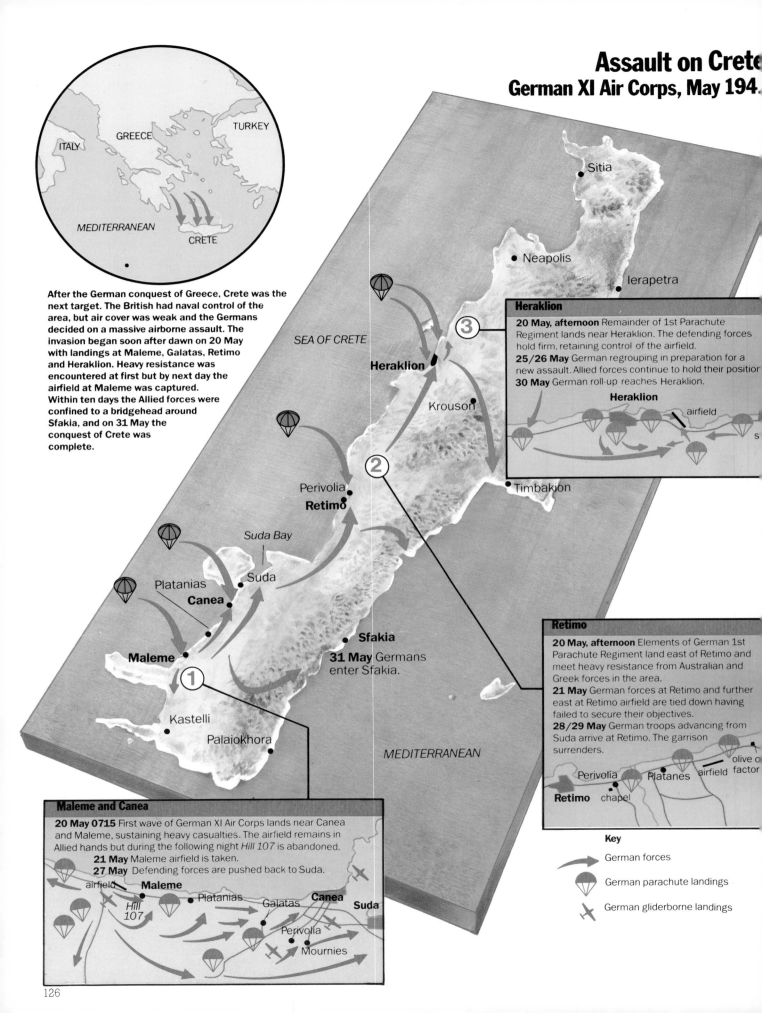

Assault on Crete
German XI Air Corps, May 194.

After the German conquest of Greece, Crete was the next target. The British had naval control of the area, but air cover was weak and the Germans decided on a massive airborne assault. The invasion began soon after dawn on 20 May with landings at Maleme, Galatas, Retimo and Heraklion. Heavy resistance was encountered at first but by next day the airfield at Maleme was captured. Within ten days the Allied forces were confined to a bridgehead around Sfakia, and on 31 May the conquest of Crete was complete.

31 May Germans enter Sfakia.

Heraklion

20 May, afternoon Remainder of 1st Parachute Regiment lands near Heraklion. The defending forces hold firm, retaining control of the airfield.

25/26 May German regrouping in preparation for a new assault. Allied forces continue to hold their position

30 May German roll-up reaches Heraklion.

Heraklion

airfield

Retimo

20 May, afternoon Elements of German 1st Parachute Regiment land east of Retimo and meet heavy resistance from Australian and Greek forces in the area.

21 May German forces at Retimo and further east at Retimo airfield are tied down having failed to secure their objectives.

28/29 May German troops advancing from Suda arrive at Retimo. The garrison surrenders.

Perivolia   Platanes   airfield   olive o factor

Retimo   chapel

Maleme and Canea

20 May 0715 First wave of German XI Air Corps lands near Canea and Maleme, sustaining heavy casualties. The airfield remains in Allied hands but during the following night Hill 107 is abandoned.

21 May Maleme airfield is taken.

27 May Defending forces are pushed back to Suda.

airfield   **Maleme**   Platanias   Galatas   **Canea**   **Suda**

Hill 107   Perivolia   Mournies

Key

German forces

German parachute landings

German gliderborne landings

SEA OF CRETE

Heraklion

Krouson

Timbakion

Sitia

Neapolis

Ierapetra

Perivolia
Retimo

Suda Bay
Suda
Platanias
Canea
Maleme
Kastelli
Palaiokhora

Sfakia

MEDITERRANEAN

GREECE
TURKEY
ITALY
MEDITERRANEAN
CRETE

asualties from the fire of the Welch Regiment and he Northumberland Hussars. In the event, the nti-aircraft battery was not found. But the company which attacked the artillery battery was more successful, overrunning the guns and capturing some 80 men. Captain von der Heydte's 1st Parachute attalion dropped in a tight formation to the south of he local prison and then advanced eastwards towards the village of Perivolia, where it encountered eavy opposition. Further to the north, the 2nd arachute Battalion dropped southwest of the village of Galatas, and, despite losing 150 men in asualties, managed to threaten the New Zealand osition on the Galatas heights. The 3rd Parachute attalion dropped in scattered groups to the east of Galatas and was immediately attacked by the New ealanders. Unable to concentrate in a battalion roup, the 3rd Battalion could not deploy as a oherent military unit. An Engineer Battalion dropped to the west of the prison encountered stiff esistance from Greek troops.

So, by mid-morning on 20 May, the first lift of General Student's XI Air Corps had landed in some onfusion and had met unexpectedly fierce resistnce. Casualties had been heavy, and although the Germans at Maleme and Canea were only eight iles apart, they were unable to make contact. A umber of senior officers had been killed, including ieutenant-General Süssman, the commander of the th Air Division, who had died with most of his eadquarters staff when their glider had crashed oon after take-off from Greece. Command at Canea ad been assumed by Colonel Heidrich. The German paratroopers at Maleme and Canea faced deeat and capture, and there was a distinct possibility hat the remainder of XI Air Corps, soon to arrive in a

second lift, would drop straight into the same cauldron of enemy firepower.

The original plans for an airborne attack on Crete had been prepared by Student in early April 1941. Student had convinced an unenthusiastic Hitler on 21 April that it would be possible to capture Crete by a lightning airborne assault. An invasion by sea was impossible because of British naval superiority, and any amphibious attack would be subordinate to an airborne attack. Student then began a frantic preparation for Operation Merkur (Mercury) which was to be launched on 15 May, but in the event was postponed until 20 May.

The airborne forces, the necessary transport aircraft, and the logistical support were brought together in a remarkably short period of time. Student's XI Air Corps consisted of the 7th Air Division, with nine battalions; the Parachute Assault Regiment of four battalions and Lieutenant-General Ringel's 5th Mountain Division. The latter had been substituted for the experienced 22nd Air Landing Division that had been deployed in Romania to protect the Ploesti oil field. Many of the paratroopers had no combat experience, and the mountain troops had not been trained for airborne operations. Nevertheless, Student had chosen mountain troops because they were used to fighting with light equipment and

'Tante Ju' (Auntie Ju) was the nickname of the Junkers 52 (Ju 52), the most successful utility aircraft flown by the Luftwaffe during World War II. Although the Ju 52 was considered obsolete by the late 1930s – its ungainly corrugated aluminium skin, fixed undercarriage and trio of air-cooled radial engines harking back to another era – it saw service in every major operation of the European and Mediterranean theatres. The aircraft first entered service in 1932 as a civilian airliner, but was then used as both a bomber and transport by the German Condor Legion and the Nationalist forces during the Spanish Civil War (1936-39). The Ju 52 only really came into its own, however, after the creation of the German parachute corps in the mid-1930s. With a maximum range of 1280km and a load capacity of either 2230kg or 13 fully-equipped paratroopers, it was well suited to airborne operations. Its debut in this role took place in the Norwegian campaign of April 1940, and the Ju 52 faced its toughest task a year later, when over 500 were used to fly elements of Fliegerkorps XI to the island of Crete.

Although the island was captured, the bitter struggle highlighted several weaknesses in the aircraft. Its speed of 265km/h was too slow, and it was too poorly armed to counter enemy aircraft. Further, its load-carrying capabilities were found inadequate for large-scale operations.

Despite these drawbacks, the Ju 52 soldiered on in a variety of roles until the end of the war. The aircraft remained in service because it was adaptable, cheap to produce and easy to fly, and unlike many more sophisticated aircraft it could fly in all but the very worst weather conditions.

Background: Hit by British anti-aircraft fire, a Ju 52 plunges to destruction. The German XI Air Corps lost 170 Ju 52s in the course of the invasion, a heavy toll for a single operation. Inset: A DFS-230 glider lies wrecked against the road embankment that brought its landing to an abrupt halt. Even so, its contents were probably used in the battle for Crete.

weapons over rugged terrain. The paratroopers' heavy weapons were to be dropped in separate containers, and until these had been opened the only weapons available were light MP-38 sub-machine guns and Luger pistols, limited in range and firepower. There was no time to provide tropical uniforms, so the paratroopers had to fight in heavy uniforms in very hot weather. But Student could rely on a hard core of experienced officers such as Koch, Meindl, Bräuer and Schulz, all of whom had served in the airborne operations in Holland and Belgium in May 1940.

To lift the airborne forces, Student had at his

AIR ASSAULT

Although British intelligence had led the defenders on Crete to expect invasion from the air, few were prepared for the harrowing experience of a full-scale airborne assault. Firstly, units manning the slit trenches around the target airfields were enveloped in clouds of thick, choking dust as the preliminary Junkers 88 bomber formations unloaded their explosives over them, while Stuka dive bombers and Messerschmitt fighter planes raced overhead.

As suddenly as they had come, the bombers disappeared, leaving the defenders reeling and deafened by the barrage. Then, as they struggled to collect themselves, they became aware of the gliders. 'Silent as ghosts...huge, black and menacing, they were sliding down from the mountains, banking in long, slow turns with a faint hiss of wings.' But then the ground fire opened up in force, and gliders were swooping in to remain still, as 'every man sat dead in his place'. Crashing into an impossible terrain of rocks and trees, frequently running in 'under the very muzzles of enemy weapons', the gliders lay shattered, surrounded by bodies.

For many of the garrison, some of whom had never seen a parachute, the spectacle of the paratroopers was equally extraordinary. To Lieutenant Thomas of the New Zealand 23rd Battalion they were:

'difficult to comprehend as anything at all dangerous. Seen against the deep blue of the early morning Cretan sky... they looked like little jerking dolls whose billowing frocks of green, yellow, red and white had somehow blown up and become entangled in the wires that controlled them.'

Fully exposed in broad daylight, the paratroopers fared no better than the gliders over the awkward terrain. Some died as they smashed down through trees, and many were picked off as they drifted in. Defenders saw Germans plummeting to earth as their parachutes caught fire or failed to open, and others who met death together as their parachutes became entangled. That the airborne invaders could recover from such a disastrous and costly start to fulfil their mission was a remarkable achievement.

Safely landed in Crete, the surviving paratroopers organised quickly, often under heavy fire. Left: Filing out under cover. Below: With a Ju 52 in the background, Paras check their armament. Centre left: Paradropped containers are broken open in a rocky defile. Centre right: Burdened by supplies collected from cargo gliders and containers, paratroopers fan out from the landing zone. Bottom: Out of danger, paratroopers improvise a hasty meal. Far left: One German fully prepared to fight for victory in Crete.

disposal about 500 Junkers 52s and 80 DFS-230 gliders. In support, there was a considerable number of fighters and bombers. German intelligence reported that there were only some 5000 British and Greek troops on Crete, and that these were spread out to defend the airfields along the northern coast. There was an airfield at Maleme in the west, another at Retimo to the east of Canea, and one at Heraklion further east.

Student's final operational plan for Operation Mercury was shaped as much by logistical constraints as by objectives or his assessment of the British defensive capability. Two thirds of his force were the 14,000 troops of the 5th Mountain Division, and they could be air landed only after an airfield had been captured or one had been improvised. The initial assault therefore had to be undertaken by the 8100 paratroopers of the 7th Air Division and the Parachute Assault Regiment. There were insufficient aircraft to take all these paratroopers in one lift, so Student settled for two lifts, which meant that Lift Two could in theory be dropped eight hours after Lift One. The latter was to consist of a Western Group made up of Meindl's Parachute Assault Regiment, except for two companies whose objective was Maleme airfield. The Centre Group, commanded by Süssman, consisted of the 3rd Parachute Regiment, divisional anti-aircraft and engineer battalions, and the two companies from Meindl's Parachute Assault Regiment. Its objective was to capture the area around Canea and Suda Bay. Lift Two, eight hours later, would consist of a remaining element of the Centre Group, two battalions of the 2nd Parachute Regiment which would land at Retimo, and the Eastern Group. This latter comprised the 1st Parachute Regiment and one additional battalion, and its task was the taking of Heraklion airfield, to enable the 5th Mountain Division to be air landed.

The Black Watch had a pheasant shoot as the paratroopers descended, then picked off the survivors on the ground

As German intelligence had concluded that there were relatively few British troops in Crete, it was assumed that resistance would be limited and the initial glider and parachute landings would quickly secure the main objectives. Unfortunately for Student and the men of XI Air Corps, this intelligence was a serious underestimation of the garrison on Crete. On 20 May there were some 27,500 British and Dominion troops and 14,000 Greek troops, the majority of whom had been evacuated from the Greek mainland. Although these troops had few heavy weapons, little armour and inadequate signals equipment, they were a determined force under the command of Major-General Bernard Freyberg, VC. These were the troops amongst whom the German paratroopers landed.

For several hours on 20 May, Student in his Athens headquarters had no clear idea of the critical situation on Crete. Lift Two began late because of the confusion produced by the clouds of dust on the dirt runways in Greece, and this gave the garrison on Crete a further opportunity to strengthen its defences. The air drop at Heraklion was a disaster, as the Ju 52s arrived piecemeal and circled over the drop zones in confusion. Soldiers of the Black Watch had a pheasant shoot as the paratroopers descended, then picked off the survivors on the ground. The 2nd Battalion of the 1st Parachute

Regiment suffered over 400 casualties when it landed to the west of the airfield. The surviving paratroopers of the battalion then had to contend with tanks and bren-gun carriers which they were unable to destroy without heavy weapons. The Black Watch soon realised the importance of the dropped containers, and many paratroopers were shot attempting to secure their heavy weapons.

The 3rd Parachute Battalion of the 1st Regiment dropped to the west of Heraklion and met less opposition, but soon found itself fighting a fierce battle with British and Greek troops in the centre of the town. The 2nd Parachute Battalion of the 2nd Regiment landed further west without opposition, blocking the coastal road. Colonel Bräuer, commander of the 1st Parachute Regiment and responsible for securing Heraklion airfield, landed with the 1st Battalion to the east of the airfield, close to its wireless station. But he was unable to move quickly to the assistance of his 2nd Battalion in securing the airfield as elements of the 1st Battalion were delayed in their drop and did not eventually reach the airfield until midnight. Bräuer, picking up scraps of information, realised that his scattered and badly mauled battalions were in no position to secure the airfield.

At Retimo, after many delays, the 2nd Parachute Regiment under Colonel Sturm had to jump over a strong defensive position held by Australian and Greek troops, and by Cretan police in Retimo itself. The Australians and Greeks were dug in on the hills along the coast road, overlooking the airfield. The 3rd Battalion dropped east of Retimo over a wide area but missed the main Australian positions. It immediately formed up and attempted to occupy Retimo. Further east, the Regimental Headquarters of the 2nd Parachute Regiment landed at the foot of the main Australian position and came under heavy fire, and over 80 paratroopers were taken prisoner. The 1st Battalion jumped and landed in a dispersed formation to the east of this debacle and was also brought under fire by the Australians. By late afternoon, the 3rd Battalion was slowly clearing the Cretan police from Retimo, but to the east scattered

Above: Cretan villagers are rounded up by paratroopers. When the German offensive began, a significant number of Cretan partisans fought alongside the garrison to defend their homes, often seizing weapons from German containers.

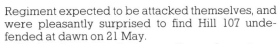

nits from the 1st Battalion were desperately attempting to drive the Australians off the hills dominating the airfield.

In the course of the afternoon and early evening, tudent in Athens began to piece together reports rom the Luftwaffe and signals from Crete which ndicated that his operational plan had gone seriously wrong. In the late evening he concluded that the ituation at Heraklion was bad, and feared the worst t Retimo because there was no news. He knew that the Assault Regiment held part of the Maleme irfield, and so hesitantly decided to reinforce this imited success by switching the main effort from the ast to the west. Maleme airfield had to be secured, nd then it could receive the 5th Mountain Division nd the British defences on Crete would be 'rolled p' from the west.

At this stage, the decisions taken by the British and Dominion field commanders on Crete influenced the

Paratrooper, Battle for Crete, May 1944

Due to a logistical failure the paratroopers landing in Crete were wearing a uniform designed for the rigours of the campaign in Norway of 1940 rather than for the intense dry heat of the island. This man wears the paratrooper's olive green, loose-fitting gabardine jump-smock, over heavy serge battledress. The boots are a special rubber-soled variety with high side-lacing, issued only to paratroopers. The helmet has a much smaller rim than the standard pattern and is held on by a chinstrap. Under its cloth cover the steel helmet bears the Luftwaffe eagle on the left side. Visible at the paratrooper's back is his green bread-bag and water-bottle with cup. His weapon is the Kar 98K rifle.

course of the battle. Freyberg, lacking proper communications, could not really control the battle from his headquarters, so initiative rested with the local commanders. During the night of 20/21 May and early the following morning, the defenders had the opportunity to counter-attack the paratroopers, and f this had been undertaken vigorously the paratroopers would have been destroyed and Student's revised plan made irrelevant. But although the Australians at Retimo did launch a strong counterattack, effectively preventing the paratroopers from capturing the airfield, elsewhere the defenders were lethargic, and at Maleme they withdrew precipitously. The commander of the New Zealand battalion holding the vital Hill 107 covering Maleme airfield withdrew his men in the night, believing that his exhausted soldiers would be overwhelmed by the Germans in the morning. In fact, the much depleted and exhausted paratroopers of the Assault

Centre left: Colonel Brauer, commander of the 1st Parachute Regiment, issues directions to one of his paratroopers on the battlefield. Bottom left: General Student, the planner of the airborne invasion of Crete and commander of XI Parachute Corps, confers with staff officers. Student directed the early stages of the operation from the Greek mainland, where his chief difficulty was in gaining accurate reports of progress on the island.

Regiment expected to be attacked themselves, and were pleasantly surprised to find Hill 107 undefended at dawn on 21 May.

Student began to fly in supplies and paratroop reinforcements to Maleme west of the Tavronitis river. Although the defenders continued to put up a stiff fight around Maleme, the paratroopers were able to push eastwards towards Canea, and by early evening the first battalion of the 5th Mountain Division had landed at Maleme. The airfield was covered with burning and damaged Ju 52s and it took considerable organisation to sort out supplies and reinforcements under heavy fire. Student replaced the wounded Meindl with the tough, impulsive and ambitious Colonel Ramcke.

Whilst the paratroopers at Retimo and Heraklion continued to fight, tying down the defenders and awaiting relief from Maleme, throughout 22 May battalion after battalion of mountain troops were air landed at Maleme airfield and immediately deployed to the east. Ringel, the commander of the 5th Mountain Division, was made operational commander on Crete, and with Maleme secured it was only a matter of time before the British positions to the east were 'rolled up'. The British, Dominion and Greek troops fought a series of hard battles to hold Galatas, Canea and the Suda Bay area, but by 24 May Freyberg had given up any hope of holding Crete, and on 27 May the decision was made to evacuate the island. The German paratroopers and mountain troops slowly pushed eastwards to relieve the survivors of Lift Two at Retimo and Heraklion, and then began the pursuit southwards across the wild Cretan mountains.

The Germans suffered nearly 4000 men killed and about 2400 wounded, as well as having 170 Ju 52s and 40 combat aircraft destroyed in the attack on Crete. The British and Dominion troops had 4000 killed, 2500 wounded and 11,800 taken prisoner. The majority of the Greek troops and Cretan police were captured. For the German paratroopers, the battle for Crete was a hard, bloody affair. Casualties were particularly heavy amongst the paratroopers of Lift One who were unprepared to find such heavy resistance. Many senior officers were killed, wounded or captured, and with the wide dispersal of units, command devolved upon junior officers and NCOs. The paratroopers had to fight in blazing weather wearing heavy uniforms, and they were often without heavy weapons as these were lost in the special containers. Student was flexible enough to change the focus point of his operations, and lucky enough to succeed when the enemy provided an opportunity for him to reinforce Maleme. But without the overwhelming air superiority of the Luftwaffe, the German operations on Crete would have been impossible.

Despite the victory on Crete, Hitler was disturbed by the heavy paratroop casualties, and decided that never again would they be used for such a large airborne operation. Although German paratroopers were air dropped for small-scale operations, the future role of German paratroopers was that of an elite ground force.

THE AUTHOR Keith Simpson is senior lecturer in War Studies and International Affairs at Sandhurst. A member of the Royal United Services Institute for Strategic Studies, he has a specialist interest in modern warfare.

Since the 1948 War of Independence, the paras of the Israeli Defence Forces have acquired a formidable arsenal of modern weapons

SINCE THE creation of an independent Jewish homeland in the late 1940s, Israel's military planners have had to face the harsh fact that, in any conflict, they might have to fight numerically superior enemy forces, attacking from several directions simultaneously. The reality of the situation was rammed home during the War of Independence (1948-49), when the Israelis' armed forces were attacked from all sides. Only by greater mobility and application of firepower, allied to a more skilful, unified command structure, were the Israelis able to defeat their Arab adversaries.

These early lessons were not forgotten: during the 1956 Sinai campaign and, above all, in the Six-Day War of 1967, the Israeli Defence Forces (IDF) used speed and firepower to inflict catastrophic defeats on the frontline Arab states. Later, the retaliatory actions of the War of Attrition (1969-70) and the rearmament drive following the disastrous initial losses of the Yom Kippur War of 1973 showed that the IDF was more than able to adapt existing weapons and introduce new equipment to keep pace with the demands of modern warfare.

Trained as a rapid deployment force, able to engage in conventional or unconventional warfare under a variety of battlefield conditions, the Israeli paras have always needed weapons that are light, easily transportable, and capable of defeating larger forces of enemy troops or tanks. Aside from their air and ground transport, the modern paras require smallarms as well as support and anti-tank weapons to fulfil their role as the spearhead of the IDF. However, in the beginning the Israelis bought or filched equipment from sympathetic countries, or the British Army, which was stationed in Palestine

PARA FIREPOWER

Right: Training for rapid deployment, an Israeli para fights to get his 'chute under control. In the early days, the Israeli armed forces used what weapons they could lay their hands on and equipment such as the old British Lewis machine gun (top) was pressed into service. For personal smallarms, the Israelis used Sten guns and Lee-Enfield rifles (above) and many of these weapons were still part of the armoury during the 1956 Sinai campaign (right). The basic Sten sub-machine gun, however, was replaced by the home-designed 9mm Uzi (far right).

EARLY MORTARS

During the bitter battles of the War of Independence, the fledgling Israeli armed forces made considerable use of weapons and equipment appropriated from British Army units stationed in Palestine during the run up to partition, scheduled for May 1948. Although generally under-equipped in comparison with their Arab opponents, the Israelis did hold a small, but valuable stock of light support weapons that included 2in and 3in mortars of World War II vintage.

The lightweight (4.75kg) 2in mortar had been developed as a platoon weapon in the 1930s from a Spanish design. In many ways obsolete by the end of the next decade, it was still a valuable addition to the Israeli armoury. Capable of firing a variety of bombs, including high-explosive and illuminating rounds, out to a range of some 450m, it was primarily used against enemy troop concentrations. Operated by a trained crew, the mortar was capable of eight rounds per minute.

The history of the larger 3in mortar dated back to the Stokes of World War I. Modernised during the inter-war period, it weighed around 50kg and was served by a crew of three.

The improved Mark 2 version of the weapon had a top range of 2560m, and could fire both high-explosive and smoke rounds at a rate of 10 per minute.

As the stocks of support weapons available to the Israelis were small, they established their own weapon-producing industry, producing rough but serviceable copies of British hardware, such as the 2in mortar. However, in the battles of the War of Independence, it was the skilful deployment of scarce resources that overcame the obvious material advantages of the opposition.

Over the next four decades the Israelis were to show, through their victories in the field and the creation of a home-grown armaments industry, that the lessons of the late 1940s had been taken to heart.

until the eve of independence in May 1948.

It was the British 6th Airborne Division that was stationed in Palestine at that time, and when the Israeli Army formed its first parachute units much of their tactical doctrine was based on British practice. Many Jews had also served with the British Army and large numbers of British weapons remained in Palestine after 1948. As a result, the first paras carried Sten guns and Lee-Enfield rifles, with 2in mortars and Bren light machine guns for their immediate support and 3in mortars and six-pounder anti-tank guns, drawn by jeeps, as their heavy support.

The War of Independence, when Israel fought for its very existence, highlighted the need for a reliable sub-machine gun and, in response to this, the Uzi 9mm weapon was produced. Built first with a wooden stock, a more compact folding-stock version rapidly followed, and this was immediately adopted by the

Left inset: The 52mm IMI mortar, the Israeli version of the British 2in weapon. Left: Israeli paras in action on the northern front during the 1967 Six-Day War with a jeep-mounted 106mm recoilless rifle. Below: Paras work to improve their smallarms skills on the firing range. The men kneeling are armed with the 9mm Uzi sub-machine gun, while the soldier lying prone puts the heavy-barrelled version of the FN FAL through its paces.

paratroopers in place of their ageing Sten guns. The Lee-Enfield gave way to the 7.92mm Mauser rifle, and in an endeavour to find a machine gun of compatible calibre, the Israelis adopted the American Johnson design of 1944, calling it the 'Dror'.

The Johnson was an unusual weapon in many ways. In the first place it operated by recoil, one of the few light machine guns to use this system. On firing, the barrel recoiled, locked to the bolt, for a short distance and then stopped; the bolt unlocked and continued rearward, then drove forward again to strip a round from the magazine and fire it. The magazine was inserted on the left side of the gun and it was possible to 'top-up' a partly emptied magazine through a door in the right side of the weapon, using either loose rounds or clips of five cartridges. The barrel could be removed rapidly and the whole weapon could then be packed into a compact space, an ideal configuration for airborne use. The system of operation was sound and the weapon was well made, but its main drawback was the movement of the recoiling barrel, which had to pass through bushings in the outer barrel jacket. This constant movement, coupled with the abrasive dust of the Middle East, soon wore away the faces of barrel and bush to the

extent that the barrel became loose and accuracy deteriorated. The Dror was removed from service after only a few years' use.

In the late 1950s, it was decided to standardise the NATO 7.62mm cartridge in Israeli service and the FN FAL semi-automatic rifle was adopted as the general service weapon for all forces. To accompany this, in the light-machine-gun role, the heavy-barrelled (HB) version of the FAL was adopted. This, as its name implied, was no more than the standard rifle mechanism with a heavy, fixed barrel and a bipod. Versions of both the rifle and the HB rifle with folding metal stocks were adopted for use by the paratroopers.

The six-pounder anti-tank gun could no longer be relied on to damage modern tanks

The support and heavy weapons also underwent revision in the late 1950s. The British 2in mortar was being manufactured in Israel as the 52mm IMI mortar, and this continued in service since it was light and effective. However, the six-pounder anti-tank gun could no longer be relied on to damage modern tanks and ammunition was no longer available from Britain or any other supplier, so the gun was dropped and replaced by the American 106mm recoilless (RCL) rifle. For lighter anti-tank defence, required by the paratroops during the early stages of an assault before heavy weapons could be brought up, the Swedish 84mm Carl Gustav recoilless gun was adopted. The Finnish company Tampella, expert in mortar design, was approached for a new 81mm mortar and this was eventually produced in Israel by the Soltam armaments company.

The M40 106mm recoilless (RCL) rifle is, in fact, of 105mm calibre; its name was deliberately chosen in order to distinguish it from an earlier 105mm model which was less than successful. Like all RCL guns it relies upon ejecting a proportion of the propellant gas to the rear to counterbalance the recoil, and, although rifled, it fires a fin-stabilised, shaped-charge anti-tank shell which is very effective against modern tanks, though no longer capable of penetrating the frontal armour of the heaviest types. Firing in the anti-tank role, it has an effective range of about

It is during the initial period after landing, before heavy support weapons can be brought up, that airborne forces are at their most vulnerable, and Israel has adopted the man-portable 84mm Carl Gustav rocket launcher (below) to cover the paras during this precarious phase of operations. Primarily an anti-tank weapon, the Carl Gustav can fire 2.6kg HEAT (high-explosive anti-tank) rounds (bottom) at a rate of six rounds per minute, but can also provide support with high-explosive, smoke and illuminating ammunition.

1200m, but it is also provided with an anti-personnel shell of conventional spin-stabilised type which has a maximum range in excess of 7000m. The gun is fitted with a 50-calibre spotting rifle on top of the barrel. This sighting weapon fires a special explosive bullet which produces a vivid flash and puff of smoke on impact and is ballistically matched to the anti-tank projectile. The gunner takes aim and fires the spotting rifle until he obtains a hit on the target, then fires the main gun. The shell follows the same trajectory and strikes home in the same place as the spotting rifle's bullet.

The 84mm Carl Gustav RCL gun is a much smaller weapon and can be fired from a man's shoulder. It fires a shaped-charge shell which is drag-stabilised in flight and has a maximum effective range of about 500m. It can also fire anti-personnel, high-explosive, smoke and illuminating shells, making it an extremely versatile support weapon. It weighs just over 14kg and can be carried by a trooper during a parachute descent, thereby giving the force an immediate anti-armour capability that is effective against all but the heaviest tanks.

By the end of the 1960s the Israeli airborne force had amassed a useful volume of combat experience and, consequently, they began to re-assess their weapon requirements. The most basic need was to integrate the personal weapons, both to simplify ammunition provision and to provide each soldier with one weapon which could function as a close-in personal defence or as a longer-range offensive armament. Early in 1972 the Galil rifle was adopted to

Right: Armed with an RPG-7 rocket launcher, an Israeli para moves in to engage a PLO (Palestine Liberation Organisation) gun position in Beirut.

Top: Armed with the Galil assault rifle, the weapon brought in to combine the functions of the Uzi sub-machine gun and the FN rifle, a group of paras patrols the war-torn streets of Beirut.
Below: Bristling with spare ammunition, a para prepares to loose off a rifle grenade.

Above: The simple, but extremely effective RPG-7 rocket launcher. Although a Soviet-built weapon, the Israelis have captured a substantial number of RPGs and placed them in service with their airborne forces. The launcher weighs only 6.3kg and can engage targets at up to 500m. The 2.2kg PG-7V HEAT round is fitted with a rocket motor that fires after it has been launched and boosts its velocity to 300mps.

replace the FN FAL and the Uzi sub-machine gun as the para's personal weapon.

The Galil is a 5.56mm calibre automatic rifle, the design of which leaned heavily on the Soviet Kalashnikov AK-47 for its basic mechanical principles. Israeli experience of the Kalashnikov in Arab hands had clearly demonstrated its reliability in harsh conditions. The Galil is gas-operated, with a rotating bolt, and is fed from a 30-round magazine. Fitted with a bipod and a 50-round magazine, it also functions as the squad automatic. Since it has a folding stock, it is compact for carriage and air-dropping; its automatic-fire capability and short overall length makes it a good substitute for a sub-machine gun. Thus one weapon replaced two, although, as is often the case, the replacement did neither job quite as success-

fully as the two weapons it superseded. The Uzi, with its 9mm Parabellum bullet, had perhaps a better knock-down power at short ranges, while the FN FAL in 7.62mm calibre had a longer effective range and a heavier bullet. However, the combat role of the Israeli airborne force suggests that neither of these two drawbacks was really very vital and certainly not sufficient to prevent the adoption of the Galil across the board.

Another weapon which has confronted the Israelis is the Soviet RPG-7 anti-tank rocket-launcher. This shoulder-fired lightweight weapon has a formidable punch against armour and there are few Western equivalents which have the same favourable combination of weight, range and power. As a result of their several successful offensives against Soviet-supplied Arab states, the Israelis amassed a con-

PARA MOBILITY

Primarily deployed as either a spearhead force, capable of attacking targets in advance of more conventional units, or as a commando-type group, able to carry out punitive cross-border raids, the Israeli paras have always relied on a great deal of mobility to fulfil their functions.

On the ground, the paras have made use of jeeps and M3 half-tracks from World War II, as in the Mitla Pass action during the 1956 Sinai campaign and the battle for Jerusalem in 1967. More recently, the paras have been mounted on US-supplied M113 armoured personnel carriers, known to the Israelis as 'Zeldas'. In all these cases, the vehicles have been fitted with machine guns and anti-armour weapons such as the 106mm recoilless rifle.

The creation of a transport wing within the Israeli Air Force in the 1950s added a new dimension to the means of para deployment.

The first parachute jump, over Mitla Pass, was from war-surplus DC-3 Dakotas. Other large transporters used by the paras have included the twin-boomed Nord Noratlas and Lockheed's C-130 Hercules. Following the war in 1956, the IAF acquired a number of helicopters. The first batch of choppers, purchased from West Germany, consisted of Sikorsky S-58s. Capable of airlifting 16 men, these were first used by the paras in the Six-Day War during a night attack on Egyptian positions at Abu Aweigila. The S-58s were replaced by Bell AB-205 attack and light transport helicopters. To give the paras a heavy-lift capability, the IAF has purchased Aérospatiale Super Frelons which were used in a raid to destroy 14 civilian airliners at Beirut airport in December 1968, and Sikorsky CH-53s. The Israeli version of the CH-53, known as the Jasoor-Frigate, saw service during the 1982 invasion of Lebanon.

siderable quantity of these weapons and most of them appear to have been earmarked for use by airborne forces, generally replacing the Carl Gustav RCL gun. The weapon itself is little more than a tube with a sight, and weighs half as much as the Carl Gustav. Each rocket weighs slightly less than a round of 84mm ammunition, but although there is an anti-personnel rocket, there is no smoke or illuminating warhead available. Nevertheless, the anti-armour performance is what counts, and with the capability of penetrating 320mm of armour plate at a maximum effective range of 500m, the RPG-7 is an extremely useful addition to the airborne armoury.

In order to augment the RPG and to replace the ageing 52mm mortar, the Israelis have adopted a range of rifle grenades for use with the Galil. The muzzle of the rifle was designed with 22mm-diameter bearing rings, so that there is no need to fit an auxiliary grenade-launcher to the rifle, a common practice in the past. The grenades are fin-stabilised and have a hollow tail-boom carrying the fins, ahead of which is the warhead. The hollow tail slips snugly over the rifle muzzle, and the trooper loads a special blank cartridge which is supplied with the grenade. He clips to the grenade tail a disposable plastic sight, takes aim, and then fires the rifle. The gas generated by the special cartridge propels the grenade from the muzzle, the sight falls off, and the rifle is immediately ready for another grenade or for normal use.

Three basic grenades are issued to airborne forces. The AP-30 is a general-purpose anti-personnel grenade which is, as a bonus, capable of penetrating up to 8mm of steel, so that it can be used against vehicles; it has a maximum range of 300m. The AP-65 is heavier, another dual-purpose design, capable of piercing 13mm of steel, and has a maximum range of 250m. The AT-52 is purely an anti-armour grenade using a shaped-charge warhead, and will penetrate 150mm of armour or even greater thicknesses of concrete, making it effective against light field defences. It has a maximum range of 275m and its penetrative capabilities are effective up to this distance.

He then drops a bomb into it and pulls a trigger on the breech end of the tube to send the bomb off

The replacement of the 52mm mortar with the rifle grenade has proven only a partial success: it has made the distribution of ammunition rather easier and has given individuals the capability to project fire out to 300m without having to call for mortar support. But the old 52mm did shoot out to 450m and the loss of 150m of range has been sorely missed on some occasions. Soltam, however, produced a weapon which would not only replace the 52mm model (which was, after all, a design from the 1930s) but would also give the airborne section an ever

greater power-projection ability.

Soltam already manufactured a conventional 60mm mortar which had been adopted by the Israeli Army as a standard infantry platoon weapon. This was the usual form: a barrel resting on a heavy baseplate and mounted on an adjustable bipod. It fired a one-and-three-quarter kilogramme bomb to a range of 2550m, but was a heavy weapon, weighing 16.5kg ready to fire. The company then produced a 'Commando' version of the mortar which is simply a short barrel with a small baseplate, a handgrip and a rudimentary elevation lever. In action, the soldier merely grips the handle, places the baseplate on the ground, looks along a line painted on the barrel to give him direction and tilts the barrel until the level on the side indicates that it is correctly angled for the desired range. He then drops a bomb into it and pulls a trigger on the breech end of the tube to send the bomb off to a maximum range of 900m. Moreover, the entire weapon weighs only six kilogrammes and is only 533mm long.

It would be a bold prophet who attempts to foresee the Israelis' next move, but one obvious area which requires attention is the anti-armour field. While the modern weapons described above are good, they are simply not good enough in view of the enormous number of modern Soviet tanks which Israel's potential enemies can muster, and the Israeli

High mobility is the key to the success of hard-hitting para and commando-style operations, and the Israelis have equipped their airborne forces with helicopters (far left) and armoured personnel carriers, for use once the paras are on the ground (below). However, despite these motorised additions to their inventory, paras do not escape the rigours of a tough foot slog with full kit (below left). Left: The new B-300 portable anti-tank system undergoes trials. An extremely powerful weapon, the B-300 is presently still in the developmental stage but is likely to become a front-line element in the para arsenal.

Army, not only the airborne forces, is looking for a portable anti-tank weapon capable of dealing with this armoured threat. A great deal of work went into a missile project called 'Picket', which had several advanced features, including a gyroscopically stabilised flight line which made aiming much easier. But this appears to have failed and has been abandoned.

Presently, much developmental work is being put into the 'B-300' system, a shoulder-fired semi-disposable weapon which projects a powerful rocket to a range of 400m. The warhead is said to be capable of penetrating armour in excess of 400mm thickness at an impact angle of 65 degrees, which suggests that it will defeat the frontal armour of any existing tank. The weapon, with three rockets, weighs 16kg and separates to form a package less than 750mm long. With a weapon of this nature, airborne forces will be secure against armoured attack at any landing zone in the vulnerable period before their heavy weapons can be brought up, and it is, therefore, highly likely that B-300 will see its first deployment in the hands of the paras.

THE AUTHOR Ian V. Hogg is an authority on small-arms, modern weapon systems and equipment, and the technology of warfare. His recent work includes *The British Army in the 20th Century*.

1ST CANADIAN PARACHUTE BATTALION

On 1 July 1942, the War Committee of the Canadian Cabinet authorised the organisation of a parachute battalion, to be used as a mobile reserve in the defence of North America. The men were trained at the US Army Parachute Training School at Fort Benning, Georgia, and some received additional training in England.

By the spring of 1943 it seemed unlikely that the American continent would come under threat, and it was proposed that the battalion should be included in the British 6th Airborne Division, which was then forming up. The paratroopers arrived in England in July and were immediately put through a conversion course in British parachuting techniques: they also participated in complex field exercises, progressing from company to battalion and brigade level.

One of the exercises conducted during training, simulating a widely dispersed landing, was of great value to the Canadians on their first airborne operation. Dropping to the northeast of Caen on D-day, the battalion was scattered over an area 10 times that of the DZ, yet it still secured its objectives. In the three months following D-day the battalion remained in Normandy and half its strength was lost in the fighting, with 25 officers and 332 other ranks killed, wounded or captured. After returning for a 90-day refit, the battalion sailed from England on Christmas Day as the 6th Airborne was rushed to help contain the Ardennes offensive. The division was withdrawn from the front in February 1945, and on the 21st the Canadians returned to England to begin preparations for the crossing of the Rhine.

AIRBORNE ASSAULT

In the vast Allied air-drop over the Rhine in 1945, no men fought better than the Canadian paras

THE HORIZON WAS cloudless, providing virtually unlimited visibility as the leading C-47 Skytrains of IX US Troop Carrier Command approached the Rhine. Flying nine abreast, the aircraft descended to jump height amid a growing storm of flak bursts and lines of tracer arcing skyward from the river's east bank. To ease the problem of locating Dropping Zones (DZs) and to ensure that the paratroopers landed in tight concentrations, the drop had been scheduled for 1000 hours. Yet now, as pilots and stick commanders strained anxiously to locate landmarks, smoke and haze caused by the massive Allied bombardment set up to neutralise German anti-aircraft batteries was obscuring much of the objective. In rapid succession, the leading paratroopers of the British 8th Battalion, The Parachute Regiment (8 Para) leapt from their aircraft, followed by headquarters personnel of Brigadier James Hill's 3rd Parachute Brigade, of the 6th Airborne Division. Only minutes later, green lights flashed on aboard the 35 aircraft carrying some 600 officers and men of the 1st Canadian Parachute Battalion. For the force of almost 22,000 American, British and Canadian airborne troops flying in aboard 1696 transport aircraft and 1348 gliders, this was the beginning of Operation Varsity, the largest single-day's airborne operation of the war. For the Canadian paratroopers it was their second jump into battle and their third strike at the enemy.

Field Marshal Sir Bernard Montgomery, commander of 21st Army Group, planned to employ the 6th Airborne Division as part of a two-phase operation designed to breach the formidable defences along the lower Rhine and launch his armies deep into Germany's industrial heartland. Operation Plunder was the codename for an assault crossing of the Rhine between Rheinberg and Rees, using Lieutenant-General Sir Miles Dempsey's Second Army on the left, and General W.H. Simpson's Ninth US Army on the right. In the area chosen for the crossing, the Rhine was between 400 and 500yds wide, with a broad floodplain on either bank. On the eastern side of the river the Germans had prepared an elaborate trench system, protected by extensive barbed-wire entanglements and minefields, while further back virtually every house concealed anti-tank or machine-gun emplacements. The defence of the Rhine in the Plunder sector was the responsibility of the German First Parachute Army, consisting of II Parachute Corps, LXXXVI Corps and LXII Corps, which were deployed along the river with XLVII Panzer Corps held in reserve.

Of particular concern to Allied planners was the one significant feature on the east bank, the Diersfordter Wald, a thick forest rising 65ft above the level of the river. The dense trees would offer ample cover from which the Germans could threaten the crossing of the British XII Corps in the Allied centre. Therefore, to prevent enemy artillery from using this vital ground and to protect the bridgehead from a counter-attack, Major-General Matthew Ridgway's XVIIIth US Airborne Corps, consisting of the veteran British 6th Airborne Division and the com

paratively inexperienced American 17th Airborne Division, was given the task of seizing the Diersfordter Wald.

Planning for Operation Varsity took into account the wealth of experience gained in the Allied and German airborne operations of previous years. Planners were particularly conscious of the hard lessons learned during the Arnhem tragedy of September 1944. Unlike at Normandy and Arnhem, where the airborne operation had preceded the attacking ground forces, the airborne forces at the Rhine would not begin dropping until 1000 hours on 24 March, almost 15 hours after the first units of XII Corps had begun to cross the river. It was hoped that a daylight assault would allow the airborne troops to land in a tight concentration on the Dropping Landing Zones located north and east of Diersfordter. The paratroopers would then immediately attack

Above left and centre: Combat training for the Canadian paras. Advancing through open ground, troops push on undeterred by grenades and ground charges exploding around them, while smoke bombs recreate the scent of battle. Below left: Airborne troops embark onto the transports that will carry them across the Rhine.

t: Hundreds of paras and lies descend into the zone. Allied planners red that the drop was ded by heavy shelling emy positions. Above 155mm 'Long Tom' ery piece lets loose.

Crossing the Rhine
March 1945

Early in March 1945, the British 2nd Army and the Canadian 1st Army, under the overall command of Montgomery's 21st Army Group, were established in Germany on the west bank of the lower Rhine. The next phase of the war in this sector – Operation Plunder – was to consist of a crossing in force to the east bank of the Rhine and an advance through Germany's strategically vital industrial heartland, the Ruhr district.

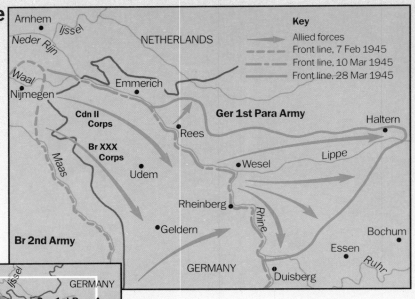

Above: The determined features of Corporal Frederick Topham, who was awarded the coveted Victoria Cross for bravery under fire. Topham's beret bears the badge of the Canadian Parachute Corps.

designated objectives which were located well within range of supporting artillery on the west side of the river. The stipulation of only one airlift meant that both divisions would be landed complete in only three hours. To ensure that the lightly armed airborne troops would not be isolated for too long without armoured support, the link-up with ground units was scheduled to take place on the first day of the operation.

The American 17th Airborne was to seize the southern half of Diersfordter Wald, the area to its southeast, and three bridges over the River Issel. The task of 6th Airborne was to take the northern half of the woods, the village of Hamminkeln and the three bridges crossing the Issel in their sector. Brigadier Hill's 3rd Parachute Brigade would be the first unit to land; 8 Para would secure the DZ to the north of Diersfordter, while the Canadians captured the northwest corner of the woods and 9 Para the area further south. The objective given to the Canadians, consisting of the western edge of the woods, a length of the main road running north from Wesel to Emmerich, and a number of houses in the southern area, was believed to be strongly held by troops of the tough German 7th Parachute Division. Although the outcome of the war was by now certain, no-one doubted that those tough German paratroopers would fight to the death to defend their homeland.

At 0445 hours on the morning of 24 March, as the Canadian troopers clambered aboard the lorries which would take them to the RAF airfield at Chipping Ongar, the leading battalions of the 15th Scottish Division had established a bridgehead opposite Diersfordter, and Royal Marines of the 1st Commando Brigade were fighting a vicious street battle for control of Wesel. By 0730 the American C-47s carrying the Canadians had taken off to join the vast air armada which was to converge over Belgium and then proceed to the Rhine. At 0955 Private J.A. Collins, a C Company sniper, was among the first to jump:

esides its obvious strategic
mportance, the Rhine
epresented a symbolic
rontier behind which lay the
erman heartland. Allied
lanners were thus well
ware that the enemy would
efend their positions in the
hine sector with the utmost
enacity. Carried in C-47
kytrain' transport aircraft,
e Canadians swooped down
ito German territory and
lenced many of the enemy
trongpoints. Below: Their
arachutes abandoned, two
irborne troops advance
arily through the mist with
hompson sub-machine guns
t the ready.

'We were somewhat apprehensive; many of us remembered our sister Div at Arnhem and the mauling it had taken... I was 19th man of a 20-man stick. I was quite calm by now and it seemed like a normal exercise jump. The aircraft bounced a few times and I could hear the anti-aircraft burst quite close. The most vivid thing I remember on the descent was a burning Dakota passing me, going back towards the Rhine.'

The battalion's war diary noted tersely, 'Flak was fairly heavy over the Dropping Zone and several aircraft were seen to go down in flames.' Collins landed unscathed, but others in C Company were not as fortunate. The company commander, Major Hanson, who had won a Military Cross in Normandy, suffered a broken collar-bone on landing, while the aircraft carrying Captain J.A. Clancy, the company second-in-command, was hit over the Dropping Zone.

As the crew struggled to maintain control of the burning aircraft, the paratroopers baled out. Scattered over a wide area, many of the troopers remained cut off from their unit for the rest of the day. Captain Clancy landed amid German troops and was immediately taken prisoner. With most of their officers out of action, it fell upon the company NCOs to take control of the situation. Gathering what men they could, Sergeants Miles Saunders and William Murray charged directly onto the company's objective on the edge of the Dropping Zone. The ferocity of the attack had already overwhelmed the German gun crews before many of the C Company troopers could make their way from the DZ to assist.

The intensity of the enemy flak had forced the C-47 transports to cross the Dropping Zone at speed, and consequently the brigade's sub-units, although generally on the DZ, were scattered over a wider area than had been anticipated. Inevitably, a number of parachutists, including the Canadians' commanding officer, Lieutenant-Colonel Jeff Nicklin, landed among the trees bordering the DZ. Although Colonel Nicklin had escaped a similar landing in Normandy, on this occasion he was trapped immediately above a German machine-gun team and was killed as he struggled to get out of his parachute harness. Most of the men of A Company landed on the eastern end of the brigade's DZ, yet within 30 minutes more than two-thirds of the company had made their way to the yellow smoke which marked the battalion's rendezvous on the western edge of the DZ.

When word reached Battalion Headquarters of Colonel Nicklin's death, Major G. Fraser Eadie, the battalion's second-in-command, assumed control. As the first of the gliders began to land at 1100 hours, Brigadier Hill ordered the Canadian battalion and 9 Para to attack their objectives. Wasting no time, Major Peter Griffin led A Company against the cluster of houses on the western edge of the Diersfordter Wald, but withering fire from the German defenders soon checked their progress. Covered by Bren and rifle fire, Company Sergeant Major George Green led an assault against the first house and captured it after a vicious firefight at close quarters. CSM Green's group then methodically cleared the remaining houses on the objective.

As A Company was clearing the buildings, B Company was moving through the woods towards the group of farm houses at the Bergenfurth junction further to

the south. Under the command of Captain Sam McGowan, who was bleeding badly from a head wound received on the DZ, the company formed up along a fence at the edge of the farm. Covered by Bren guns, the Company swept forward, firing as they ran, and quickly cleared the position with hand grenades and Sten guns. While the remainder of the company began to dig trenches, patrols were sent out to clear the surrounding woods. One patrol of seven men returned with 98 prisoners to add to those already taken. By mid-afternoon the battalion found it had more than 400 prisoners on its hands.

By 1200 hours all three rifle companies could report that they were firm on their objectives and digging in to resist any possible enemy counter-attacks. Overhead, gliders still swooped towards the Landing Zones to the north and east of the Diersfordter Wald, and the noise of battle could be heard from all directions. Brigadier Hill moved his headquarters into a small school-house within the Canadian peri-

meter, while an advanced dressing station was set up by the 224th Field Ambulance. Throughout the afternoon the battalion was subjected to sporadic shelling from enemy artillery and tanks, and A Company repelled two counter-attacks with little difficulty. Particularly troublesome were some German paratroopers in houses to the north, who were raking the western half of the DZ and C Company's positions with mortar and machine-gun fire. It was in this area that Corporal Frederick Topham, a medical orderly of the battalion, won the Victoria Cross. Seeing two medics from the Field Ambulance killed by machine-gun fire as they moved to help a wounded trooper, Corporal Topham ran to the man's aid. Although shot through the nose, Topham continued dressing the man's wound and carried him to the shelter of the woods. Two hours later, having refused to seek medical attention, Topham managed to rescue three wounded men from a blazing Bren-gun carrier which was loaded with mortar ammunition

and in danger of exploding.

Around the battalion's perimeter, sniper rifles and medium machine guns were used to pick off any Germans rash enough to break cover. At about 1400, fire from the Vickers guns of the Machine-Gun Platoon wiped out a group of some 40 enemy approaching the battalion's positions from the direction of the Rhine. Troopers who had landed wide of the DZ continued to make their way to the battalion's position; one was Lance-Corporal Real Aubert, a Battalion Provost Corporal. Before leaving England, Aubert had wrapped around his waist the Canadian flag which had flown outside Battalion Headquarters at Carter Barracks. Now, with the help of several prisoners, he fixed the flag to the longest pole he could find and raised it over the Canadian position.

'The airborne drop in depth destroyed enemy gun and rear defensive positions in one day'

By early afternoon, the 15th Scottish Division had secured its bridgehead on the eastern bank, and the Carrier Platoon of the 8th Battalion, The Royal Scots, was despatched to make contact with 6th Airborne Division. Sent forward with a patrol, one Canadian paratrooper described the meeting:

'We heard the rattle of an armoured vehicle and were prepared for a German tank, but as we cautiously crept forward through scrubby undergrowth a platoon of Germans suddenly ran towards us. I was towards the rear of the group but the lead troops opened fire. Only minutes after they began cheering, and pushing between them I saw Bren carriers trundling along a track towards us. The sense of relief was overwhelming and certainly I, at least, felt intense relief that we weren't going to be isolated as had been the troops at Arnhem.'

The 6th Airborne Division maintained its positions throughout the night of 24/25 March as the Second and Ninth Armies continued to expand their bridgehead. At first light the German paratroopers who had been harassing the Canadians from the houses on the northwest of the DZ, launched a final desperate counter-attack against the Canadian position, but they were driven off by C Company. Although shelling continued throughout the day and forward positions had still to be manned, the Canadians were now able to collect their casualties. On the previous day the battalion had lost two officers and 22 other ranks killed and one officer and 32 other ranks had been wounded. The 6th Airborne Division had lost 347 men killed and 731 wounded, while the 17th Airborne lost 359 men with a further 522 wounded. Of the transport aircraft, 22 C-46s, 12 C-47s and more than 80 gliders had been destroyed by anti-aircraft fire. Although casualties had been much greater than anticipated, Operation Varsity was a complete success. General Ridgway summed up the results:

'The airborne drop in depth destroyed enemy gun and rear defensive positions in one day – positions it might have taken many days to reduce by ground attack. The impact of the airborne divisions at one blow shattered hostile defence and permitted the prompt link up with ground troops.'

In the weeks following the Rhine crossing the 6th Airborne Division advanced on Montgomery's left flank until on 2 May, after covering 275 miles, the 1st Canadian Parachute Battalion led the division into Wismar on the Baltic Coast and there halted to await the arrival of the Red Army. The paratroopers were still in Wismar when Germany capitulated three days later.

The 1st Canadian Parachute Battalion had made two drops into battle and accumulated a total of seven months of frontline service. As the first Canadian unit to land in Normandy and the first Canadian unit to cross the Rhine, it was only appropriate that the Canadian paratroopers should be the first unit to be sent home, arriving in Halifax to a tumultuous welcome on 21 June. The battalion was subsequently disbanded at Niagara-on-the-Lake on 30 September. However, the value of the airborne tradition and the reputation which the battalion had established were not lost, as the Canadian Army decided to train one battalion in each of its regular infantry regiments in the airborne role.

THE AUTHOR Lieutenant Ian Kemp, a former member of both the British and Canadian Armies, graduated from the Department of War Studies, King's College, London, and is a researcher at the Royal United Services Institute for Defence Studies.

Above: An M36 tank destroyer, one of the first to link up with airborne troops following their lightning advance; in the background, a group of German prisoners awaits transportation to POW camps. Below: Objective secured, all aboard for Hamminkeln. Crack paras take two more prisoners as they prepare to enter the ravaged town using a transport jeep and trailer.

EAGLES OF BAS

Surrounded by German panzers, the US 101st Airborne Division faced its greatest ever test at Bastogne during the Battle of the Bulge

ON THE MORNING of 22 December 1944, a week after the Ardennes offensive began, men of Company F, 2nd Battalion 327th Glider Infantry Regiment (2/327th), a component unit of the US 101st Airborne Division, were occupying forward defensive positions around Remoifosse to the south of Bastogne. At about 1130 hours they were surprised to see a small group of Germans (two officers and two soldiers) approaching under a white flag of truce, and even more surprised when their spokesman, Leutnant (2nd Lieutenant) Hellmuth Henke of the Panzer Lehr Division, announced in English, 'We are parlementaires.' A rumour quickly spread through the American lines that the enemy was about to surrender, but in fact Henke's intention was to negotiate quite the opposite. He carried a typed message from General Heinrich von Luttwitz, commander of the XLVII Panzer Corps, which demanded 'the honourable surrender' of the encircled town of Bastogne within two hours, otherwise overwhelming German forces would 'annihilate the USA troops'.

Henke and his fellow officer, Major Wagner of XLVII Panzer Corps staff, were led blindfold to the command post of Company F and the message was immediately passed up the chain to divisional headquarters in Bastogne. Delivered by Colonel Joseph Harper, commanding officer of the 327th Glider

Infantry Regiment, it was initially regarded as something of a joke by the acting divisional commander, Brigadier-General Anthony McAuliffe. His reaction was merely to laugh and say, 'Aw, nuts!' and when he came to compile a written reply, neither he nor his staff could think of anything more appropriate. Harper was therefore handed a slip of paper on which was written: 'To the German Commander: NUTS! The American Commander' and directed to deliver it to the German officers still waiting at Remoifosse. Hardly surprisingly, when he received the reply at 1330, Henke had no idea what it meant and Harper had to spell it out:

'If you don't understand what "Nuts" means, in plain English it is the same as "Go to hell". And I will tell you something else – if you continue to attack we will kill every goddam German that tries to break into this city.'

This was 'fighting talk', only to be expected from an elite formation such as the 101st Airborne – nicknamed the 'Screaming Eagles' – but in reality McAuliffe was in an unenviable position. For the past

Below: A PzKpfw IV blown apart on the outskirts of Bastogne. By the time General Patton's 4th Armored Division had forced its way through to relieve the encircled garrison, the surrounding countryside was littered with such evidence of the fierce battles fought to defend the town. Below right: a US 57mm anti-tank gun is hauled through the Ardennes mud in preparation for a German counter-attack. Right: Brigadier-General McAuliffe (on the right), commanding officer of 101st Airborne at Bastogne, confers with General Patton after the siege. Background: An air-drop of desperately-needed medical supplies and ammunition to the defenders of Bastogne.

OGNE

24 hours the forces under his command had been cut off and besieged in Bastogne. They faced elements of four German divisions – 2nd Panzer, Panzer Lehr, 26th Volksgrenadier and 5th Fallschirmjäger – and were already running short of supplies. Their morale may have been high (the airborne spirit was epitomised by the slogan 'The Germans have got us surrounded – the poor bastards!') but the security of Bastogne was by no means guaranteed.

Hitler's attack on 16 December had come as a complete surprise to the Allies. The 130km front was held by weak or inexperienced divisions of Major-General Troy Middleton's VIII Corps and, although individual units held out for longer than expected, the initial German assault formations made significant progress. Their aim was to punch holes in the American defences preparatory to a concerted thrust which would strike deep into Allied lines, crossing the Meuse river and recapturing Antwerp before the Anglo-American commanders could react. But to do this, the panzers and their support units had to control the roads. Communication centres such as St. Vith in the north and Bastogne in the south of the developing salient became of crucial importance. In the event, the defence of St. Vith, which had delayed the Germans for a week, had to be abandoned on 23 December and this increased the need of the Allies to defend Bastogne. With seven major roads radiating from its centre (to Houffalize in the north, St. Vith in the northeast, Wiltz in the southeast, Arlon in the south, Neufchâteau in the southwest and Marche and La Roche in the northwest) the town was a serious block to the enemy.

The American commanders in the line of the

When World War II began the US Army had no airborne troops, and it was only after the spectacular successes of Germany's airborne forces that their organisation was put in hand. On 16 August 1942 the newly-reformed 82nd Infantry Division was divided into the 82nd 'All American' and the 101st 'Screaming Eagles' Airborne Divisions (the Eagles' shoulder flash is shown above). After initial parachute training at Fort Bragg, the 101st transferred to Tennessee and practised mass jumps and glider runs in preparation for the war in Europe.

On 6 June 1944 (D-Day) the Eagles parachuted into the Cotentin peninsula in Normandy. Although their landing pattern was severely disrupted by flak they cleared the coastal sector assigned to them, and some units won the Presidential Unit Citation for their part in the capture of the town of Carentan. As part of the First Allied Airborne Army, the Eagles were dropped just north of Eindhoven in Holland as part of the Market Garden Operation. With great courage their transport pilots maintained their course in heavy flak and this time the paras' landing pattern was concentrated and orderly. Meeting only light opposition the Eagles secured all their objectives. However, the defensive battles that followed against German reinforcements were probably the most vicious in the division's history.

Market Garden was the Eagles' last airborne operation of the war and thereafter the division fought as ground troops. In recognition of their heroic defence of Bastogne in December 1944 the entire division was awarded the Presidential Unit Citation.

M1 Carbine

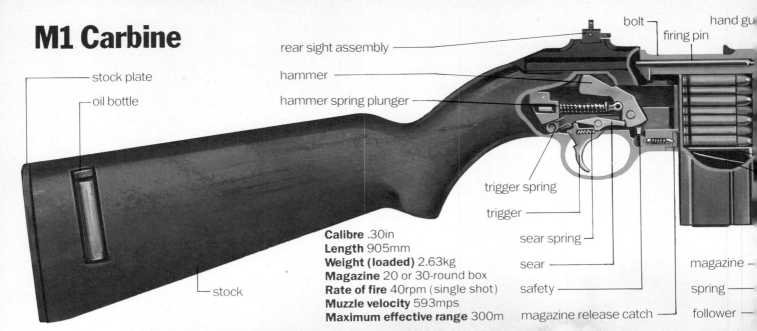

stock plate

oil bottle

stock

rear sight assembly

hammer

hammer spring plunger

bolt

firing pin

hand gu...

trigger spring

trigger

sear spring

sear

safety

magazine release catch

magazine

spring

follower

Calibre .30in
Length 905mm
Weight (loaded) 2.63kg
Magazine 20 or 30-round box
Rate of fire 40rpm (single shot)
Muzzle velocity 593mps
Maximum effective range 300m

advance had recognised this as early as 16 December, when Middleton committed his only mobile reserve, Combat Command R (CCR), 9th Armored Division, to the east of Bastogne to establish roadblocks. The Supreme Commander, General Dwight Eisenhower, then ordered the 10th Armored Division to rush north from Third Army to reinforce the town. When Combat Command B (CCB) of the 10th Armored arrived early on 18 December, it too was despatched to the east of the town, setting up an arc of defensive positions that stretched from Noville (Team Desobry), through Longvilly (Team Cherry) to Wardin (Team O'Hara). This move coincided with probing attacks by 2nd Panzer and Panzer Lehr. by the end of the day the CCR road-blocks had been outflanked or overwhelmed and the CCB Teams were all that stood between the Germans and Bastogne.

When the German offensive began on 16 December, Eisenhower's only strategic reserve was the US XVIII Airborne Corps, commanded by Major-General Matthew Ridgway; its European-based divisions, the 82nd and 101st Airborne, resting near Rheims in northern France after the Arnhem operation, were alerted for movement to the Ardennes late on 17 December. Major-General James Gavin, commanding officer of the 82nd and acting corps commander while Ridgway was in England, received the orders at 1930 hours and, after a hectic night of preparations, his division set out in trucks just after dawn on the 18th. unsure of its precise destination. The 101st, temporarily under the command of McAuliffe (in the absence on leave of both Major-General Maxwell Taylor and his deputy Brigadier-General Gerald Higgins), followed at 1400 hours, by which time Gavin had received new orders to concentrate around Werbomont on the northern shoul-

Above: The US M1 0·3in carbine. As early as 1938 the US infantry was requesting a light rifle for such personnel as machine-gunners, mortar crews, drivers and service units who might require an effective weapon to defend themselves while carrying out their tasks. In 1940 arms manufacturers were asked to submit designs suitable for the 0.3in Short Rifle Cartridge, a round developed from the Winchester .32in Automatic sporting rifle cartridge. The successful design, submitted by Winchester, incorporated a modified Garand bolt and a short-stroke gas piston, and it was finalised in late 1941. An estimated six-and-a-quarter million carbines were manufactured in the war. Servicemen issued with carbines found them light, reliable and simple to operate, but beyond short range their accuracy and stopping power was unsatisfactory and they were eventually superseded by sub-machine guns.

der of the bulge. McAuliffe expected to join him there, but while still on the road the 101st wa diverted to Bastogne. Rerouting some 380 trucks i the dark, on unfamiliar and icy roads already choked with traffic, was a nightmare of confusion. Neverthe less, by risking the use of headlamps right up to the Belgian border, the 11,000 strong Eagle Division made the journey of 160km in well under 24 hours.

Batteries of guns dug into the hillsides overlooking the village pounded the paras without mercy

There was no time for detailed briefings or recon naissance, for the situation to the east of the town wa desperate. During the night, spearheads of 2n Panzer had captured Allerborn and struck north westwards, isolating the CCR road-block at Ant niushaff and brushing against the Sherman tanks of Team Desobry at Noville, while Panzer Lehr ha moved under cover of dense fog to drive a wedge between Teams Cherry and O'Hara further south 1/506th Parachute Infantry was hurriedly despatch ed to reinforce Desobry. arriving at 1200 hours on 1 December. Their initial reaction was to mount counter-attack, but when that took place two hour later it clashed with a panzer assault coming th other way. The fighting was confused, with neithe side giving ground. Batteries of guns dug into th hillsides overlooking the village pounded the para troopers without mercy and their defensive pos tions were repeatedly overrun by the tanks' heav onslaughts. In the sustained artillery storm the commanding officer, Lieutenant-Colonel Jame LaPrade, was killed. It was a cruel introduction to th Ardennes battle, and worse came when 2nd Panze renewed its attack at 0530 hours on 20th. Noville fe.

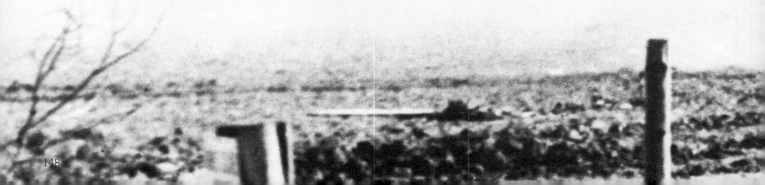

Diagram labels (top):
- gas port
- locking spring
- barrel
- front band
- front sight assembly
- piston
- operating slide
- operating slide spring and guide

forcing the Americans to withdraw into lines established by the 502nd Parachute Infantry to their rear at Foy. However, although it was unknown to them at the time, 2nd Panzer had been deterred by the resistance from a direct assault on Bastogne, and had decided to push westwards to the Meuse.

Elsewhere, a similar pattern had begun to emerge. The thrust by Panzer Lehr that had isolated Team Cherry at Longvilly was blunted by a spirited counter-attack by all three battalions of the 501st Parachute Infantry at Bizory, but this did not prevent the destruction of the Longvilly pocket. At 1300 hours on 19 December German artillery pounded the road between Longvilly and Mageret, destroying over 200 American vehicles and leaving the remnants of Team Cherry to escape by foot into lines held by the 501st. By then Team O'Hara had been forced out of Wardin towards Marvie, perilously close to the eastern outskirts of Bastogne, but had been reinforced by 2/327th Glider Infantry. When this combined force proved too stubborn for Panzer Lehr reconnaissance patrols early on the 20th, they too diverted westwards, taking Lutrebois and cutting the Arlon road. Twenty-four hours later, when elements of the 5th Fallschirmjäger captured Sibret in the west, Bastogne was effectively encircled. Late on 21 December, as snow began to fall, McAuliffe was given responsibility for the defence of the town soon to be called 'the Alamo of Europe'.

The men of the 101st Airborne had therefore achieved a great deal even before the direct siege

Soldier, 101st Airborne Division, Bastogne 1944

This soldier wears an M1943 combat jacket and a ragged pair of trousers from the M42 airborne uniform. Gloves, a scarf and rubber overboots are worn to try to alleviate the bitter winter cold experienced at Bastogne. A rations box is carried under his left arm and slung over his right shoulder is a 0.3in Garand M1 rifle, the standard weapon of the US infantryman during World War II.

HITLER'S LAST THROW

The Battle of the Bulge, otherwise called the Battle of the Ardennes, was the largest pitched battle ever fought by the US Army. On 16 December 1944 Hitler launched what was to be his last great offensive on the Western Front. In a repetition of the strategy that had led to his lightning conquest of Western Europe in 1940, 200,000 German troops with heavy armoured support burst into the snow-covered Ardennes, rapidly destroying or overrunning the units of Eisenhower's thin defensive front line and pouring west. However, American forces that were stationed to the north and south of the penetration made successful tactical withdrawals and then stood firm to contain the onslaught. The invading force was channelled into a narrowing corridor along which the leading elements of Hitler's army strove to reach the River Meuse.

Within the territory occupied by the Germans (the bulge) two essential crossroads, the Belgian towns of St Vith and Bastogne, remained in Allied hands, and these were to be disastrous stumbling blocks to Hitler's campaign. Denied access to the only major roads north to Liège and south into Luxembourg, the leading German units were ordered to bypass the two Allied strongholds on minor roads and tracks, while large detachments remained to beat the towns into submission. The progress of the offensive slowed and, whereas Hitler's blitzkrieg of 1940 had swept all before it, the invaders now had to deal with enemy outposts in their rear which had the potential of disrupting their supply lines and the flow of reinforcements to the front. As the days passed the capture of the towns became increasingly imperative if the Nazis were to succeed.

The Battle of the Bulge
101st Airborne Division, Bastogne, December 1944

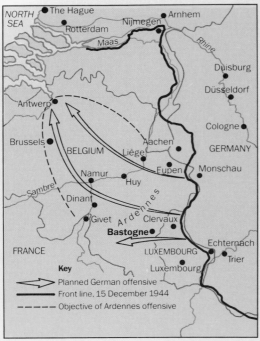

In December 1944, 24 German divisions were thrown into a final offensive against the advancing Allied armies on the Western Front. Hitler's plan called for a breakthrough in the Ardennes, splitting the Allied armies in two, and pushing on to Antwerp. The offensive took the Allies by surprise and from 16 – 20 December the German divisions pushed forward to Stavelot, St Vith, Houffalize and Bastogne. General Eisenhower committed the 101st Airborne Division to the defence of Bastogne, which was situated on a vital crossroads controlling movements north-south and east-west. By 20 December Bastogne was surrounded but the 101st held out, imposing delays on the exploitation of the 'bulge' that were to prove fatal to the German offensive.

Key

⇨ Planned German offensive
— Front line, 15 December 1944
--- Objective of Ardennes offensive

got under way. Their arrival at Bastogne was opportune, enabling the Americans to bolster up the thin defensive ring when it mattered most. It was now up to McAuliffe and his airborne troopers to hold on, tying down enemy units which should have been well on the way to Antwerp, and granting Eisenhower the opportunity to organise a strong defence on the two shoulders of the bulge, preparatory to eventual counter-attack.

Meanwhile, the Germans began to subject Bastogne to a ceaseless barrage of artillery and night bombing that eventually reduced the town to rubble. The wounded sent from the front positions lay helpless in an inferno of exploding shells, while medics worked frantically with their fast-diminishing stocks of supplies. One bomb hit a hospital and only two patients survived. Trench foot and frozen limbs became common as the troops stayed interminable periods at their posts.

If Bastogne was to hold out, however, it had to receive supplies. As the weather cleared, McAuliffe turned to the only possible solution – aerial resupply. At 0935 hours on 22 December – two hours before the Germans demanded a surrender – a pathfinder team from the divisional base unit parachuted in to positions held by the 327th Glider Infantry and set up radar beacons. Ninety minutes later the men of the 101st Airborne were much relieved to see the first

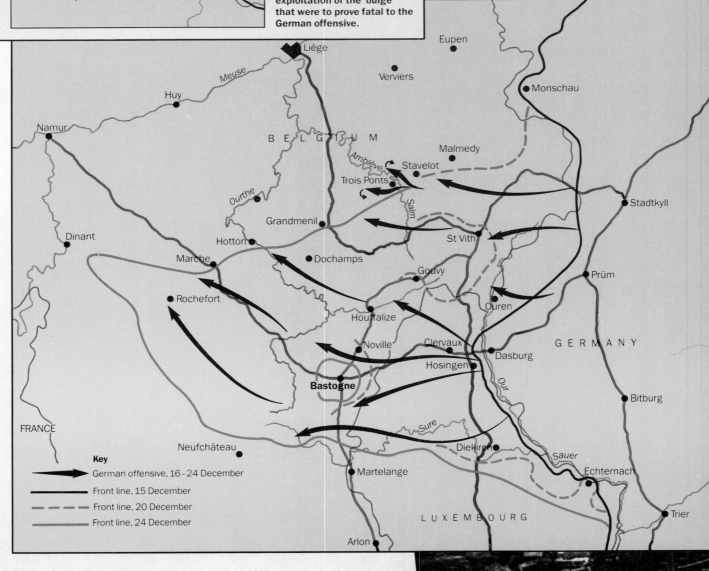

Key

▶ German offensive, 16 - 24 December
— Front line, 15 December
--- Front line, 20 December
— Front line, 24 December

C-47s (known in the US as Skytrains) arrived over the drop zone; by 1400 over 240 aircraft had delivered .44 tonnes of supplies, the bulk of which was artillery ammunition. But the weather could still be fickle; despite another successful delivery on 24 December, by Christmas Day the C-47 bases in England were shrouded in fog, forcing the Americans to use gliders flown in from France. The first glider run took place on 26 December and encountered a hail of German anti-aircraft fire: 11 gliders reached the 101st, shot full of holes but containing urgently-needed medical supplies and surgical teams. A second run the following day was less successful and 15 gliders and 17 C-47 tugs were lost.

Despite a comparative lull in the fighting on 22 December the battle was far from over. At 1725 hours on the 23rd, positions held by 2/327th Glider Infantry around Marvie were hit by heavy artillery and tank fire, and this was closely followed by a wave of armour and supporting infantry. A platoon of Company G, commanded by Lieutenant Stanley Morrison, was dug in on Hill 500, to the south of the town, and bore the brunt of the assault. Colonel Harper spoke to Morrison over the field telephone. 'What's your situation?' The reply came, 'I see tanks just outside my window. It looks like they have us.' Then the line went dead: Company G had been overwhelmed, and the Germans had opened up a route into Marvie itself. Company A of 1/501st Parachute Infantry was rushed forward to plug the gap, arriving only just in time. As they entered the action, German tanks were less than 50m from the edge of the town, and although the American line held, a second German attack that night broke through to gain positions actually inside Marvie. By now the roads and surrounding countryside were littered with the wreckage of Allied and enemy armour and equipment, and as the fog lifted Allied P-47s flew in to strafe and dive-bomb the German force. Further round the perimeter to the northwest, 3/327th Glider Infantry had succeeded in blunting a

Below: An Eagles corporal drags a case of medical supplies across the snow after an air drop. He carries its parachute under his arm. Bottom: A US patrol passes shattered buildings in Bastogne. Large areas of the town were reduced to rubble by bombing and artillery barrages during the siege.

similar attack at Flamierge, but with the defensive ring now contracted to a circumference of less than 25km and Bastogne subject to nightly Luftwaffe bombing raids, the situation did not look good.

By 23 December, however, the panzer divisions had diverted most of their forces to the west, trying desperately to reach the Meuse, and responsibility for taking Bastogne had been delegated to the 26th Volksgrenadiers, under Generalmajor (Major-General) Heinz Kokott, reinforced by elements of 115th Panzergrenadier Division, newly-arrived in the front line. Christmas Eve was quiet as Kokott prepared for what he hoped would be the final assault, and McAuliffe took the opportunity to tighten his defences, placing his four airborne regiments on the perimeter, backed by all-arms teams from his other available units. It was a sensible move.

The attack began before dawn on Christmas Day, when Captain Wallace Swanson, commanding Company A of 1/502nd Parachute Infantry, reported enemy tanks coming over his positions outside Champs, on the northwestern edge of the perimeter. Company B was ordered to move to his aid, although nothing could prevent the Germans entering Champs, and bitter house-to-house fighting broke out. But this action proved something of a diversion, for soon afterwards a force of 18 tanks and assault guns, each with panzer grenadiers clinging to the hull, attacked further south, aiming for the gap between 1/502nd Parachute and 3/327th Glider Infantry. By 0715 hours the command post of the 3/327th had been overrun. As the panzers swung round to approach Champs from the rear, however, they passed positions manned by Allen's Company C and these men poured fire onto the German column with everything they had, sweeping the panzer

grenadiers from their perches on the armour. Tank destroyers of the 705th TD Battalion moved up to engage the tanks and all 18 vehicles were destroyed. The German advance ground to a halt.

This was the turning point of the Bastogne battle. At 1650 hours the first vehicle of General Patton's 4th Armored Division crossed the lines of 101st Airborne's perimeter defence. The scenes in Bastogne and the outlying villages told a terrible story of destruction, suffering and misery. The garrison, now known as 'the battered bastards of Bastogne bastion', had tenaciously defended a key strongpoint against overwhelming odds.

THE AUTHOR John Pimlott is Senior Lecturer in War Studies and International Affairs at the Royal Military Academy, Sandhurst. He has written *Strategy and Tactics of War* and edited *Vietnam: the History and Tactics.*

PARA KIT

A whole series of weapons and new equipment was developed for the German airborne forces of World War II

WHEN Germany's paratroop arm came into being in June 1938, its personnel were armed with the standard weapons of the German Army: the 7.92mm bolt-action Mauser rifle, the 7.92mm MG34 machine gun and the 8cm mortar. However, the particular design of parachute harness adopted by the Germans – together with the difficulty of exiting from the Junkers Ju 52 aircraft (it required a peculiar forward dive) – meant that none of these weapons could be carried by the man but had to be dropped in containers. Consequently, the parachutist was unarmed on the ground until he could find his weapon container.

To counter this potentially fatal limitation, pistols (the standard Luger Pistole '08) were lavishly issued, as was the MP38 sub-machine gun which became the standard personal weapon for most troops. The MP38 was a highly effective short-range gun and was distinctive in being constructed entirely of metal and plastic, featuring a folding metal stock in place of the heavy wooden type. Firing a 9mm Parabellum round, the MP38 had a 32-round box magazine and a cyclic rate-of-fire of 500rpm. Expensive to manufacture in war conditions, the MP38 was subsequently replaced by the MP40; virtually the same weapon as its predecessor, it was, however, far easier to mass produce by virtue of its simpler construction and extensive use of steel pressings.

In an attempt to provide the paratroops with handy weapons of superior range, experiments were performed on a folding version of the standard Kar 98 Mauser short rifle. Two versions were developed, one of which simply had a hinge at the small of the stock, whereby the stock could be folded sideways to lie alongside the body of the rifle, whilst a more complicated design broke and hinged in front of the chamber, using a bayonet joint to lock the barrel and chamber together for firing. Both of these weapons folded up satisfactorily and could be carried on the paratrooper's harness but neither proved to be satisfactory from a ballistic point of view; either the folding stock came loose or the bayonet-jointed barrel leaked gas. As a result the folding Mauser rifle never went into service.

More important was the paratroopers' demand for long-range fire support. The standard 8cm mortar was something of a handful but with a range of 2000m it gave the air-landed force a means with which to beat back the inevitable counter-attack or to soften-up an objective during an offensive. But what was lacking was a weapon with the ability to fire on a flat trajectory, a lightweight field gun which would also be capable of dealing with tanks and other armoured vehicles.

Had the matter remained within the domain of the Army Weapons Bureau, the airborne troops would have had nothing more than what the Army pro-vided: the standard 3.7cm PAK 36 anti-tank gun. While capable of dealing with light armoured vehicles, it had a minute high-explosive projectile and was thus useless as a general support weapon. But the airborne troops were not part of the Army, they were part of the Luftwaffe; and their master was Hermann Göring, who also controlled a powerful consortium of munitions companies, the *Hermann-Göring Werke*. Moreover, the Luftwaffe was not bound by the Army's decree in the matter of arma-ment and could – provided they were able to obtain the necessary priorities in materials – have whatever they wished manufactured for their own use. And with a name like Hermann Göring to conjure with, the magic priorities were easily obtained in Hitler's pre-war Germany.

During the 1930s two arms manufacturers, Krupp and Rheinmetall, had been experimenting with re-coilless guns and by 1938 both had workable pro-totypes; the airborne troops heard of these, tested them and selected the Rheinmetall design. The recoilless gun relied upon Newton's law that action and reaction are opposite and equal; in its simplest form the gun could consist of two opposite-facing barrels connected to a single chamber. One barrel was loaded with the projectile, the other with a similar weight of lead shot and grease. When the

Bottom Left: German paras leap onto motorcycle combinations as part of the rapid response to the Allies landing at Anzio in 1943. Below: Para artillerymen load a well-camouflaged anti-tank gun during the fighting in Tunisia.

The Germans had begun experimenting with self-loading rifles in the late 1930s and a couple of models – the Gewehr 41 and 43 – saw limited service on the Eastern Front, but both were heavy to use and complex to manufacture. The FG42 represented a major advance over these earlier designs, making full use of the manufacturing advances made in other areas of small arms production. Gone was the heavy wooden stock and handguard, replaced by steel pressings and laminates which could be produced and assembled by semi-skilled labour with comparative ease. The FG42 had a straight-line layout which made it easy to control when fired as a single-shot hand-held rifle but as a bipod-mounted automatic it was too light and tended to 'walk away' from the line of fire, moving to the right despite the bipod. Below: the side-mounted magazine and bolt assembly of the FG42.

central charge was fired, the shot and counter-shot were blasted down their respective barrels at similar speeds, the projectile proceeding to the target, the countershot simply dispersing in the air. But since the weights and speeds were equal, the two barrels recoiled equally, so that the entire weapon would remain at rest. This economised on weight; there was no need for a strong carriage to withstand the recoil, nor for a complicated hydro-pneumatic system to absorb the recoil force and save wear and tear on the carriage.

The equal-weight and equal-speed equation could be taken further, since it was possible to have the countershot half the weight of the projectile but move it at twice the velocity. Provided that weight × velocity for the shot and the countershot always remained the same, recoil was cancelled out. And to take it to the ultimate, a stream of gas could be discharged at very high speed and still balance the weight and velocity of the projectile.

The 7.5cm Light Gun 40 (LG 40) – designed by Rheinmetall and built by several manufacturers under contract – had a short rifled barrel with a sliding-block breech; in the breech block was a hole, and behind this hole was a venturi and a cone-shaped gas exhaust. The firing pin was suspended in the centre of the hole by two steel arms.

The cartridge case had a base of heavy plastic, with the primer in the centre. On firing, the plastic base held together long enough to allow the shell to engage in the gun's rifling and begin moving, after which it shattered and allowed the propellant gas to escape through the venturi. The gun could fire a 5.5kg shell to a range of over 6500m, an acceptable performance for airborne troops. Besides the standard 7.5cm high explosive round, it was also provided with a useful armour-piercing shell.

The LG 40 was first used during the invasion of Crete. The ability of a parachute-landed force to deploy artillery of this calibre and performance came as an unpleasant surprise to the Allied defenders; and the utility of the weapon was not lost on the Germans. A 10.5cm version, a scale-up of the 7.5cm but with some minor improvements, was put into production and plans for a 15cm weapon were also put in hand. Moreover, it was the impact of this

Above: The Para's 'secret' weapon on Crete: the 7.5cm LG 40 recoiless rifle, mounted on a lightweight carriage.

weapon which led both the British and Americans to develop their own recoilless guns.

The German forces which assaulted Crete did not have everything their own way, however, and one of their principal complaints was that well-directed rifle fire from the Allied defenders pinned them down at ranges their sub-machine guns could not

FG42

- rear sight assembly
- firing pin
- bolt
- barrel extension
- buffer spring
- operating rod
- stock
- grip
- trigger sear
- trigger
- piston
- cocking handle

Above: The two separate sections of a para Mauser Kar 98 rifle, revealing its interrupted screw thread joint.

Above: covered by an MG34 machine gun German paras race towards an assembly point immediately after landing.

Below: A side-view of the Mauser Kar 98 incorporating the hinged stock.

gas port

barrel

bayonet

fore sight assembly

fore grip

gas cylinder

bipod (folded)

flash eliminator/compensator

Calibre 7.92mm
Length 94cm
Weight 4.5kg
Magazine 20-round box
Rate of fire (cyclic) 750rpm
Muzzle velocity 762mps

LG40 Recoilless Gun

breech block — — frangible base — shell — rifling
breech ring — — cartridge case
venturi nozzle — firing mechanism — barrel

1 Explosion of cartridge generates gas. Shell starts to move forward and rotate because of the rifling.

2 After the explosion, the frangible plastic base of the cartridge breaks, allowing the gases to escape through the hollow breech block.

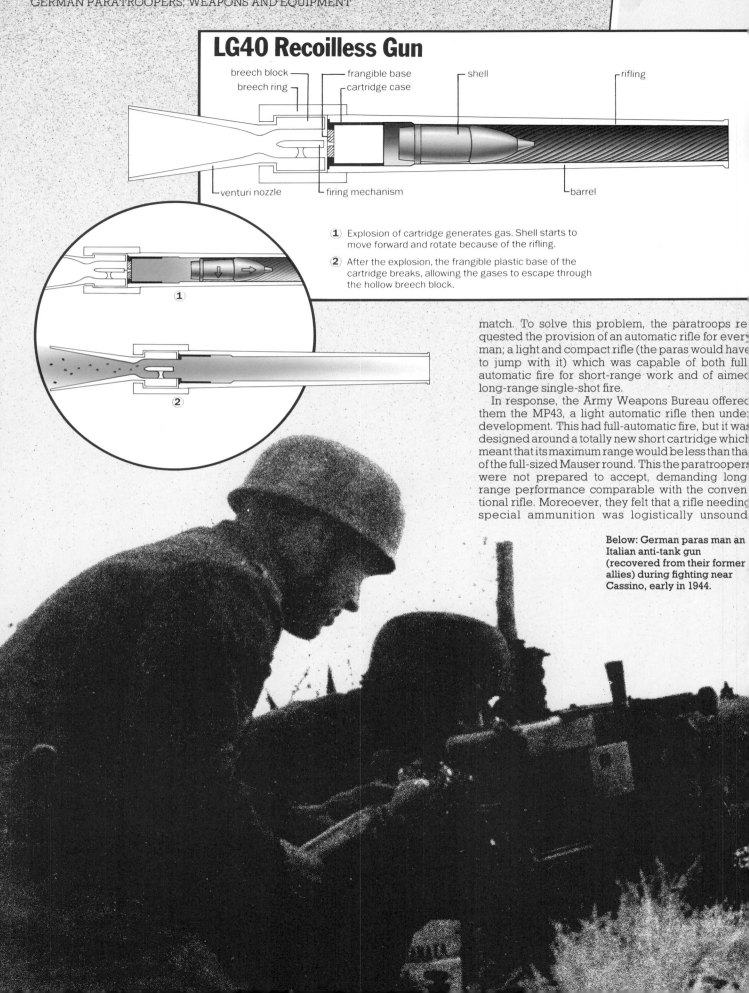

match. To solve this problem, the paratroops re quested the provision of an automatic rifle for ever man; a light and compact rifle (the paras would have to jump with it) which was capable of both full automatic fire for short-range work and of aimed long-range single-shot fire.

In response, the Army Weapons Bureau offered them the MP43, a light automatic rifle then unde development. This had full-automatic fire, but it wa designed around a totally new short cartridge which meant that its maximum range would be less than tha of the full-sized Mauser round. This the paratrooper were not prepared to accept, demanding long range performance comparable with the conven tional rifle. Moreoever, they felt that a rifle needing special ammunition was logistically unsound

Below: German paras man an Italian anti-tank gun (recovered from their former allies) during fighting near Cassino, early in 1944.

Left: Perched on a 'Kettenrad' half-tracked motorcycle, German paras tow a recoilless gun towards the battle front. Both the Kettenrad and recoilless gun were lightweight items, ideal for airborne troops. Below: Paras take cover behind an SdKfz 251 half-track during fighting for the city of Rome in September 1943. The soldier on the right has an MP40 slung over his back. Bottom: As part of defensive measures in Italy, paras lay Teller mines to slow the Allied advance.

very hard to control in automatic fire. The FG42 saw its first use in the successful raid to free Mussolini in September 1943 but as only 7000 were manufactured, it supplemented rather than replaced the existing weapons available to the German paratroopers.

Once on the ground the paratroopers became infantrymen, relying on their legs for transport; if they were to operate effectively they required some degree of motorised transport. While air-dropped paras were expected to utilise any vehicles encountered on the ground, provision was made to supply them with lightweight vehicles which could be carried by gliders or by transport planes once an airstrip had been secured. The Kübelwagen was a simple four-wheeled car which was sufficiently rugged to endure the conditions encountered on the battlefield. A later variant – the Schwimmwagen – had an amphibious capability and an optional four-wheel drive which made it a highly versatile vehicle. Motorcycle combinations were widely used by Germany's paratroopers, especially for reconnaissance purposes, although they had only limited cross-country mobility.

ammunition supply was a major problem for air-dropped units and to have two separate rounds in use would only increase difficulties. The Army was not interested in such a weapon, and so the paratroops turned again to the Luftwaffe, submitted a demand through that channel, and had it approved. By the middle of 1942 Rheinmetall had a prototype ready for testing. In fact, eight companies had been approached, but only the Rheinmetall design was considered worth following up.

The eventual weapon, the Fallschirmgewehr 42 (FG42) was a sound design, based on well-tried principles. It was gas operated and the bolt mechanism was so designed that for single-shot fire the bolt closed and locked on the cartridge; and after each shot a new round was automatically re-chambered, ready for firing. When automatic fire was selected, however, the bolt remained open after the release of the trigger, so that air could circulate through the barrel and chamber to cool them between bursts of fire. Much of the rifle was fabricated from steel pressings, while laminated plywood or plastic was used in the construction of the stock and handguard.

The FG42, though technically a success, was a difficult and demanding weapon to use. Due to its lightness (4.5kg) the power of the full-sized 7.92mm cartridge made for a heavy recoil force, and it was

One noteworthy piece of paratroop equipment was the SdKfz 22 Kleinkettenrad half-tracked motorcycle which utilised a tracked suspension unit with half a motorcycle frame at its front end. Between the tracks lay the engine and transmission, and above this unit were seats and cargo stowage. The driver sat on the saddle and steered by handlebars, although the drive went via a five-speed gearbox and differential into the tracks. The SdKfz 22 could carry 350kg and tow a further 450kg on a small trailer. Alternatively the SdKfz was used to tow the paras' recoilless guns.

As the war progressed, Germany's paratroop units were assigned the role of elite infantry and consequently the need for air-transportable weapons and equipment no longer applied. Nevertheless, the paras had been instrumental in the development of some of the most influential weapons of the war.

THE AUTHOR Ian V. Hogg is an authority on smallarms and modern weapon systems, and has written many books on the technology of warfare.

WEST GERMAN PARATROOPERS

It was Germany which made the first major tactical use of paratroopers during World War II, and in the early stages of the war these men achieved several spectacular coups as the spearhead of Blitzkrieg offensives. Their largest airborne operation, the invasion of Crete in 1941, proved very costly in men, however, and henceforth they were deployed as ground troops. Nevertheless, the German High Command fully recognised the value of the airborne forces' training and light scale of equipment, and the parachute formations were expanded continually up to the end of the war and the dismantling of the German Army.

Today's paratroopers came into being when the Bundeswehr was formed in the late 1950s. They were trained by a number of regular officers experienced in airborne operations at the re-opened Parachute Training School at Stendal, near Berlin. The number of units proliferated and West Germany now has three airborne brigades, incorporating both parachute and helicopter-borne units.

The German Feldheer (Field Army) comprises 12 divisions, formed into three corps (I, HQ Munster; II, HQ Ulm; III, HQ Koblenz). The Feldheer is responsible for the defence of NATO's Central Europe Region, and the three Luftlandebrigaden (airborne brigades) of the airborne division are stationed within the Region, each one attached to a corps. Allocated to I, II and III Corps respectively are 27 Brigade, based at Lippstadt, 25 Brigade at Schwarswald, and 26 Brigade at Saarlouis. In the event of an armoured threat within its own Corps Area, the appropriate airborne brigade would be rapidly deployed to neutralise the enemy incursion.

Tasked with the defence of the Central Europe Region, the paras of the West German Army are put through a rigorous and demanding programme of physical training and weapons instruction

ON NATO'S FRONT LINE

jäger battalions, each of which in turn is split into two airborne infantry companies (Fallschirmjäger) and two airmobile anti-tank companies (FallschirmPanzerAbwehr). Both types of company are capable of rapid aerial deployment, either from the C-160 Transall aircraft or the CH-53 helicopter.

When engaged in their primary anti-tank role, the airborne infantry companies drop in by parachute or land in Bell Huey helicopters. They then secure the landing zone (LZ) for the arrival of the anti-tank

Far left: Rapid deployment: a flight of CH-53 helicopters swoops in to deliver its cargo of Fallschirmjäger. Left: A group of paras on exercise in the field. Below: Although highly trained in sophisticated battle arts, from tank busting to unarmed combat, paras are not exempted from traditional infantry spade work. Bottom: Under the watchful eye of their instructor, paras learn the finer points of anti-tank warfare.

THE FALLSCHIRMJÄGER, as the paratrooper of the West German Army is known, is one of the front-runners among NATO's crack airborne forces. The Germans have a proud airborne tradition that dates back to the early days of World War II and the Fallschirmjäger of today possesses many of the fine physical qualities and tactical assault skills that served his gallant predecessors on the battlefields of Eben Emael and Crete.

The German armed forces (Bundeswehr), is currently responsible within the NATO framework for the defence of the Central Europe Region and its three Luftlandebrigaden (airborne brigades) are assigned the crucial task of countering any threat from enemy armoured forces. Each Luftlandebrigade consists of a brigade HQ and three Fallschirm-

companies in CH-53 helicopters. These companies are equipped with the 'Kraka' cross-country vehicle, a small four-wheel-drive machine which is like a cross between a moon-buggy and the US Army's 'mechanical mule', and mounts either five TOW anti-tank missiles or a 20mm gun (Feldkanone). The units can then deploy into position very rapidly with their firepower and can engage a variety of targets, ranging from main battle tanks such as the Soviet T-72, and armoured personnel carriers, to slow flying aircraft; at the same time they are protected from dismounted infantry attack by their own airborne infantry elements. These are tactics the Fallschirmjäger have developed over the years, and in which they are constantly trained.

Basic training for the Fallschirmjäger is carried out at brigade level and, since approximately two-thirds of each brigade's total strength is made up of conscripts, great emphasis is placed on such training. All new conscripts undergo a series of both physical and psychological tests. Strength and physical fitness are primary requirements for the German paras, and those wishing to go on to the Luftlandebrigaden are put through a series of arduous tests: they must run 5000m in under 23 minutes, throw a shot at least 8m, be able to long jump over 4m, sprint 100m in under 13.4 seconds, and swim 200m. Having passed these initial selection tests, recruits then go on to a three-month basic infantry training course with their brigade. There the new men form up into a training company and, under the instruction of regular NCOs and officers, learn the rudiments of weapons handling, fieldcraft, infantry tactics and marksmanship.

On completion of the fourth week at Altenstadt the student paras make a total of five descents

After 12 weeks of basic training, the recruits are sent to the German Army Parachute Training Centre at Altenstadt in Bavaria. Here they spend approximately four weeks under the instruction of NCOs from the 1st German Airborne Division. At Altenstadt the training is at a very high level and, with an instructor-to-student ratio of about one to eight, the recruits are pushed hard for the first two and a half weeks of ground work. This period is spent learning parachute control and landing techniques.

During their second week the recruits practise jumping from the 'tower', and by the end of the third week they are thoroughly tested on what they have learnt. If for any reason they fail this test, they are RTU'd (returned to unit). By the time they are deemed ready to parachute for real, the recruits will have completed at least 15 tower jumps, and a number of dry runs in a C-160 Transall. During the fourth week at Altenstadt the student paras make a total of five descents: the first two are made without equipment from a height of 400m, the third is with an equipment container, the fourth is a night jump without a container, and the fifth is a standard day jump. The course is hard, both physically and mentally, and there is an average drop-out rate of between 10 and 20 per cent. Those men who pass receive the coveted wings, which are worn on the right breast of their uniform, and return to their brigade fully-fledged Fallschirmjäger. One additional incentive for the conscript soldier undergoing para training is the extra 150DM parachute pay per month, which almost doubles the basic pay of 180DM per month that the average soldier in service with the

AIR AND GROUND TRANSPORT

Many of the aircraft deployed by the Luftlandebrigaden are produced in Germany in partnership with international manufacturers. Germany's largest aerospace conglomerate, Messerschmitt-Bölkow-Blohm GmbH (MBB) has produced the Transall C-160 medium-range tactical military transport, which has a maximum capacity of 81 troops, in a co-operative project, and two American helicopters, the Bell UH-1D and the Sikorsky CH-53 were also produced under licence. The Sikorsky CH-53 is the most powerful member of that company's S-65 helicopter family, and 112 examples, designated CH-53G, were assembled by VFW-Fokker. The CH-53G carries up to 55 troops and has a range of 2076km. The smaller UH-1D takes 14 troops over a range of 512km, and 352 examples have been produced by Dornier in Germany.

For their ground transport the Luftlandebrigaden have probably the best light airborne vehicle in the world, the Faun Kraftkarren, or Kraka. This small flat-bed vehicle, weighing just 1300kg, has wheels below the load bed, and is powered by a BMW twin-cylinder engine located below the rear floor with direct drive to the back wheels. One extraordinary advantage of the Kraka is that it folds up along a transverse hinge, reducing overall length from 2.75m to 1.75m. A Transall can carry 16 Krakas folded, or 10 unfolded, while the CH-53 takes five folded ones. Since production began in 1972, the Luftlandebrigaden have received 762 of them, and they have proved an excellent solution to the traditional airborne problem of providing a vehicle which is light, manoeuvrable and compact for air transport, yet of genuine practical value to paratroopers on the ground.

On the modern battlefield mobility is crucial. Once the paras have been dropped or heli-lifted into the battle zone, they are provided with their own transport, the Faun Kraftkarren (this page), to enable them to move quickly into vital defensive positions at a moment's notice.

Bundeswehr receives.

Training in the German Army never ceases. There are two main reasons for this: first, there is a constant stream of conscripts doing their military service (the Germans take this very seriously) and second, they believe in the saying, 'Train hard – fight easy'. So, once the Fallschirmjäger joins his battalion, he spends the next 10 to 12 months receiving further training in the use of his equipment, and on tactical exercises, from platoon up to corps level.

When the German para is not out on exercise he has a full day's work in camp. The routine starts with early morning call at 0545 hours, followed by a quick wash and shave. Breakfast is at 0610 and consists of bread, meat, cheese, boiled egg and coffee. The section commander's inspection at 0630 is followed by the platoon commander's inspection at 0700hrs. The platoon is then visited by its company commander, a Hauptmann (captain), who briefs the men on their daily duties, which they then carry out until lunchtime at 1200. At 1300 they resume training until 1700, when they finish for the day, except for one night per week which they spend in the field on a night training exercise. Training is intensive, fitness and marksmanship being priorities.

The command and leadership aspects of the course are the most important and all students must graduate in these skills

Weapons training is taken very seriously in the Bundeswehr, and at least once a week the company spends the day on the range firing personal and platoon weapons. Ammunition is not a problem, and there is an above average allocation for the Bundeswehr. There is also greater availability of helicopter support for the Fallschirmjäger than for many of their NATO airborne counterparts. The two main reasons for this are the importance that the West German Army attaches to airmobile operations, and the fact that the Bell Huey and CH-53 helicopters belong to the army, and are flown by army pilots. These helicopters are tasked by Corps and the Fallschirmjäger have priority over all other units.

Apart from the conscript element, the remaining third of each brigade is made up of temporary career volunteers serving between two and 15 years, or by regular officers and NCOs. Most of these men go on for further training at the Airborne Training Centre at Schongau, Bavaria. Situated in this suitably rugged setting, the centre offers 31 different courses and an intensive 'ranger' instruction programme. Courses cover everything from junior leadership and aircrew survival techniques, to freefall parachuting.

Ten ranger courses are held every year at Schoengau, and each course lasts for four weeks. The students are divided into four 30-man platoons under the command of an experienced Hauptmann, who will have served previously as a company commander in a Fallschirmjäger battalion. Under him there are usually four NCO instructors, each with a particular speciality in skills such as combat survival or unarmed combat. Since the ranger course must be passed by all platoon leaders in the infantry, paras, mountain troops, and long range reconnaissance patrols (LRRPs), the course is designed to improve special leadership qualities, and is in no way suppressive. Much emphasis is placed on developing personal skills, and throughout the course the student is tested and graded on four main subjects: leadership, unarmed combat, obstacle

crossing and mobility, and individual survival skills. The command and leadership aspects of the course are considered the most important, and all students must graduate in leadership skills; failing to do so will mean that the NCO will never be able to command fighting troops in the field. Instructors watch the students very closely as they are given the chance to command the other members of their platoon at various stages throughout the course.

The unarmed combat taught to rangers is a standard mixture of ju-jitsu and karate, the emphasis being placed on the ability to kill quickly and silently. There are three tests held during the course, and the students are graded on their fighting skills, ability to instruct, and technique. Obstacle crossing and mobility techniques are also taught throughout the four weeks. Runs over obstacle courses are held every week, and all students must be able to abseil and climb a 120ft rope with full equipment, swim 300 yds across a river after waterproofing their equipment, and pass a series of tests, culminating in the second week with a three-mile run to be completed in under 22 minutes, carrying rifle and pack.

The final aspect of the course covers individual survival skills. Students are taught how to recognise and collect edible plants and how to catch wild

Airborne assault work: paras emplane on a Transall transport aircraft (below) and prepare to make one of their numerous training jumps (left).

animals and prepare them for eating. They also learn how to light fires and build shelters using natural materials, and how to navigate by the stars.

Apart from acquiring new skills on the ranger course, the students are constantly applying their new-found knowledge in a series of tactical exercises, which start with a four-day exercise during the second week. They practise infiltration techniques and how to pass through enemy lines undetected, while at the same time living off the land. In the third week they spend two nights in the field: the first night is spent setting up and springing an ambush, and on the second night they must raid an enemy position and capture a prisoner for intelligence purposes. There is also a 24-hour tactical exercise in the third week, during which they are evaluated on all the skills that they have learnt. This ends up with a 25-mile cross-country speed march, and is generally considered the most difficult part of the ranger course. In fact, it is only the practice run-up to the final four-day exercise held in the last week.

During the final exercise the students are under constant pressure from the instructors. They build shelters, live off the land, move at night and lie-up during the day. Each man has to take his turn in commanding the other four men in his patrol, and has to plan attacks and assign duties while being constantly evaluated by his instructor. At the end of this exercise the course is over. The instructors get together and evaluate the test results, and those who

Fallschirmjäger are well-trained to fight in built-up areas. This sequence of photographs shows a training assault. Covering each other, paras race from one building to another (top), mount a fire escape and lob in a grenade (centre above), and then crash in through the door (centre below). The whole operation is covered by a para strategically placed at the foot of the steps (bottom).

have passed receive a certificate and the green and white leaf badge of the Ranger.

The ranger course is one of the toughest of its kind in the world. There is a 50 per cent drop out rate first time round, which is high considering the standard of fitness and experience of the NCOs who go on the course. Many who have passed all but one subject are allowed to return for the final exercise, and if they pass this they then automatically qualify. Others who have failed, get one more chance to do the whole course again.

Once the Fallschirmjäger has passed his ranger course he is able to command a platoon in either an airborne infantry company or an airmobile anti-tank company. He is also able to apply for the LRRPs or the Fernspäy companies. The latter are divided into four-man patrols, capable of HALO (high altitude low opening) parachute insertion behind enemy lines and are the West German Army's equivalent to the British Special Air Service.

Training is realistic and dangerous: 'stun' grenades are used, as well as a special plastic practice round

The Bundeswehr has long since realised the importance of being able to fight in an urban area, and all Fallschirmjäger are trained in FIBUA (fighting in built-up area) tactics. Unlike GSG-9, the West German police anti-terrorist unit, the paratroopers do not have to deal with hostage situations, but train to assault and clear buildings. The possibility of intensive urban warfare in an East – West conflict has not escaped the attention of the German commanders, and Fallschirmjäger companies regularly train for this role in disused factories and other buildings set aside specifically for this purpose. Small five-man groups work in tandem, giving covering fire, flanking, and entering buildings by different means, including through the walls and the roofs. Training is realistic and dangerous: 'stun' grenades are used, as well as a special plastic 7.62mm practice round which is accurate up to 200yds.

Germany's airborne forces are highly trained and effective. Troops can be deployed rapidly by air to outflank the enemy or to support other units. Anti-tank companies can be air-landed to counter enemy armoured units, specialist teams can be used for strategic reconnaissance or to carry out raids, and Fallschirmjäger companies can be deployed to fight in an urban environment. More advanced and sophisticated weapon systems are being designed for the airborne troops, and the four-wheeled Kraka is shortly to be replaced by the 'Weasel' – a purpose-built tracked armoured vehicle. This will be capable of being air-transported and will offer the Fallschirmjäger the protection they need, and an even greater mobility on the battlefields of the future.

THE AUTHOR Peter Macdonald is a free-lance defence photo-journalist. He served with the British Army and the Rhodesian Security Forces between 1974-80, and is the author of two forthcoming books *Special Forces: A history of the World's Elite Fighting Units*, and *The 20th Century Mercenary*.

EQUIPPING THE PARAS

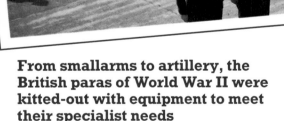

From smallarms to artillery, the British paras of World War II were kitted-out with equipment to meet their specialist needs

THE FIRST BRITISH paratroopers began training on Midsummer's Day 1940 at Ringway Airport, Manchester, and on the following day Winston Churchill demanded a force of 5000 parachutists, to include men from all over the Commonwealth and from France and Norway. In addition to initiating parachute troops, the 'Central Landing School' at Ringway was charged with the task of investigating the possibility of using gliders to carry troops and equipment. By August 1940 some 500 men were under training, but there were no aircraft available for dropping them, nor were there any gliders suitable for carrying troops. The Air Ministry and the War Office had agreed to develop four different prototype gliders and test them, the most suitable then to be put into production.

The Air Ministry favoured gliders, and argued that only one-tenth of any airborne force should be parachutists. The RAF opposed the idea of flying unarmed troop transports and insisted that parachutists should be carried only in armed bombers, while other bombers would tow the gliders. The reasoning behind these arguments is obscure at this remove of time, but it was probably simply that there were no suitable transport aircraft in existence and there was small chance of obtaining the necessary priority to design and build one. Unfortunately, the RAF's bombers – the Whitley was favoured – did not lend themselves to dropping parachutists, and it was not until the American C-47 Dakota became available in mid-1942 that the parachute force obtained an aircraft suited to its task.

Despite the initial enthusiasm for parachute troops, there was no doctrine on their employment, no role yet existed for them, and although many conflicting ideas had been put forward, there was no firm statement about how they should be used in battle. With a dearth of transport aircraft, no gliders, no glider tugs and no formal establishment, the British airborne forces throughout 1940 and 1941 were a solution looking for a problem.

As there was no firm policy on their employment, it is hardly surprising that there were no firm directives about their equipment. So far as anyone had given the matter any thought, it was assumed that once they reached the ground they would fight just like any other infantry soldier, and therefore the ordinary infantry soldier's equipment would be perfectly satisfactory.

The only drawback to this was that the necessity of delivering parachutists from bombers argued against much of this equipment. The standard method of exiting from the Whitley was through a hole in the floor, and it was difficult enough for the man to get himself through this hole without encumbering him with anything as awkward as a rifle or a light machine gun, let alone the component parts of a mortar. Anything the man carried had to be small, and the result of this was that the sub-machine gun soon became a favoured weapon. The Thompson,

and later the Sten, were sufficiently small to be carried by the man as he dropped, and they had sufficient firepower to make themselves felt on the ground.

The heavier or bulkier equipment – the rifles, heavy machine guns and mortars – had to be dropped independently of the men, and for this a variety of stores containers were devised. These could be carried in the bomb-bays or under the wings of the troop-carrying aircraft and, under control of the pilot, could be released as the parachutists were dropping. Fitted with coloured parachutes so that they could be quickly identified, these fell randomly throughout the dropping zone, and thus the first task of the parachutists was to locate the containers and obtain their heavy weapons and ammunition.

Most of the early items of equipment were direct copies of those issued to German parachute troops

Preliminary exercises with these containers soon demonstrated that while the basic idea was good, there were, however, problems involved in collecting this weaponry and one of the first pieces of specialist equipment to be provided was a simple 'para-cart', a collapsible cart made of tubular steel and canvas and fitted with small wheels, a pair of handles and drag-ropes. This was pulled from its container and expanded into working order, then piled with the contents of the containers and trundled smartly away by three or four men.

So far as equipment was concerned, most of the early items were direct copies of those issued to German parachute troops, largely because they were the only models known. Consequently, the first uniform for parachutists was an overall and a leather helmet, and even the German side-lacing parachute boots were copied; but these latter, the War Office felt, were unjustifiably luxurious and the paras were soon back in standard army boots. (Indeed, British paras have worn them ever since, unlike almost every other parachute force in the world.) The overalls were then abandoned and the Denison Smock adopted, another item which is still in use today and which has, in fact, been widely copied elsewhere. The Denison Smock is a heavy cloth

THE WELBIKE

While it was based in Welwyn Garden City the Special Operations Executive (SOE) initiated the production of a number of specialised items of equipment for the exclusive use of its paratroopers and commandos. Among them were the Welgun, (a light sub-machine gun that was supplanted by the Sten), the Welrod (a small silenced pistol), and the Welbike. The airborne formations needed a form of fast transport that could be parachuted down alongside the men in the standard long, narrow paradrop container. Consequently, the SOE's motorbike, which was manufactured in Birmingham by the Excelsior Motor Company, was set low with small wheels, and when stowed it measured only 38cm high and 56cm wide. The folding handlebar and saddle pillars were locked upright after the bike had been lifted from the container (see below).
Although several thousand Welbikes were built, they did not prove very useful in the field. No passengers or equipment could be carried, as they overworked the 98cc single-cylinder engine, and the small wheels rendered the motorbike virtually immobile on anything but a good road. Although the machine was popular with the men, it was finally decided that the extra mobility that had been gained did not justify the manufacturing effort.

Left above: An early photograph of paras on parade, wearing the canvas and rubber jumping head gear. This item of equipment was soon replaced by the rimless steel helmet which provided far more protection in battle. Left: Paras, wearing Denison Smocks, check their gear before enplaning. Below: A stores container. When it landed, the hollow end would crumple, acting as a shock absorber.

Sten MkII SMG

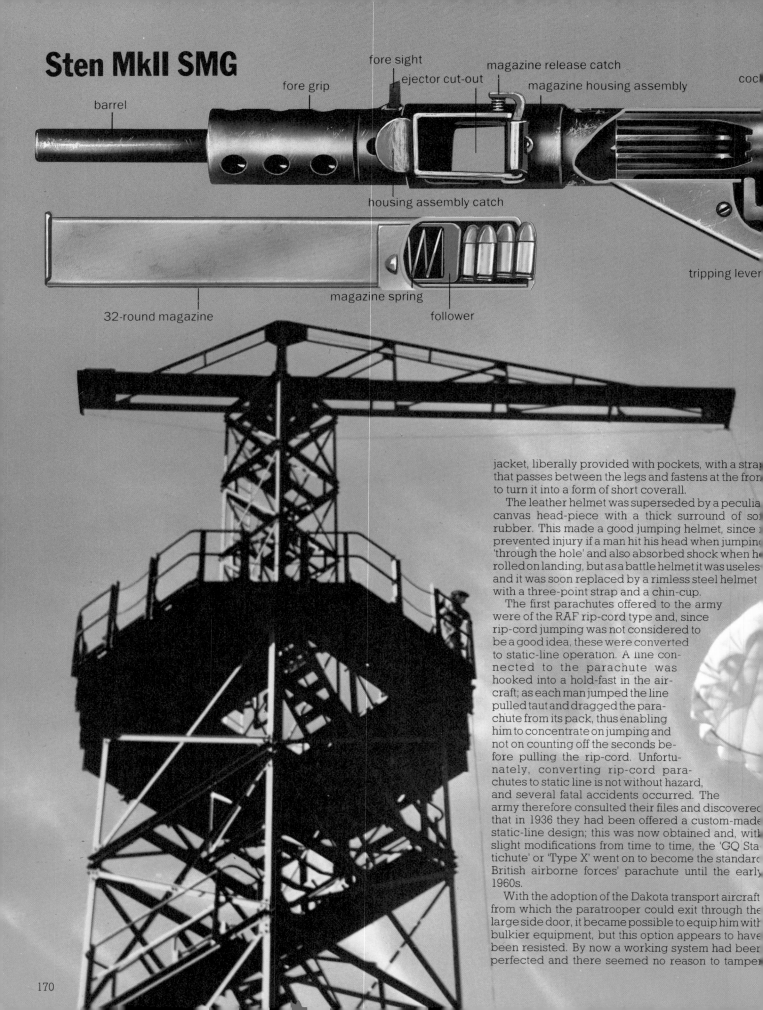

barrel

fore grip

fore sight

ejector cut-out

magazine release catch

magazine housing assembly

coc[king]

housing assembly catch

tripping lever

32-round magazine

magazine spring

follower

jacket, liberally provided with pockets, with a strap that passes between the legs and fastens at the fron[t] to turn it into a form of short coverall.

The leather helmet was superseded by a peculia[r] canvas head-piece with a thick surround of sof[t] rubber. This made a good jumping helmet, since [it] prevented injury if a man hit his head when jumpin[g] 'through the hole' and also absorbed shock when h[e] rolled on landing, but as a battle helmet it was useles[s] and it was soon replaced by a rimless steel helmet with a three-point strap and a chin-cup.

The first parachutes offered to the army were of the RAF rip-cord type and, since rip-cord jumping was not considered to be a good idea, these were converted to static-line operation. A line connected to the parachute was hooked into a hold-fast in the aircraft; as each man jumped the line pulled taut and dragged the parachute from its pack, thus enabling him to concentrate on jumping and not on counting off the seconds before pulling the rip-cord. Unfortunately, converting rip-cord parachutes to static line is not without hazard, and several fatal accidents occurred. The army therefore consulted their files and discovered that in 1936 they had been offered a custom-made static-line design; this was now obtained and, with slight modifications from time to time, the 'GQ Statichute' or 'Type X' went on to become the standard British airborne forces' parachute until the early 1960s.

With the adoption of the Dakota transport aircraft from which the paratrooper could exit through the large side door, it became possible to equip him with bulkier equipment, but this option appears to have been resisted. By now a working system had been perfected and there seemed no reason to tamper

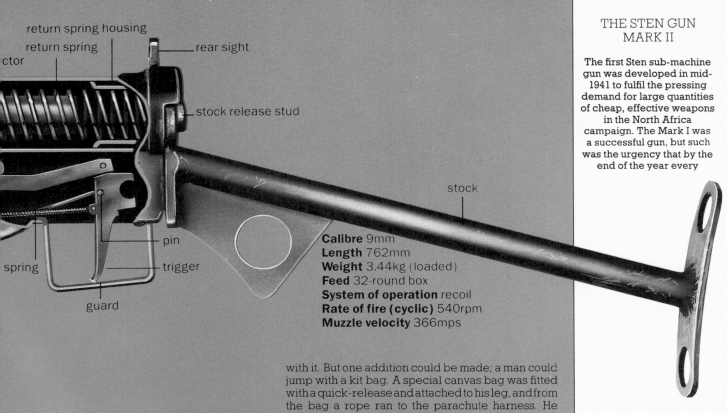

return spring housing

return spring

ctor

rear sight

stock release stud

spring

pin

trigger

guard

stock

Calibre 9mm
Length 762mm
Weight 3.44kg (loaded)
Feed 32-round box
System of operation recoil
Rate of fire (cyclic) 540rpm
Muzzle velocity 366mps

The first Sten sub-machine gun was developed in mid-1941 to fulfil the pressing demand for large quantities of cheap, effective weapons in the North Africa campaign. The Mark I was a successful gun, but such was the urgency that by the end of the year every

refinement had been stripped away to facilitate production. Consequently, the Mark II was probably the crudest weapon ever used by the British soldier, and it was soon to earn such nicknames as the 'tin Tommy-gun', the 'plumber's delight' and even the 'stench gun'.

The Mark II consisted of simple pressings of a cheap metal hurriedly welded together, and it frequently came apart if subjected to a hard shock. Its magazine caused a great deal of trouble. The lips were prone to become deformed, and then it would misfeed the rounds into the gun. The magazine also rapidly became clogged with dust, a serious problem in the desert.

Nevertheless, the Sten gun Mark II was a valuable weapon. Over two million were made, and with factories pouring them out at up to 20,000 a week they could be produced for £2.87 apiece. Despite its weaknesses the gun earned its acceptance on the battlefield, and it was extensively copied throughout the world.

with it. But one addition could be made; a man could jump with a kit bag. A special canvas bag was fitted with a quick-release and attached to his leg, and from the bag a rope ran to the parachute harness. He hobbled to the door with the large load strapped to his leg, and jumped. Once his parachute was open, he pulled the quick-release and the kit bag dropped to the end of its rope, so that it dangled beneath him. Nearing the ground, the bag landed first; this reduced the weight on the parachute, thus slowing the man's descent and making it less hazardous.

The parachutists could now land, and they could take some reasonably heavy weapons with them. One thing that remained was the provision of some means of mobility once on the ground, not so much for transporting the men – they were infantry, and were expected to march – but to allow scouts and messengers to move rapidly out of the drop zone.

The first answer to appear was the famous folding bicycle, famous not so much for its battle record but for the myriad jokes which it engendered. It was, in fact, a very practical machine, a standard bicycle with the frame hinged in the middle so that it would fold to permit the two wheels to lie one on top of the other. The handlebars and saddle also folded, and the resulting package went into a paradrop container. Once it was removed, the bicycle was unfolded and the various wing-nuts screwed up tight, after which it was a perfectly sound machine. But in the heat of the moment many a parachutist forgot one of the nuts and after a short ride, usually across rough country, the bicycle would suddenly fold up underneath him. Perhaps the most famous joke on this subject was the story of the parachutist whistling through the air underneath a failed parachute, who ruefully said: 'And when I do get down, I bet the bloody bike won't work either.'

The folding bicycle was later followed by the folding motorcycle, a very small, specially designed machine called the 'Welbike', the 'Wel' part of the name indicating that it had been designed by the Special Forces' design unit located in Welwyn Garden City. This had small wheels and a two-stroke engine laid inside a very low frame, with saddle and handlebars which folded flat and were extended

Left: The wartime parachute tower on which many an aspiring airborne soldier was put through his paces before attempting the real thing. The Parachute Training School's first home was at Ringway airport in Manchester, where Major Rock and Squadron Leader Strange set up the training of British airborne forces in June 1940. The first training establishment was known as the Central Landing School. Apart from the tower, other pieces of familiarisation equipment included a mock-up of the Whitley fuselage hole, constructed in a hangar, and a simulated Whitley hole suspended in a cage beneath a balloon. It was all very well, however, jumping through the hole while it remained static – when actually exiting from a moving aircraft it was not uncommon for the jumper to smash his face on the opposite edge of the hole as he went through. This particularly unpleasant experience was known as 'ringing the bell'.

Right: A para sergeant with 'chute and kitbag, and a few extra items stuffed into the front of his smock. A useful early discovery was that a man could drop with a substantial load in his kitbag, dangling beneath him as he descended, and, provided the bag hit the ground well in advance of its owner, he could land unscathed. Below: A para, armed with a Bren gun, training for airborne operations in the autumn of 1941.

upwards for use. It could move at 30mph, could cover 90 miles on one tank of six-and-a-half pints of petrol, and it proved very popular.

By the spring of 1942 the first Horsa gliders appeared. These could carry 28 men or, cleared of seats, they could take a jeep and a 75mm pack howitzer, thus permitting the airborne force some close support artillery and some motorised transport. Shortly afterwards came the Hamilcar glider, and this large and boxy machine was able to carry more jeeps and guns, or a 25-pounder field gun, or even a light tank.

The 75mm Pack Howitzer M8 was an American weapon which, as the name implies, had been originally intended for carriage by mules in mountain warfare. Its small size made it an obvious choice for airborne use and the British were able to acquire a large number. It fired a 14.7lb high-explosive shell to a maximum range of 9600yds, and it was also provided with a shaped-charge anti-tank shell which could defeat three-and-a-half inches of armour at even maximum range, though its practical engagement range was generally considered to be not more than 1000yds. As well as being carried in gliders, it could be dismantled into six unit loads, each of which could be dropped in a 'Paracrate' with a parachute attached. On the ground it took less than one minute for trained men to assemble the weapon once the various containers had been located and the parts brought together in one place.

The standard British 25-pounder gun could not be loaded into a glider without considerable dismantling, and therefore a special 'Mark 3 carriage' version was developed. This had a smaller shield and narrower wheel track, and the trail was hinged in the middle, which allowed it to be stowed more easily inside a glider and also gave the barrel a degree of extra elevation, a useful advantage in some tactical situations. The gun was unchanged ballistically, and still fired the standard 25lb shell to a maximum range of 13,400yds.

The ultimate piece of specialist equipment for the

Right, top to bottom: A group of Polish paras demonstrates the handy 'para-cart', a device for gathering equipment from around the drop zone; paras equipped with the legendary folding bicycle, butt of many a sour joke among its hapless users; the 75mm M8 pack howitzer, developed for mountain warfare but particularly suited to the needs of airborne forces – a compact artillery piece, the M8 could be dropped alongside the paras and provided fire support in the crucial early stages of an airborne assault); and paras await their arrival at a drop zone in the cramped fuselage of a Whitley. Below: An M22 Locust light tank emerges from a Hamilcar glider.

airborne troops was the air-portable tank. The fact that the British had one was something of an accident; the Tetrarch light tank had been designed by Vickers before the war but due to various delays did not go into production until 1940. By that time, with the experience of the French campaign behind them, the army had decided against light tanks, and the production was stopped while the matter was discussed. Then, in 1941, it was considered that the –ton Tetrarch might have a future as an airborne tank, and production was restarted, a total of 177 being built. Armed with the usual 2-pounder gun and 7.92mm Besa machine gun, it could move at 40mph and had an operational range of 140 miles.

In addition to the Tetrarch, the British were also issued with a number of American M22 Locust light tanks. This was about the same size as the Tetrarch and mounted a 37mm gun; in general form it resembled a miniature Sherman and could reach 35mph. Unfortunately, the Americans failed to design a suitable glider and could only carry it by slinging it beneath an aircraft after removing its turret. This was so impractical that the US airborne forces never used it, but since it fitted into the British Hamilcar glider a few M22s saw action during the crossing of the Rhine.

THE AUTHOR Ian V Hogg is an authority on smallarms, modern weapon systems and equipment, and the technology of warfare.

Crossing minefields

Concertina wire

Marked mine

Probe

MINEFIELDS AND WIRE

Mobility on the battlefield and speed of movement are essential to a successful assault. Troops defending an area, however, will do their best to contain an attack by setting up defensive barriers such as minefields and barbed wire. The armed forces of today field a number of specialist vehicles for dealing with such man-made obstacles, but these will not always be available to the small unit in combat. Nor can they be used when surprise is a crucial ingredient of the attack. If you are infiltrating enemy lines on a reconnaissance mission, or launching a surprise raid on an enemy position, you will have to negotiate hidden minefields or barbed-wire defences with the minimum of equipment, and often at night.

Above: The patient and methodical process of clearing a path through a minefield. Two men work in front, feeling for and clearing anti-personnel mines with their bare hands. Behind them a metal detector is used to locate more deeply buried anti-tank mines which would not be detonated by the weight of a man but still remain a potential hazard. A radio operator remains in the rear to report on the process of clearance. The area already cleared is carefully marked out with white tape.

Crossing an enemy minefield is an extremel hazardous business and the first rule is to remai calm and to approach the task methodically. Ant personnel mines are usually triggered either b direct pressure from the foot, or by a trip wir stretched across the ground and you most remai alert for both types. To minimise the possibility casualties, a three-foot wide path across th minefield should be cleared and carefully markec But first, the buried mines have to be located.

If you are not carrying an electronic mine detectc you will have to unearth any mines by probing. Th best implement for this exacting task is a stron wooden stick, sharpened at one end. Having d vested yourself of all excess equipment and ar loose objects which might fall off or catch on a tr wire, lie face down on the ground and begin to edg your way forward. Push the probe into the groun immediately in front of you as gently as possib while feeling for trip wires with your free hand. A

Bangalore torpedo

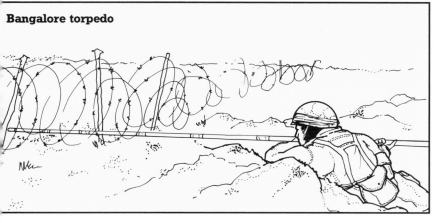

pedo will alert the enemy to your presence so you will have to cut a way through the entanglement with wire-cutters. To reduce the sharp sound of the wire snapping, wrap a piece of cloth around the strand you are going to cut and then apply a steady pressure with the cutters. Start working at the bottom of the obstacle and only cut as many strands as is necessary to create a breach you can slip through. Once you have made an opening, wriggle under the wire on your back. This will leave your hands free to push the wire upwards so that it does not snag your clothing.

The crossing of both minefields and wire defences demands a steady hand and a watchful eye. Neither obstacle should be tackled hurriedly. Although the necessary skills are fairly easily acquired, they must be second nature when you are called upon to use them under pressure.

oon as you detect a solid object, remove the probe and start scraping away the earth around the suspected mine with your fingers. If the object is indeed a mine you should leave it alone, mark it, and then report its position to the men behind you. There are many different methods of marking a mine – piles of stones, tape, pegs – but whichever system you use, make doubly sure that every man in the unit is thoroughly familiar with it. Probing and marking out a path across a minefield requires great patience and concentration. Take care not to rush the job – your first mistake will be your last!

When you have made your way across the field and staked out a clear route, a team of men should be sent over to check out and secure the far side. Your unit will be at its most vulnerable when the main body of troops reaches the middle of the minefield, so it is essential to make sure that the area ahead is clear of enemy before moving out.

The second main obstacle to troop mobility is the barbed-wire entanglement. This type of defensive measure can vary in depth and density, but usually takes the form of either a series of interlocking wire strand fences, or a pattern of 'concertina' wire barriers.

Wire can be tackled in a number of different ways, but the method you choose will depend very much on the nature of the mission you are out to perform. In an all-out assault on an enemy position you will need to breach the wire as quickly as possible in order to maintain the momentum of the attack. If armoured vehicles are not available to crash through the wire and clear a path for the infantry, Bangalore torpedoes should be used to blow gaps in the defences. A Bangalore torpedo is a long, thin explosive device, shaped like a length of pipe, which is pushed underneath the tangle of wire and then detonated.

Once a gap has been blasted, any wire left uncut by the explosion should be severed with wire-cutters. If you are expecting to encounter wire obstacles when you launch the attack, rush matting or boards can be taken in to throw onto the partially destroyed structures. This will speed up the crossing and allow the troops an easier passage. A great deal of supporting fire is necessary for infantry crossing wire defences since the enemy will have set up machine-gun positions to rake the area with fire.

Breaching wire obstacles during a clandestine infiltration operation, however, requires a very different approach. The detonation of a Bangalore tor-

Right: Using his bayonet and scabbard as wire-cutters, a soldier inches through a barbed-wire obstacle.

COMBAT SKILLS Of The Elite